The Supply-side Revolution with Chinese Characteristics

Focusing on the supply-side structural reform in China, this book investigates the impetus, implementation strategy, initial results, and theoretical underpinnings of the revolution, assessing its significance in perfecting China's socialist market economic system.

The supply-side structural reform launched in China in 2015 aims to thoroughly resolve the cyclical excess capacity and the habitual imbalance of economic structure; and form a long-term mechanism for economic stability, different from the supply-side policies under the Reagan Administration in the 1980s. Based on the analysis framework of aggregate demand and supply, combined with institutional and structural analysis, the title elucidates the reason, theory, measures, and results that ground the reform. It explicates the three-step strategy to ensure the successful outcome, countermeasures against current supply-side problems, upgrading the economic structure, and most importantly the institutional reform and innovation. The author emphasizes the importance of reforming both market and government and advances a "double-effect" model combining the effective market and government.

This title will appeal to scholars, students, and policy makers interested in economics, macroeconomic control, and the Chinese economy and economic system reform.

Fang Fuqian is Chair Professor at School of Economics, Renmin University of China. His research interests include macroeconomic theory and policy and China's economic system reform and economic development.

The Supply-side Revolution with Chinese Characteristics

Fang Fuqian

LONDON AND NEW YORK

This publication was supported by fund for building world-class universities (disciplines) of Renmin University of China.

First published in English 2023
by Routledge
4 Park Square, Milton Park, Abingdon, Oxon OX14 4RN

and by Routledge
605 Third Avenue, New York, NY 10158

Routledge is an imprint of the Taylor & Francis Group, an informa business

British Library Cataloguing-in-Publication Data
A catalogue record for this book is available from the British Library

Library of Congress Cataloging-in-Publication Data
Names: Fang, Fuqian, 1954- author.
Title: The supply-side revolution with Chinese characteristics/Fang Fuqian.
Other titles: Zhongguo shi gong ji ge ming. English
Description: Milton Park, Abingdon, Oxon; New York, NY: Routledge, 2023. | Includes bibliographical references and index. | Identifiers: LCCN 2022042353 (print) | LCCN 2022042354 (ebook) | ISBN 9781032433622 (hardback) | ISBN 9781032433691 (paperback) | ISBN 9781003367000 (ebook)
Classification: LCC HB241. F32513 2023 (print) | LCC HB241 (ebook) | DDC 338.50951—dc23/eng/20220915
LC record available at https://lccn.loc.gov/2022042353
LC ebook record available at https://lccn.loc.gov/2022042354

ISBN: 978-1-032-43362-2 (hbk)
ISBN: 978-1-032-43369-1 (pbk)
ISBN: 978-1-003-36700-0 (ebk)

DOI: 10.4324/9781003367000

Typeset in Times New Roman
by Apex CoVantage, LLC

Contents

Figures

Tables

Introduction

I. Interpretation of the title of this monograph

The supply-side structural reform of China's economy, which was initiated in November 2015, is a "supply-side revolution with Chinese characteristics" in essence.

The reform and opening up that began in 1979 was a revolution in China's economy—a revolution against the highly centralized planned-economy system, and a revolution against the closed-door policy or closed development model. The supply-side structural reform, which began in November 2015, is another revolution of China's economy—the supply-side structural reform, which itself aims to make major adjustments to the economic structure and great change in the development pattern and macroeconomic control pattern. To achieve this major adjustment and great change, and to maintain the dynamic optimization of the economic structure and the development pattern, it is necessary to push forward the comprehensive deepening of reform and to revolutionize the traditional systems and mechanisms that cause the rigidity and cyclical imbalance of China's economic structure and the extensive development pattern. If the previous revolution aimed to make China's economy stronger and richer, shorten the development gap between China and developed countries, and lift China out of poverty as soon as possible, this revolution will aim to strengthen and improve China's economy, strengthen its physique and bones, improve its development potential and international competitiveness, and make China's economy successfully cross the middle-income trap and enter the ranks of developed countries. Through reforming the traditional planned-economy system, the reform and opening up in 1979 was mainly to liberate the productivity, promote the increase in aggregate supply, eliminate the shortage economy, and continuously improve the level of national income per capita and the living standard. Through deepening the reform of productive relations and superstructure, the supply-side structural reform will be mainly to innovate systems, optimize and upgrade the economic structure, develop new impetus for supply growth, improve the quality of economic development and people's living quality and welfare, enhance the capacity for sustainable economic development, and strengthen the capacity for coordinated and balanced development of the environment, society and economy. The

DOI: 10.4324/9781003367000-1

reform and opening up that began in 1979 has dramatically changed the fate of the Chinese people, and the situation of every Chinese achieved the Pareto improvement, so that the reform has been widely welcomed and actively participated in; this round of reform will go deeper into the system, which will inevitably give rise to big change in China's existing systems and damage the "benefits" of those with vested interests. Therefore, the reform faces greater resistance and difficulty. In this sense, this round of reform is more revolutionary in nature.

Just as we named China's agricultural and rural reform the "household contract responsibility system" in the early 1980s, now we name the new round of comprehensively deepening the reform "supply-side structural reform". "Supply-side structural reform" is just the battle name of the new round of great reform. If the implementation of the household contract responsibility system was the core of China's agricultural and rural reform in 1980s, the supply-side structural reform will be the core of comprehensively deepening the reform in China at present. The process of supply-side structural reform is deemed the process of building and perfecting China's socialist market economic system.

The first supply-side structural reform was not initiated by China, and a large-scale supply-side structural reform was launched during the Reagan Administration Period in the 1980s.[1] However, China's current supply-side structural reform is not a copy of the supply reform in the United States. The supply-side structural reform of China's economy is a major issue raised by China's economic practice and an objective requirement for China's economic development to enter a new stage and a new normal. China's current supply-side structural reform is much and qualitatively different from the supply reform conducted during the Reagan Administration Period. It is a supply-side structural reform with "Chinese characteristics" or supply-side revolution with Chinese characteristics.

The supply reform during the Reagan Administration Period was launched under the background where the American economy fell into stagflation in the mid to late 1970s: economic growth stagnated, and unemployment rate rose with higher and higher inflation. The reasons for stagflation are that the two oil crises in 1970s led to a sharp increase in the cost of production and living cost in the United States, and the United States fell into the quagmire of the Vietnam War, resulting in a huge fiscal deficit and government debt, imbalance of economic structure and continuous decline in productivity growth.[2] On September 17, 1979, an article in *American Business Week* described the background of the Reagan Administration's supply reform and supply-side economics:

> Because of this decade of weak economic growth and rising inflation, during which the American economy has been suffering from goods shortages, sluggish productivity growth, sluggish capital investment, and insufficient manufacturing capacity—the main problem now is very clear. It is not how to stimulate demand but how to stimulate supply.

This economic background led to the great popularity of the supply-side economics, resulting in the great shift in the Reagan administration's economic policy: abandoning the Keynesian policy of stimulating aggregate demand that the American government had been pursuing since Roosevelt's New Deal, and shifting to supply reform and supply management advocated by the supply-side economics.

China's economy has experienced a decline in growth rate since the first quarter of 2010, and the growth of labor productivity and total factor productivity (TFP) has declined. However, the main problems the Chinese economy faces are not a shortage of goods and insufficient manufacturing capacity, but rather the relative surplus of production and absolute surplus of low-grade products. More importantly, China's economic growth rate has suffered from deflation rather than inflation since it declined in the first quarter of 2010.[3] This shows that the main problems of China's economy at present are insufficient growth impetus and cold market demand, which is quite different from the economic situation during the Reagan Administration Period.

The supply reform implemented by the Reagan Administration mainly aimed to enable the American economy to get rid of the stagflation predicament, restore the TFP growth and economic growth of the United States, and increase supply. The main purpose of China's supply-side structural reform is to transform the past "inefficient, high-speed, and unstable" economic growth mode into an "efficient, medium-high-speed, and stable" economic growth mode, and increase effective supply under the new normal.

The main contents of Reagan Administration's supply reform are about reducing taxes, cutting excessive and outdated regulations, and carrying out reindustrialization and remarketization. The main contents of China's supply-side structural reform are about "cutting overcapacity, reducing excess inventory, deleveraging, lowering costs, and strengthening areas of weakness", adjusting, optimizing, and upgrading the economic structure, deepening the industrialization, further carrying out marketization, transforming the kinetic energy of economic development, and comprehensively deepening the reform of the economic system.[4]

The Reagan Administration implemented the supply reform on the theoretical basis of then-popular supply-side economics and monetarism, and mainly adopted the supply management and structural adjustment policies of the supply-side economics and monetarism policy of stabilizing the money supply in terms of the reform measures. The supply-side structural reform proposed by the Chinese government is mainly based on the crux of the main economic problems in China at the present stage and the needs of deepening reform and further development of China's economy, rather than originating from a certain ready-made economic theory, and has nothing to do with Say's Law, supply-side economics and Reaganomics. In fact, since the reform and opening up, the major reform measures and important policy adjustments introduced by the Chinese government have all started from China's national conditions and actual needs at that time, rather than from a certain ready-made theory. China's reform and opening up, as well as the establishment of a socialist market economy based on the breakup of the planned economy, are unprecedented initiatives. This round of supply-side structural reform also has "Chinese style" or Chinese characteristics.

II. A basic analytical framework

China's supply-side structural reform is launched mainly against the background of excess production and excess capacity, which can be analyzed through the basic analytical framework for macroeconomics, namely, the aggregate demand–aggregate supply model (AD-AS Model).

The macroeconomic situation of a country or an economy can be measured by such indicators as aggregate output (GDP or GNI) and its growth, commodity prices and growth (inflation), employment rate or unemployment rate, foreign trade surplus or deficit, and the values of these indicators are the results of the interaction of various forces in the economy. These forces can be divided into two categories: one factor of affecting aggregate supply and the other factor of affecting aggregate demand. Therefore, we build a basic framework for analyzing macroeconomic operation, namely, the AD-AS Model.

Aggregate demand (AD) is the total amount of goods and services that all economic entities (economic sectors) in an economy willingly spend in a given period, which is a function of the aggregate price level (e.g., CPI) and also depends on monetary policy, fiscal policy, consumer and producer expectations and confidence, and other factors.

Structurally, AD consists of four components: household consumption, enterprise investment, government expenditure and net exports (the difference obtained from exports minus imports). According to China's statistical criteria, AD consists of three components: consumption (including household consumption and government consumption), investment (including enterprise investment and government investment) and net exports, which Chinese media call the "troika of the economy factors" driving AD.

Aggregate supply (AS) can be distinguished into actual AS and potential AS. The actual AS refers to the total amount of various goods and services that production units in an economy willingly produce and provide for the market in a given period, and also serves as a function of the overall price level. The actual AS level or scale depends on the potential AS and cost of production. The so-called potential AS refers to the maximum production capacity or potential aggregate output level of an economy, which depends on the technical level, the management level, the quantity and quality of resources (mainly labor resources and capital) and the efficiency of the economic system in a given period. The nature and condition of economic system affect the enthusiasm of consumers and producers, the efficiency of government, and the allocation of resources, thus affecting the productivity and the efficiency of resource allocation.

The equilibrium between AD and AS determines the macroeconomic condition of an economy: the actual level of aggregate output, commodity prices, employment or unemployment (see Figure 0.1).

In Figure 0.1, the vertical axis represents the overall price level P, and the horizontal axis represents the actual aggregate output y (e.g. GDP or GNI adjusted by a given price index); when AD and AS are in equilibrium, the price and aggregate output as determined by the intersection point of AD curve and AS curve are

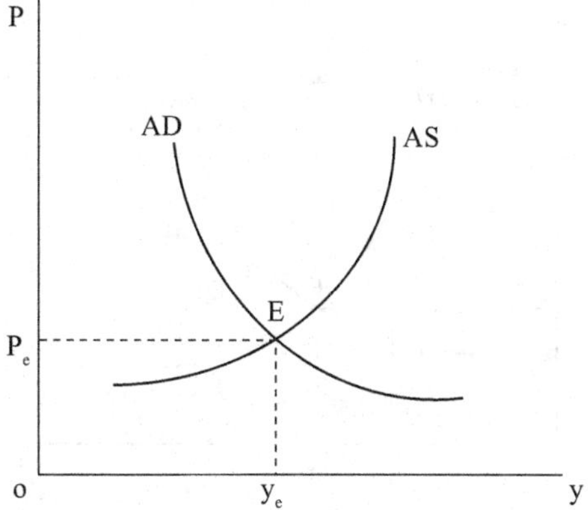

Figure 0.1 AD-AS Model

equilibrium price P_e and equilibrium output y_e, respectively, that is, the overall price level actually presented and aggregate output actually realized in an economy in a given period. There is no sign indicating the employment or unemployment condition in Figure 0.1. However, in a short term, the capital stock K is certain, and the aggregate output mainly serves as the function of employment quantity (N), $y = f(N, \bar{K})$); thus a certain aggregate output corresponds to a certain employment quantity, that is to say, the horizontal axis y implies the employment quantity N.

When the actual overall price level is higher than the equilibrium price in an economy, the quantity of various goods and services that all producers willingly produce and provide for the market will be greater than the quantity of such goods and services that all demanders willingly buy, that is, AS > AD, at which point the excess production will appear. In Figure 0.2, when $P_1 > P_e$, the quantity of AS y_b and the quantity of AD y_a are determined by point B on the AS curve and point A on the AD curve, respectively, at which point $y_b > y_a$, and $y_b - y_a$ represents the quantity of excess production, namely, the quantity of goods and services that cannot be sold at the prevailing price level (P_1). From a microcosmic view, such excess production is manifested as the unexpected increase in enterprise inventory, and the enterprise inventory exceeds the normal inventory level, that is to say, the production unit appears as excess inventory. On the contrary, if the actual price is lower than the equilibrium price, insufficient production or supply will appear in the economy, that is, the supply falls short of the demand, at which point the enterprise inventory is lower than the normal inventory level.

Over the longer term, the aggregate output of an economy is determined by actual factors (quantity and quality of resources, technology, systems, etc.) and is independent of changes in the overall price level, and thus the potential AS curve is a straight line perpendicular to the horizontal axis in the long run (see LS in

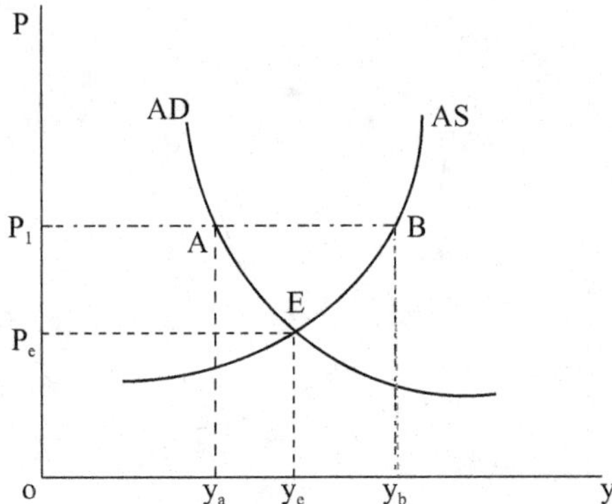

Figure 0.2 When AS is greater than AD, the excess production will appear

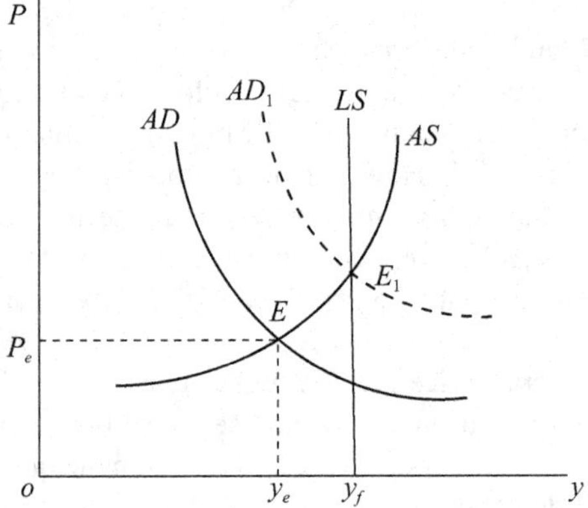

Figure 0.3 Potential output and actual output

Figure 0.3). When the equilibrium point at which AD and AS are in equilibrium in an economy is located on the left side of the potential AS curve (see point E in Figure 0.3), it suggests that the production capacity in the economy is underutilized. At this time, the total amount of goods and services actually produced is less than the total amount of goods and services that can be produced by the maximum production capacity of the economy, and there are some idle resources (mainly labor resources and capital) that fail to be utilized for actual production. Figure 0.3 shows that, under the existing conditions, the aggregate output that the economy can produce with its maximum production capacity is y_f, while the aggregate output that the economy actually produces is y_e. $y_f - y_e$ represents the quantity of goods and services that are not produced because resources are idle, that is, the idle production capacity. The potential aggregate output y_f is also called as the aggregate output of full employment or the natural rate level of output, so $y_f - y_e$ can also measure the quantity of involuntary unemployment. If the potential AS curve is located on the left of point E in Figure 0.3, that is to say the macro-economic equilibrium point E is located at a certain point on the right of LS curve, indicating that the production capacity in the economy is overutilized, and the economy is overheated, with the result that the inflation will appear.

$y_f - y_e$ is also known as "output gap". In theory, the output gap may be either positive or negative. When $y_f - y_e > 0$, it suggests that the production capacity (or resources) of the economy is underutilized; when $y_f - y_e < 0$, it means that the production capacity is overutilized. Generally, when the market economy develops to a certain stage, the normal state of economic operation is $y_f - y_e > 0$.

Strictly speaking, "overproduction or excess production" and "excess production capacity or excess capacity" are not two completely equivalent concepts. Excess production mainly refers to that the aggregate output (actual AS) produced at a certain price level is greater than the actual AD (effective demand), and some goods and services that have been produced are unsalable because they cannot be digested by the market; while excess capacity refers to excess production capacity, to be specific, part of the production capacity cannot be effectively utilized due to excessive product inventory or other reasons.[5]

Although excess production and excess capacity are not exactly the same, there are many connections between the two: (1) Excess production is often the prelude or introduction to excess capacity. The part of the output corresponding to the original AD level will be surplus due to the substantial reduction of effective demand caused by internal reasons or external shocks; with the unexpected increase of enterprise inventory (stock) and the stockpiling of unsold products, enterprises pursuing profit maximization will reduce output and employment, part of production capacity will be idle, and excess production will be transformed into excess capacity. (2) Both are the result or economic manifestation of the imbalance in quantity and the mismatch in structure between AS and AD. Excess production may be caused by insufficient effective demand, or by over-investment and/or over-production due to previous optimistic expectations of producers. Therefore, excess production is usually a relative surplus—compared with the effective demand level at that time, some goods are overproduced and become surplus. Excess capacity may be the result of reduced effective demand, or the growth of effective demand lagging behind the growth of production capacity, because the largest capacity is usually formed during the period of economic prosperity (the peak of the economic cycle); however, when the economy changes from the peak to the downside and the growth rate of effective demand slows down, some capacity will become surplus.

For the convenience of narration, this monograph sometimes refers to excess production and excess capacity as supply surplus.

This monograph distinguishes three cases of excess capacity.

In the first case, the production capacity is greater than the market demand capacity, where the potential production scale of a product is larger than the scale that the market can digest and absorb such products; that is, the potential production scale is larger than the scale of its effective demand. For example, assume that the domestic and foreign market demand for the steel of a country is 200 million tons every year, and this country can produce 300 million tons of steel every year; if all the 300 million tons of steel are produced, the 100 million tons that cannot be unsold will be deemed as excess capacity. This kind of excess capacity can be called "excess capacity in aggregate or scale".

In the second case, the supply and demand of some products used to be in balance, but now due to the changes of demand structure and demand quantity, the supply of some products exceeds the demand, leaving some of the production capacity of these products idle. For example, assume that an economy used to use 1 billion tons of coal, 1.2 billion cubic meters of natural gas and 300 million kWh of electricity every year, and the economic production capacity can meet such energy demand; however, with the change of the energy demand structure of the economy and society, 800 million tons of coal, 1.1 billion cubic meters of natural gas and 420 million kWh of electricity are needed now every year, which will lead to the surplus of the production capacity of some coal and natural gas and the shortage of electricity production capacity. This kind of excess capacity can be called "structural excess capacity".

In the third case, the quantity of goods and services actually produced in the economy is less than the quantity of goods and services that can be produced by the maximum production capacity (under the condition of full employment); that is, the actual output is less than the potential output or the natural rate level of output, while some production capacity is not utilized and some resources are left idle. This can be called "underutilized excess capacity".

Underutilization of production capacity[6] may be deemed as excess capacity from another point of view. In Figure 0.3, the reason why $y_e < y_f$ is that the quantity of effective demand is at point E on the AD curve, compared with the AD at point E, the production capacity of $y_f\, y_e\, (= y_f - y_e)$ cannot be utilized, that is, compared with the current quantity of effective demand, this part of production capacity becomes surplus. If the AD curve moves to AD_1 due to the change of policy or some exogenous factors, the effective demand at point E_1 will make the production capacity y_f to be fully utilized and the production capacity will disappear.

Excess capacity can be divided into absolute excess capacity and relative excess capacity: if a part of production capacity that should be eliminated by the market from the perspective of technical standards and economic efficiency principles is not eliminated, this part will be deemed as absolute excess capacity. The reason why such absolute excess capacity has not been eliminated often lies in the failure of market mechanism, weak market mechanism and improper or excessive government intervention, that is, the reasons can be found from the system factors. For example, for some reason, the government protects enterprises that have suffered losses for many years from bankruptcy, resulting in these enterprises becoming "zombie firms". Under the condition of strong and effective market mechanism, absolute excess capacity is difficult to exist for a long time. Relative excess capacity refers to such excess capacity that is unable to be effectively utilized due to the temporary contraction of effective demand or the slowdown of effective demand growth caused by some reason (such as the international financial crisis), while this part of capacity is reasonable and necessary in terms of technical standards and economic efficiency principles; when the market recovers and the demand turns strong, this part of capacity will be fully utilized. Therefore, relative excess capacity can also be called "temporary idle capacity". It can be seen that what we need to eliminate or clear is absolute excess capacity, but not all the excess capacity.

Excess capacity can sometimes be called excess capital. The so-called excess capital refers to the excessive capital stock accumulated in the economy according to a certain standard. The capital surplus here refers to the excess of physical capital or capital stock, not monetary capital, financial capital or investment capital (liquidity).

Production capacity is the ability of an economy to produce a certain kind of and a certain quantity of products by combining capital, labor, technology and other resources in a certain period of time. Therefore, the long-term production capacity of an economy is determined by the volume and technical content of capital, the quantity and quality of population or labor force, and institutional conditions, or mainly by the volume (or scale) of capital, especially the volume of fixed capital, under fixed technical and institutional conditions. This is not contradictory to the fact that the short-term aggregate output y is a function of employment quantity N. In the short term, the capital stock is fixed. How much the capital stock can be utilized and whether it can be fully utilized depends on the size of N. The size of short-term N is mainly determined by the effective demand, which determines the quantity of employment the existing capital is willing to use. Therefore, although labor is an active factor to promote capital, the amount of labor employed is determined by capital. Therefore, the scale of capital stock containing certain technology has corresponding production capacity; that is, if the technical level of capital is fixed, then the scale of capital stock corresponds to a production capacity, excess capacity means excess capital, and excess capital is a form of excess capacity.

According to the definition of Marxist political economy, excess capital refers to the excess capital that can no longer be multiplied at the general profit rate. Therefore, the gap between the profit rate obtained by capital and the general profit rate of the industry can be used to judge whether there is excess capital.

The methods of measuring excess capital in modern economics mainly include

1. The capital marginal product (physical flow) or capital marginal revenue (financial flow) is used to measure whether there is excess capital. If the capital marginal product or capital marginal revenue is zero or negative, these capitals are excess capital. From a macro perspective, if the growth rate of capital marginal product (marginal productivity of capital) is lower than the economic growth rate, it indicates that there is excess capital in the economy.

At present, the incremental capital-output ratio (ICOR) is usually used to judge whether the capital is excess or not. ICOR = Δ K/Δ Y, 1/ICOR = Δ Y/Δ K, where

ΔK and ΔY are the increase in capital (or investment) and increase in (aggregate) output, respectively. When ICOR increases, it indicates that the increase in capital required for increasing one unit of aggregate output is increasing, which means that the efficiency of investment decreases. At the same time, as ICOR increases, the average productivity Y/K of capital will decline, and the overall efficiency of capital will also decline, which indicates that some capital is excess.

2. In the Slow-Swan model,[7] when capital accumulation exceeds its Golden-rule level of capital,[8] capital accumulation is excessive, which is also called "dynamic inefficiency". When there is technological progress, the Slow-Swan model can be expressed by formula (1)

$$sf(k) = (\delta + n + g)\ k \tag{1}$$

Wherein s is the savings rate or accumulation rate, $f(k)$ is per capita income, so $sf(k)$ is per capita savings or per capita accumulation; δ is capital depreciation rate; n is population or labor force growth rate; g is technological progress rate or TFP growth rate; and k is per capita capital. Therefore, $(\delta + n + g)\ k$ represents per capita capital required in the presence of capital depreciation, population growth, and technological progress. If (1) is satisfied, the economy will achieve steady state. The so-called steady state means that the variable quantity of per capita capital stock (dk) is equal to zero, the per capita capital of efficient workers remains unchanged, and the economy reaches a long-run equilibrium state.[9]

Phelps proposed another method to judge whether capital is excess on the basis of Slow-Swan model in 1961.[10]

In a steady state, per capita consumption (c) of per efficient worker is equal to per capita income (y) minus investment (I), assuming that investment is equal to savings, namely, $I = S$. I.e.

$$c = y - I \tag{2}$$

According to the Slow-Swan model, formula (2) can be written as

$$c = f(k) - (\delta + n + g)k \tag{2A}$$

The Golden-rule level of capital with technological progress is defined as the state of maximizing the consumption of each efficient worker, namely, the maximum of formula (2A). Taking the first derivative of (2A) can obtain

$$MPK = \delta + n + g \tag{3}$$

Wherein MPK is the marginal output of capital.

Because the marginal output of capital determines the actual interest rate (r), Phelps put forward the following methods to judge excess capital: When the actual interest rate is less than the growth rate of investment with expenses and receipts on balance, that is, $r < (n + g + \delta)$; or if there is no depreciation ($\delta = 0$), $r < (n + g)$; or if there is neither depreciation nor technological progress ($\delta = g = 0$), $r < n$; under any of the previous three circumstances, the capital is excess.

3. According to AMSZ Criterion put forward by Abel and other scholars in1989, whether capital accumulation is excess or not is judged.[11] The main contents of AMSZ Criterion are as follows: (1) Under certain conditions, an economy is in a balanced growth path, so the long-run growth rate of an economy can be regarded as the growth rate of investment with expenses and receipts on balance (that is, the per capita increase in capital $dk = 0$). If the marginal product of capital in the balanced growth path is less than the long-run growth rate of the economy, it will show that the capital accumulation in the economy is excessive or the economy is dynamic-inefficient. (2) Under uncertainty, if the total return of capital in t period is less than the total investment, that is, the net return of capital is less than zero, and the capital is excess.

The AD-AS Model can be used not only to analyze the decision on equilibrium output and equilibrium employment quantity in a certain period, but also to analyze the dynamic process of economic growth or macroeconomic operation.

Economic growth is a macroeconomic problem analyzed from a very long-run perspective.[12] The process of economic growth is a dynamic process in which the production capacity of the economy (potential AS) is constantly growing. This process can also be described by the AD-AS Model.

Figure 0.4 describes the process of economic growth.

In the very long run, the amount of labor and capital in an economy will continue to increase with continuous improvement in technology, and the economic system will undergo adjustment and change. The changes of these supply-side factors will lead to the growth of potential output, that is, the potential AS or long-run AS (LS) curve will move parallel to the right. Figure 0.4 shows the potential output levels y_1, y_2 and y_3 of an economy for three different years in over 60 years from 1953 to 2015. In Figure 0.4, AS_1 and AD_1, AS_2 and AD_2, and AS_3 and AD_3 represent the AS curve and AD curve of the three years respectively, and E_1, E_2 and E_3 represent the short-run equilibrium points of the three years respectively. Because of the increase in cost of production, the short-run AS curve is constantly moving up; the expansion of production will cause the expansion of demand, so the AD curve is constantly moving up, which shows that the overall price level is constantly rising in the long run. One curve connecting E_1, E_2, and E_3 constitutes the long-run economic growth path (see the dotted line in Figure 0.4). For example, as far as China's economy is concerned, at constant prices, the GDP in 1953, 1978, and 2015 was RMB 82.44 billion, RMB 367.87 billion, and RMB 68,905.2 billion respectively, and the GDP in 2015 was 835.8 times and 187.3 times higher than that in 1953 and 1978 respectively! The per capita GDP in 1953, 1978, and 2015 was RMB 142, RMB 385, and RMB 49,992 respectively, and the per capita GDP in 2015 was 352 times and 129.8 times higher than that in 1953

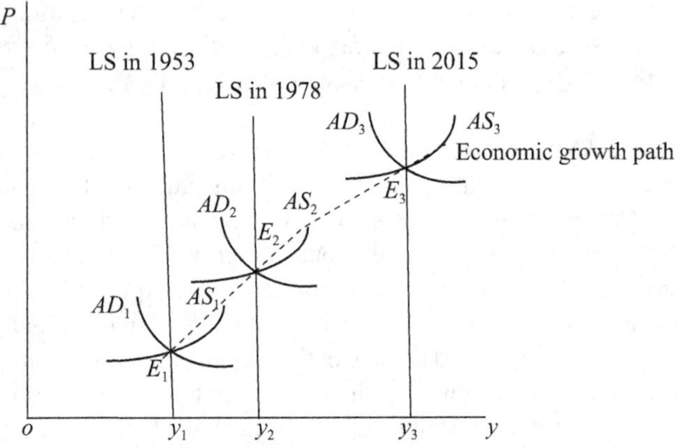

Figure 0.4 Supply is the main determinant of long-run economic growth

and 1978 respectively! The overall price level of China's economy is measured based on the consumer price index (CPI). If the CPI in 1978 and 2015 was 100 and 615.2 respectively, it will indicate that the commodity price level increases by about 5.2 times.

It is the result and manifestation of the imbalance between AD and AS (including quantity imbalance and structural imbalance) regardless of excess production or excess capacity, thus the AD-AS Model can be used for analysis. As for the reason for the imbalanced relationship between AD and AS, it is necessary to analyze the determinants of the demand side and supply side to find the answer. Both the determinants of the demand side and the determinants of the supply side are restricted and influenced by the current economic system and political system of an economy. Therefore, the imbalance of relationship between AD and AS of an economy needs to be rooted from the economic system.

Of course, there are limitations in using the AD-AS Model to analyze supply surplus, for which the main reasons are as follows: (1) We can only analyze supply surplus from the comparative relationship or gap between AD and AS in terms of quantity, but cannot conduct such analysis from the structure, that is to say, the mismatch between AD structure and AS structure may also lead to supply surplus, and this structural imbalance is manifested by the coexistence of supply surplus and insufficient production (supply). The nature and severity of structural imbalance cannot be directly judged by using the AD-AS Model. Our AD-AS Model can only analyze the excess capacity under the first and third circumstances mentioned earlier, but is not suitable for analyzing the excess capacity under the second circumstance. (2) Excess capacity can be divided into absolute excess capacity and relative excess capacity. The former is considered from the perspective of technical and economic efficiency principles. This part of capacity is excess, because it lags in technology, or it is uneconomical to use these capacities from the perspective of economic efficiency principle. Therefore, these capacities should be eliminated. For the latter, which is considered from the perspective of technical and economic efficiency principles, these capacities need to be retained, and are temporarily excess compared with the current economic downturn and sluggish market demand, but, when the economy picks up and the market demand increases, this part of capacities can be effectively utilized. Therefore, from the perspective of the AD-AS Model, we can only judge the supply surplus according to AS capacity > effective demand, but we cannot judge whether the excess capacity belongs to absolute excess capacity or relative excess capacity based on this model. (3) The system reasons behind supply surplus and structural imbalance cannot be directly analyzed by using the AD-AS Model.

Therefore, we also need to conduct additional analysis, such as system analysis and structural analysis, on the basis of the AD-AS analysis framework.

An analysis will be conducted by this logical way of thinking in the rest of this monograph.

Notes

1 Fang, F. Q. (2019). *Main Schools of Modern Western Economics*. 3rd Ed. Beijing: China Renmin University Press, 194–197.

2 In the 1950s and 1960s, the average annual rate of economic growth of the United States was 4.2%, while it dropped below 3% in the late 1970s; the annual inflation rate was 2%–3% in the 1960s, while it soared to over 8% in the late 1970s; the annual average (labor) productivity growth reached 3% in the first 20 years after the end of World War II, and then continuously declined to 1%, and began to show negative growth in 1977.

3 The Producer Price Index (PPI) of industrial producers in China's economy did not turn from negative to positive (on a year-on-year basis) until September 2016.

4 The content is about "cutting overcapacity, reducing excess inventory, deleveraging, lowering costs, and strengthening areas of weakness". The so-called "cutting overcapacity" is to eliminate outdated and excess capacity in the real economy; the so-called "reducing excess inventory" is to reduce the excessive product inventory of the enterprise, especially to reduce the excessive vacant commercial housing inventory in the real estate industry; the so-called "deleveraging" is to reduce the financial leverage ratio or liabilities level of the enterprise and government; the so-called "lowering costs" is to lower production and operation costs of the enterprise through tax and fee cuts, and to lower institutional transaction costs through deepening reform; the so-called "strengthening areas of weakness" is to strengthen and improve some weak links in the industrial chain, supply chain, and economic structure, especially some "troublesome" technologies and products.

5 "Production capacity" and "excess capacity" may involve an enterprise, an industry or an economy. This monograph mainly uses these two concepts at the industrial and macroeconomic levels, and occasionally at the enterprise level.

6 What people generally call "underutilization of production capacity" seems to mean that some capacity is left idle and the capacity utilization does not reach the maximum output under the given conditions. This is the understanding of excess capacity from the perspective of microeconomics. According to the theory of three stages of production or the theory of reasonable input interval for production factors in microeconomics, the aggregate output under the existing resources and technical conditions will reach the maximum at the turning point from the second stage to the third stage

of production. The production capacity is utilized insufficiently before this point, but excessively after this point. From the perspective of macroeconomics, it is impossible to have production capacity beyond the maximum (aggregate) output, that is, beyond the potential aggregate output, and it may only have the production capacity beyond the maximum consumption or the current effective demand scale. Therefore, from the perspective of AD-AS analysis framework, the underutilization of production capacity can be understood as excess capacity from another perspective. Assuming that the actual capacity utilization rate of an industry is only 63%, which is lower than the moderate capacity utilization rate of 79%–82% (American Standard), we can determine that the industry has excess capacity. However, we can also say that the capacity utilization of this industry is insufficient, because its capacity utilization rate does not reach 79%–82%. If the actual aggregate output of an economy is less than its potential total output, it means that some resources are left idle or the production capacity is underutilized, but this situation can also be understood as excess capacity—the existing production capacity exceeds the scale of effective demand, that is, from the current effective demand, some production capacity becomes surplus. Therefore, according to the excess capacity discussed in this monograph, there are two ways to solve excess capacity: one is to reduce capacity ("reduction of capacity"), and the other is to improve capacity utilization ("utilization of capacity"), both of which can make the actual utilization rate of capacity equal to or close to the optimal utilization rate of capacity, but the former is implemented by reduction, and the latter is by addition (increasing effective demand). It should be emphasized that "underutilization of production capacity" does not mean "insufficient capacity" or "capacity shortage", and "underutilization of production capacity" and "excess capacity" are not opposite concepts.

7 Solow, R. M. (1956). "A Contribution to the Theory of Economic Growth", *Quarterly Journal of Economics*, 65–94.

8 The Golden-rule level of capital (accumulation) is also called the optimal level of capital accumulation, which refers to the level of capital accumulation that can maximize the per capita consumption of social members.

9 Technological progress is first reflected in the improvement of labor efficiency (E) of laborers. If the number of laborers is L, ($L \times E$) is the number of efficient workers.

10 Phelps, E. S. (1961). "The Golden Rule of Accumulation: A Fable for Growthmen", *The American Economics Review*, 638–643.

11 Abel, A., Mankiw G., Summers, L., & Zeckhauser, R. (1989). "Assessing Dynamic Efficiency: Theory and Evidence", *The Review of Economic Studies*, 1–20.

12 The very long-run analysis focuses on the growth of production capacity of the economy by assuming that the available resources (natural resources, capital, and labor) and technology are variable. Both long-run analysis and short-run analysis assume that the available resources and technologies are certain, but the former holds that the actual aggregate output is mainly determined by the AS side, while the latter holds that the actual aggregate output is mainly determined by the AD side.

Part I

Cause

Why is it imperative to launch the supply-side structural reform? What has gone wrong with the supply side of China's economy? When did the supply surplus in China begin? What is the status of the surplus? More importantly, what are the main causes of the supply surplus? This part will provide answers to these questions.

DOI: 10.4324/9781003367000-2

1 The great transformation of China's economy

From supply shortage to supply surplus

From the comparative relationship between AD and AS, since 1949, China's economy has undergone a great transformation from acute shortage of supply to relative surplus of supply, which can be divided into four stages. Due to the changing relationship between AD and AS, the focuses of China's economic work and economic policy were different in these four stages: from 1949 to the 1980s, China's economy was in high shortage, with the focus of economic work and economic policy on "developing production and guaranteeing supply" during that period; from the late 1980s to the mid-1990s, the supply shortage gradually eased, and China's economy gradually realized the relative balance between AD and AS, with the focus of economic work and economic policy on "stability" and "growth" during that period; China's economy experienced a relative surplus of supply around 1998, and, until 2015, the implementation of "proactive fiscal policy", "expansion of domestic demand", and "steady growth" served as the main focus of economic work and economic policy; from 2015 to now, the overall pattern of macroeconomy is still relative surplus of supply, but the focus of economic work and economic policy has shifted to supply-side structural reform, and simultaneously attention are paid to demand-side management, with the focus of economic work and economic policy on "high-quality development".

I. From acute shortage of supply to relative surplus of supply

For a long time after the founding of the People's Republic of China in October 1949, China's economy has been a supply-shortage economy: AS < AD, with a high shortage of many consumer goods and means of production, and the government had to force a balance between AD and AS through the deployment of tickets and material supply plans.

China implemented a highly centralized planned-economy system shortly after the founding of New China; due to the high shortage of grain and consumer goods, the government had to implement an allotment system. In 1953, the Chinese government began to implement planned state purchase and planned supply of grain and other major agricultural products, i.e., the implementation of the system of state monopoly for purchase and marketing. On August 25, 1955, the State

DOI: 10.4324/9781003367000-3

Council promulgated the Interim Measures for Quantitative Supply of Grain in Small Towns, stipulating that grain rations for residents in small towns, grain for industry and commerce, and grain for livestock feed should be issued with supply vouchers according to the approved supply quantity, and units and residents must purchase grain with supply vouchers. According to these Interim Measures, the quantitative standards for grain ration supply in areas where rice serves as the staple food were as follows: for ordinary residents and children over 10 years old, they were provided with 11 to 13 kg per person per month, with the average not exceeding 12.5 kg; for staff of government agencies and organizations, employees of State-owned and private enterprises, shop assistants and other mental workers, they were provided with 12 to 14.5 kg per person per month, with the average not exceeding 14 kg; for heavy workers, they were provided with 17.5 to 22 kg per person per month, with the average not exceeding 20 kg. At the same time, the Interim Measures also stipulated that residents and the floating population should eat or buy rice or cooked wheaten food sold by the cooked food industry, and dried noodles, cut noodles, rice noodles, and rice cakes sold by the reproduction industry in small towns with local grain tickets (tickets for purchasing grain and grain products) or national grain tickets. Even by 1978, China's per capita share of grain was only 319 kg, and the grain supply was still in short supply. Urban residents still needed to buy grain with grain tickets for their meals.

Since the "three-year (1959–1961) natural disasters" had led to a significant reduction in production in China's agriculture and light industry, the supply of grain and general consumer goods became even more scarce. Therefore, since October 1961, tickets for purchasing manufactured goods (or consumer goods) for daily use were issued once again throughout China based on the population and wage standards, and more than 60 kinds of daily industrial products were included in the scope of tickets for purchase. In addition to grain tickets, there were also cloth tickets, sugar tickets, cooking oil tickets, paraffin tickets, meat tickets, salt tickets, soap tickets, match tickets, pastry tickets, and otherwise. Some regions even required that relevant tickets should be used to buy tofu, enamel cups, batteries, handkerchiefs, shoes, and electric bulbs.

There was also a serious shortage of many materials and means of production. Steel, timber, cotton, medicines, coal, electricity, petroleum, and diesel oil were often in short supply; many thermal power plants often had "no overnight coal", and water and electricity cuts were commonplace; many households still needed kerosene lamps for lighting at night. In the rural areas of central Anhui Province, where the author's hometown is located, electricity was not introduced until the mid-1980s, and many means of production had to be "rationed" through government planning departments because demand exceeded supply.

Although not all goods needed to be purchased with tickets, many of them were "unavailable" or "unaffordable" because they were in short supply. Before the 1990s, those who worked in the planning, commercial, material supply, grain supply, and food supply departments of the Chinese government were persons having "real power" and obtaining "benefits". Their jobs were enviable occupations, because they "enjoyed the benefits of a favorable position", and could buy goods in short supply that others could not buy. They became the targets, via whom people "made use of social relationships" or "secured advantages through influence" to buy goods in short supply. At that time, people "made use of social relationships" or "secured advantages through influence" mainly for the purpose of buying scarce materials and consumer goods.

In 1980s, with the great development of production brought about by the reform and opening up, the supply of raw materials, fuels, and other production materials became increasingly tight. As a result, the phenomenon of "buyers surging all over the place" emerged in China, and "official speculation" of illegal dealings of approval documents on scarce materials and "private speculation" of illegal dealings of scarce materials emerged.

The reform and opening up, which began in 1979, gradually relaxed the control of the planned-economy system over economic activities through system reform, opened up and enlivened the economy, introduced market mechanism, broke the "big-pot" distribution system, and reformed the distribution system, which greatly mobilized the enthusiasm of individuals, enterprises, and local governments, and released the vitality of the economic system, resulting in the rapid development of industrial and agricultural production and the economy.[1]

The implementation of the household contract responsibility system in rural areas had greatly mobilized farmers' enthusiasm for producing grain and other economic crops. From 1979 to 1984, China's agriculture experienced a "supernormal" growth, and the gross output value of agriculture grew at an average annual rate of 8.29%, which was the highest growth rate in history since 1950. The gross output of grain increased to 407.305 million tons in 1984 from 320.555 million tons in 1980, and the per capita output of grain increased to 392.84 kg in 1984 from 326.7 kg in 1980; the cotton output increased to 6,258,400 tons in 1984 from 2,207,350 tons in 1979, and the per capita output of cotton increased to 6.04 kg in 1984 from 2.28 kg in 1979; the output of oil-bearing crops increased to 15,784,200 tons in 1985 from 6,435,400 tons in 1979, and the per capita output of oil-bearing crops increased to 15 kg in 1985 from 6.64 kg in 1979; peanut output increased to 6,663,600 tons in 1985 from 2,822,400 tons in 1979; the gross output value of agriculture, forestry, animal husbandry, and fishery increased to RMB 401.301 billion in 1986 from RMB 169.76 billion in 1979. After just five years of reform, opening up and development, the shortage of grain and other agricultural products in China was greatly alleviated. In the early 1980s, the Chinese government issued a circular to abolish cloth tickets; since then, other tickets have been gradually cancelled, and the last coupon-grain coupon in China was cancelled in 1992.

With the focus of reform shifting to cities, price reform, state-owned enterprise reform, and investment and financing system reform are conducted in an all-round way, especially the reform of the production and operation system and mode of state-owned enterprises, and the rise of township enterprises, private enterprises and individual business; with the development of opening to the outside world, capital accumulation and technological progress have been promoted by introducing foreign capital, foreign advanced equipment and technology; these reform and opening-up measures have greatly improved the potential AS capacity and actual output of China's economy. By the 1990s, the circumstance of supply shortage gradually disappeared in China. With the abolition of grain tickets in 1992, the era of purchasing consumer goods with tickets in China finally came to an end. This showed that China's consumer market entered a state of relative balance between supply and demand from a state of supply shortage. In 1979, China's per capita GDP was only RMB 423 (about USD 272.90), but it had surpassed RMB 1,000 and reached RMB 1,123 (about USD 301.88) by 1987, and it had risen further to RMB 6,481 (about USD 781.79) by 1997.[2] China has completely broken the "vicious circle of poverty" and successfully leapt over the "poverty trap". Since the second half of 1997, China's macroeconomy had experienced a major historical transition from "supply shortage" to "relative surplus of supply". According to the annual survey on 600 major consumer goods conducted by China's Ministry of Commerce, the AS and AD in the Chinese consumer market were generally in balance from 1995 to the first half of 1997, but, by the second half of 1997, nearly 32% of the major consumer goods in the Chinese market were oversupplied. The outbreak of Southeast Asian financial crisis in the summer and autumn of 1997 caused a strong external impact on China's economy, and the shrinking export market worsened the relative excess production of China's economy. After 1999, the surplus rate of consumer goods in China's market soared to over 80% (see Table 1.1). Since then, China's economic development has been plagued by

Table 1.1 Changes in supply and demand of (600) goods in China's consumer market (%) (1995–2004)

Year	*Demand exceeding supply Proportion of goods*	*Balance between supply and demand Proportion of goods*	*Supply exceeding demand Proportion of goods*
First half of 1995	14.4	67.3	18.3
Second half of 1995	13.3	72.3	14.6
First half of 1996	10.5	74.5	15.0
Second half of 1996	6.2	84.7	9.1
First half of 1997	5.3	89.4	5.3
Second half of 1997	1.6	66.6	31.8
First half of 1998	0.0	74.2	25.8
Second half of 1998	0.2	66.1	33.8
First half of 1999	0.2	27.6	72.2
Second half of 1999	0.0	20.0	80.0
First half of 2000	0.0	21.6	78.4
Second half of 2000	2.0	18.4	79.6
First half of 2001	0.2	19.3	80.5
Second half of 2001	0.0	17.0	83.0
First half of 2002	0.0	13.7	86.3
Second half of 2002	0.0	13.0	87.0
First half of 2003	0.0	14.5	85.5
Second half of 2003	0.0	15.2	84.8

Source: Annual survey on supply and demand of 600 major consumer goods conducted by China's Ministry of Commerce

insufficient effective demand. This led to a great shift in the Chinese government's economic work and macroeconomic policy thinking—from the policy tone of "developing production and guaranteeing supply" implemented during the period of the Anti-Japanese War (1931–1945) to the policy tone of "expanding domestic demand and stabilizing (economic) growth"; that is to say, the emphasis changed from promoting supply increase to promoting demand growth, and the focus changed from the supply side to the demand side.

A large surplus of supply in the consumer market led to a part of the production capacity of enterprises being idle and a part of the workforce unemployed; that is, excess production in the economy led to excess capacity of enterprises. According to a survey conducted by the relevant authorities at the time on the production capacity of 67 major industrial products in key enterprises nationwide, in 1997, 33.3% of key enterprises had an operating rate above 80%, 32.8% of key enterprises had an insufficient operating rate (60%–80%), and 33.9% of key enterprises had a serious insufficient operating rate (below 60%); in 1998, affected by the insufficient market consumption demand, the low operating rate of enterprises further deteriorated.[3] In other words, only one third of industrial products had normal capacity utilization rate, while two thirds of industrial products had insufficient capacity utilization rate due to relative surplus.

In response to the impact of the Southeast Asian financial crisis on China's economy, the Chinese government has introduced its first proactive fiscal policy aimed at expanding domestic demand. On August 29, 1998, the Fourth Session of the Standing Committee of the Ninth National People's Congress deliberated and adopted the central budget adjustment plan. Such a plan adjusted the deficit in the central budget to RMB 96 billion (RMB 56 billion in 1997), and issued RMB 100 billion of long-term treasury bonds for construction, together with an additional bank loan of RMB 100 billion. All of these amounts were used for infrastructure construction. From 1998 to 2004, the Chinese government issued a total of RMB 910 billion of long-term treasury bonds for construction, and major state-owned commercial banks issued corresponding amounts of matching funds; the People's Bank of China has reduced deposit and loan interest rates seven times and lowered the legal deposit–reserve ratio twice, increasing the money supply and credit scale; the Chinese government terminated the welfare housing system that had been implemented for more than 40 years, implemented the monetization of housing distribution, opened up the real estate market, and implemented the reform of education and the medical system at the same time; it also reformed the foreign trade system, opened up the import and export autonomy of foreign trade, and allowed private enterprises to operate their own exports. These reforms and initiatives have effectively pulled the "troika of the economy factors" on the demand side of China's economy, greatly eased the relative excess production of China's economy, and enabled China's economy to recover quickly, with economic (GDP) growth rate increasing from 7.7% in 1999 to 8.5% in 2000 and 8.3% in 2001. After China became a member of the WTO in 2001, China's international market space was greatly expanded, and China's import and export costs were reduced, which strongly promoted the development of China's foreign trade. The expansion and sustained growth of external demand allowed the potential AS capacity of China's economy to be fully utilized, and the economic growth had made great strides: in 2002, economic growth exceeded 9% (9.1%). From 2003 to 2007, China's economy grew at an annual rate of more than 10%, with the growth rate in 2007 reaching a very high 14.2%.

In the first half of 2007, the subprime mortgage crisis broke out in the United States, which was called a "financial tsunami" because of its size and fierceness, and subsequently evolved into an international financial crisis. After ten years from the outbreak of the Southeast Asian financial crisis, China's economy once again suffered a major external shock. This round of impact hit the external demand of China's economy first, and then hit the domestic demand of China's economy, causing the demand-side "troika of the economy factors" to slow down at the same time, thus highlighting the excess production as the main contradiction of China's economy.

To cope with the impact of the international financial crisis, stabilize economic growth and stabilize employment, China has implemented a new round of proactive fiscal policy aimed at expanding domestic demand, the main element of which is the RMB 4 trillion investment expansion plan introduced by the State Council in November 2008.[4] This expansion plan focuses on the construction of major infrastructure, such as railways, highways, airports and water conservancy, and the transformation of urban power grids, with an investment of about RMB 1.5 trillion, accounting for 37.5% of RMB 4 trillion investment.

This expansion plan has an obvious, quick and good effect on the recovery of China's economy: China's GDP growth rate rebounded rapidly from a low of 6.2% in the first quarter of 2009 to 8% in the second quarter, and continued to rise to 10.4% in the third quarter (see Figure 1.1a).

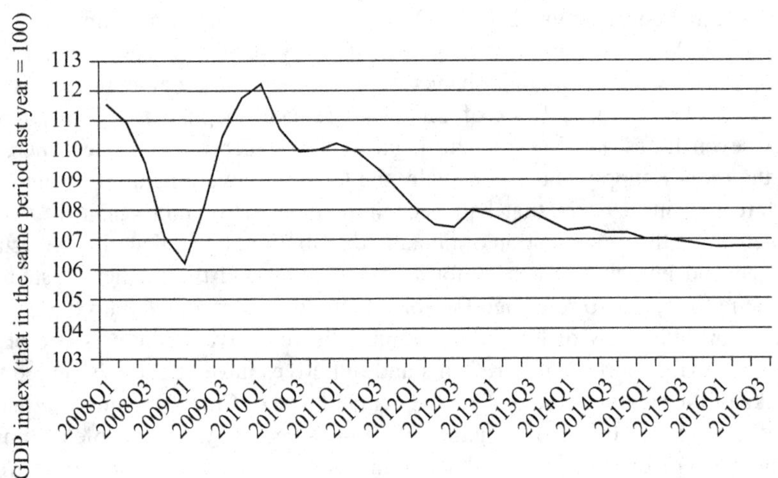

Figure 1.1a China's economic growth (first quarter of 2008–fourth quarter of 2016)

Source: China Statistical Yearbook (2017) compiled by the National Bureau of Statistics of China

II. China's economy stepping in a downward cycle

After peaking at 12.2% in the first quarter of 2010, China's GDP growth rate began a downward cycle, falling below two important hurdles, 10% and 8%, and even below 7% (6.9%) in the third quarter of 2015, with GDP growth of 6.8% and 6.0% in 2016 and 2019 respectively. (See Figure 1.1a and Figure 1.1b).

As economic growth continues to decline, excess production has gradually evolved into excess capacity. The economic downturn that has lasted for many years has made the problem of excess capacity bigger and more serious, just as the sea level continues to lower, making more and more rocks expose to the surface of water and become bigger and bigger.

In which industries does excess capacity in China's economy appear? What is the severity of the surplus? It seems that answers to aforesaid questions are not very clear, and there is no uniform statement from Chinese academic circles and government authorities. However, the following two sets of data should be authoritative.

One set of data is sourced from a special survey research on the excess capacity conducted by a research group, the Development Research Center of the State Council of China in the second half of 2013. The research group conducted field research in provinces and municipalities directly under the Central Government, including Hebei, Shandong, Henan, Zhejiang, Jiangsu, Shanghai, and Beijing, and obtained the following data and relevant information: In 2012, China's steel capacity reached about 1 billion tons, with the output of 720 million tons, accounting for about 46% of the global output, and the capacity utilization rate of 72%; in 2012, China's cement production capacity reached 3.07 billion tons, with the output of 2.21 billion tons and the capacity utilization rate of 73.7%. If

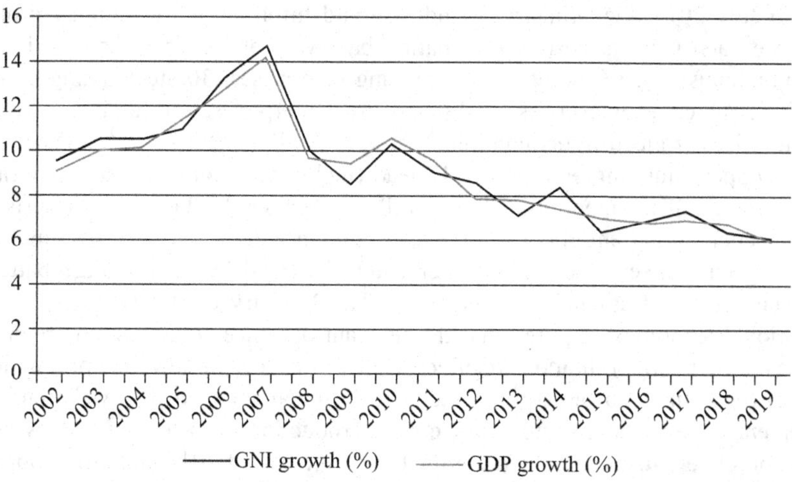

Figure 1.1b China's economic growth (2002–2019)

Source: China Statistical Yearbook (2021) compiled by the National Bureau of Statistics of China

we consider that about 290 new dry-process cement production lines are under construction, after all of them are completed and put into operation, the cement capacity will reach 3.63 billion tons, and the capacity utilization rate will drop further; in 2012, China's electrolytic aluminum output was 19.88 million tons, with the capacity of 27.65 million tons and the capacity utilization rate of only 71.9%, and the capacity of the electrolytic aluminum industry was still increasing rapidly; in 2012, the capacity of flat glass industry was 1.04 billion weight cases, with the output of 760 million weight cases, accounting for about 50% of the global output, and an average capacity utilization rate of 73.1%. If all of the 32 float lines under construction are completed, the total capacity will reach 1.13 billion weight cases, and the capacity utilization rate will further decline. In 2012, the capacity of China's shipbuilding industry was about 80.1 million deadweight tons, with the completion of ships of 60.21 million deadweight tons and the capacity utilization rate of 75.2%. However, if the capacity with no output for more than three years and some capacity transferred to maritime work and ship repair are included, the capacity of the shipbuilding industry can reach 120 million deadweight tons, and the capacity utilization rate will be even lower.[56]

The other set of data is sourced from the Ministry of Industry and Information Technology of the Chinese government in charge of industrial production. The 2015 catalogue of key industries to eliminate backward and excess capacity published in the Circular on Effectively Carrying out the Work Related to Elimination of Backward and Excess Capacity (GXTCYH [2015] No. 900) issued by the Ministry of Industry and Information Technology on December 28, 2015 included 14 industries: ironmaking, steelmaking, coke, ferroalloy, calcium carbide, electrolytic aluminum, copper smelting, lead smelting, cement, flat glass, papermaking, leather making, printing and dyeing, and lead storage battery.

In July 2014, the Ministry of Industry and Information Technology promulgated a list of enterprises eliminating backward and excess capacity in 15 major industries, including 44 ironmaking enterprises, 30 steelmaking enterprises, 44 coke enterprises, 164 ferroalloy enterprises, 40 calcium carbide enterprises, 7 electrolytic aluminum enterprises, 43 copper (including secondary copper) smelting enterprises, 12 lead (including secondary lead) smelting enterprises, 381 cement (clinker and mill) enterprises, 15 flat glass enterprises, 221 papermaking enterprises, 27 leather making enterprises, 107 printing and dyeing enterprises, 4 chemical fiber enterprises and 39 lead storage battery (polar plate and assembly) enterprises.[7] The Ministry of Industry and Information Technology required that the relevant provinces (autonomous regions and municipalities) should take effective measures to shut down the production lines (equipment) of enterprises included in the announced list by the end of September 2014, and should ensure such production lines (equipment) would be completely dismantled and eliminated by the end of 2014 and might not be transferred to other regions.

The aforementioned can be regarded as industries and relevant enterprises with excess capacity confirmed by the Chinese government.

III. Decline in the efficiency of capital utilization

As mentioned earlier, supply surplus means excess capital, which is manifested by a decline in the capital utilization efficiency.

By measuring the changes in incremental capital–output ratio (ICOR), we can see the changes in investment effect or capital efficiency in China's economy since the 21st century.

Figure 1.2 shows the changes in ICOR in China's economy from 1996 to 2015, wherein ΔY represents the annual increase in gross national income (GNI) and ΔK represents the annual increase in gross fixed capital formation (GFCF). It can be seen that the ICOR in China's economy has risen since the international financial crisis in 2008, with the ICOR in 2008–2013 significantly higher than that in 2005–2007.

Looking at Figures 1.2, it seems that the capital efficiency in China's economy has not changed much. This may be because Figure 1.2 reflects the changes in ICOR for China's economy as a whole. The ICOR in some industries (such as some industries in the secondary industry) may rise, while the ICOR in other industries (such as some industries in the tertiary industry) may decline. Their rises and declines cancel each other out, making the comprehensive ICOR change insignificant.

If we look at the industrial sector alone, the changes in ICOR are somewhat surprising.

Figure 1.3 shows the ICOR of China's industrial sector, wherein ΔY represents is the annual industrial added value and I represents the annual investment in the industrial sector. There are no indicators for "total industrial investment" or "gross capital formation in the industrial sector" in the national data provided by the National Bureau of Statistics. To represent the total industrial investment, the

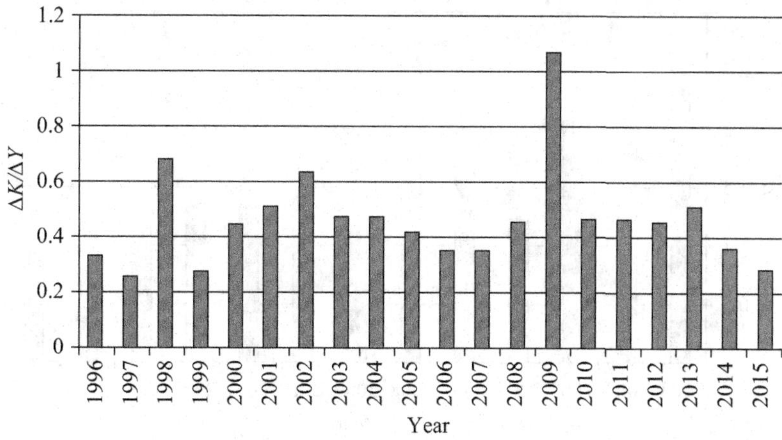

Figure 1.2 ICOR in China's economy (1996–2015)

Source: Relevant data of the China Statistical Yearbook (2016) compiled by the National Bureau of Statistics

author uses the data table of "fixed assets investment in different industries" in the national data by summing up "total investment in fixed assets in mining industry", "total investment in fixed assets in manufacturing industry", and "total investment in fixed assets in electricity, gas, and water production and supply industries".

From Figure 1.3, we know that the ICOR in the industrial sector has been rising continuously since the 21st century. The industrial ICOR in 2015 (0.93) is 2.51 times higher than that in 2003 (0.37); that is to say, to obtain the same industrial added value, the investment spent in 2015 is 2.51 times higher than that spent in 2003!

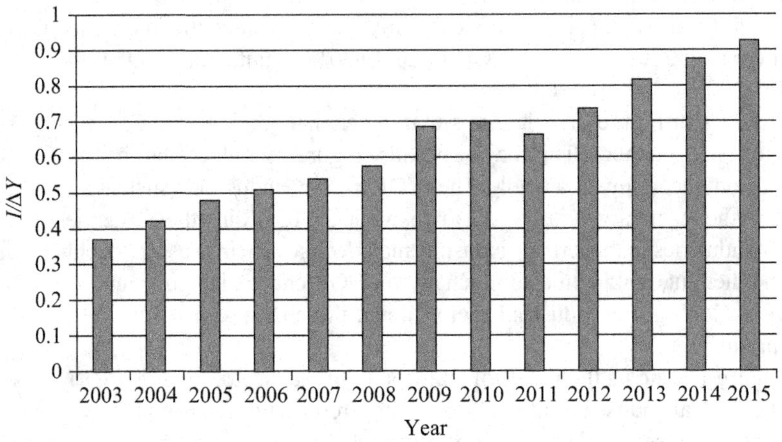

Figure 1.3 ICOR of China's industrial sector (2003–2015)

Source: "2003–2015 National Data" issued by the National Bureau of Statistics

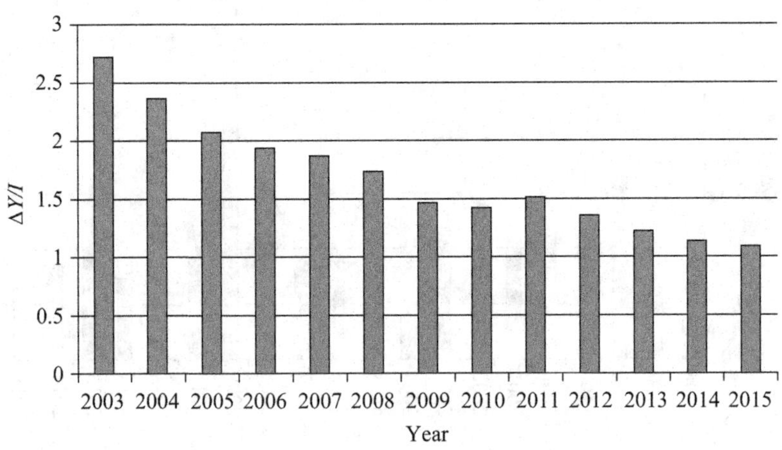

Figure 1.4 Investment effect of China's industrial sector (2003–2015)

Source: Relevant data of the *China Statistical Yearbook* (2016) compiled by the National Bureau of Statistics

Figure 1.4 reflects the changes in the effect of investment in the industrial sector from 2003 to 2015, that is, the changes in $\Delta Y/I$. During this period, the effect of industrial investment is declining: if the industrial investment of RMB 1 could bring RMB 2.71 of industrial added value in 2003, the industrial investment of RMB 1 would only bring RMB 1.07 of industrial added value by 2015!

Figures 1.3 and 1.4 confirm why China's excess capacity mostly occurs in some industries and enterprises in the industrial sector.

The aforementioned is the background under which Xi Jinping, General Secretary of the CPC Central Committee, put forward "strengthening supply-side structural reform" at the 11th meeting of the Central Leading Group on Financial and Economic Affairs on November 10, 2015.

Notes

1 Unlike many western market economy countries, local governments in China have been one of the leading forces or subjects of economic development since the establishment of the People's Republic of China.

2 The annual average exchange rates for RMB against USD in 1979, 1987 and 1997 were RMB 1.55, RMB 3.72, and RMB 8.29 per USD, respectively.

3 Jin, R. Q. (2006). *Scientific Development and Fiscal Policy in China*. Beijing: China Financial and Economic Publishing House, 78.

4 From the fourth quarter of 2008 to the end of 2010, China's central government arranged RMB 1.18 trillion of investment by increasing central capital construction investment, central government fund investment, other central government public investments, and post-disaster reconstruction investment, plus RMB 2.82 trillion of local government supporting and social investments, forming an investment scale of RMB 4 trillion.

5 Research Group of "Policy Research on Further Resolving Excess Capacity", the Development Research Center of the State Council. Research on the Characteristics, Risks and Countermeasures of Current Excess Capacity in China—Based on Field Research and Micro-data Analysis. Management World, 2015 (4): 3.

6 This research group believed that although many studies usually adopted 75% or 79%–82% as the standard of reasonable capacity utilization rate, research found that there are great differences in reasonable capacity utilization rate among different industries. For example, for flat glass, steelmaking, and ironmaking industries, their production processes are so unique that their whole production line cannot be stopped easily once it starts the production, otherwise huge economic losses will occur. Therefore, the industries believe that the reasonable capacity utilization rate of flat glass should be about 90%, while that of steel industry should be about 80%–85%. Thus it can be judged that the excess capacity in these industries is quite serious.

7 Ironmaking, steelmaking, coke, ferroalloy, calcium carbide, electrolytic aluminum, copper (including secondary copper) smelting, lead (including secondary lead) smelting, cement (clinker and mill), flat glass, papermaking, leather making, printing and dyeing, chemical fiber, and lead storage battery (polar plate and assembly) industries.

2 Cause of excess capacity

Demand analysis

China's excess capacity is the result of many causes that have accumulated for a long time. These causes can be generally divided into demand-side causes, supply-side causes, and system causes. This chapter starts with an analysis on the demand-side causes.

I. Objectively looking upon the "RMB 4 trillion" investment expansion plan

It seems simplistic and impractical to entirely impute excess capacity to the RMB 4 trillion investment expansion plan, which was implemented by the Chinese government from the fourth quarter of 2008. In fact, as early as around 2005, there was massive and serious excess capacity in China's economy.

On May 8, 2006, China Economic Weekly published an article co-written by Wu Zaiping and Zhu Jianfeng with the title of "Considerable Excess Capacity and Low Capacity Utilization Rate in China's 13 Industries". The article revealed the excess capacity situation in China's 13 industries as follows:

Steel industry: In 2005, the total capacity was 470 million tons, but only 370 million tons were produced, with an excess capacity of 100 million tons. At present, there are 70 million tons of production capacity under construction and 80 million tons of proposed production capacity.

Electrolytic aluminum industry: In 2005, the total capacity of electrolytic aluminum industry was 10.3 million tons, with only 6.02 million tons of domestic demand, 1.02 million tons of external demand, and 3.26 million tons of idle capacity. At present, there are 11 projects under construction and 14 proposed projects.

Ferroalloy industry: By the end of September 2005, the capacity was 22.13 million tons. After the projects under construction and proposed are put into production, the total capacity will reach 24.97 million tons. However, the domestic demand in 2005 was only 12 million tons, and the current operating rate is only 40%.

Coke industry: In 2005, the national coke output was 243 million tons, domestic demand and external demand totaled 232 million tons, and the capacity

DOI: 10.4324/9781003367000-4

exceeded the demand by 11 million tons. At present, there are 240 new and expansion projects and 390 coke ovens in China, and the production capacity will increase by about 100 million tons.

Calcium carbide industry: In 2005, the national calcium carbide output was 10.426 million tons, and the average operating rate of domestic calcium carbide manufacturers was maintained at about 60%. At present, the projects under construction and proposed have a capacity of 12 million tons to 22 million tons.

Automobile industry: In 2005, the output of automobiles was nearly 8 million units, while the sales volume was only 5.7 million units. At present, there are more than 2 million units in surplus. In case of no restriction on the investment, the automobile capacity at the end of "the 11th Five-Year Plan" period will reach 20 million units, more than double the actual demand.

Copper smelting industry: The total construction capacity reached 2.05 million tons by the end of 2005, 1.3 times that of the end of 2004. It is estimated that the capacity will reach 3.7 million tons by the end of 2007, far exceeding the national copper concentrate guarantee capacity and the quantity of copper concentrate that may be provided by the international market. The copper smelting industry will go the way of electrolytic aluminum, provided that the macroeconomic control fails to be strengthened in a timely manner.

Cement industry: In 2005, the cement capacity was 1.287 billion tons, and the output was 1.038 billion tons, with the remaining capacity of 249 million tons.

Textile industry: Among the 84 kinds of textiles and garments monitored by the Ministry of Commerce, the supply of 86.9% of the goods exceeds demand. By the end of 2005, the comprehensive textile processing capacity was surplus by 15%–20%.

Electric power industry: By the end of 2005, the installed power generation capacity in China was 510 million kilowatts. At present, the installed power generation capacity of projects under construction are about 200 million kilowatts. It is estimated that by the end of 2006, the total installed capacity will reach nearly 600 million kilowatts, and power surplus will appear in some areas; By the end of 2007, the installed capacity will be surplus by 10%.

Coal industry: In 2005, the output of raw coal reached 2.19 billion tons which had already been close to China's projected coal consumption target of 2.2 billion tons in 2010. At present, another 400 million tons of capacity is under construction.

Container industry: At present, the capacity of dry cargo containers has reached 4.5 million TEU (i.e. Twenty-foot Equivalent Unit), while the annual demand is only 2.4 million TEU. The supply–demand ratio is as high as 2:1. The previously given capacity is expected to reach 5.8 million TEU in 2007, and the excess capacity will be even more serious.

Mobile phone industry: In 2005, China's mobile phone capacity has reached more than 500 million units, while the domestic market volume is only about 70 million to 80 million units a year, and it is difficult to have another large growth.

As early as March 12, 2006, the State Council of China issued the Circular on Stepping up the Promotion of the Restructuring for Industries with Excess Capacity (Guo Fa [2006] No. 11), requiring relevant ministries and commissions under the State Council and local governments to step up the restructuring for industries with excess capacity. The Circular emphasizes:

> At present, the reckless investment and inefficient expansion of certain industries have created excess capacity, which has quickly become a major economic problem. If not resolved in a timely manner, this problem may further aggravate the underlying conflict arising from the irrationality of the industry structure and affect the fast, sustainable, balanced, and sound development of the economy.

Judging from the Circular issued by the State Council, we learnt that the condition of excess capacity and economic structure imbalance at that time was as follows: The obvious excess capacity has already appeared in steel, electrolytic aluminum, calcium carbide, ferroalloy, coke, automobile and other industries. As for the cement, coal, electric power, and textile industries, although production and demand has, for the moment, struck a balance, the scale of projects under construction is so large that the potential for excess capacity is there. Under the current circumstances, some regions and enterprises still insist on initiating new projects in the aforementioned sectors; thus, without a doubt, the inherent conflict of production capacity outstripping demand will be further aggravated. Moreover, besides the gross overproduction in these sectors, they are exhibiting other serious problems including irrationality in the enterprise organizational structure, industrial technical structure, and product configuration. Currently, the unfortunate consequences stemming from the excess capacity of some sectors are visible in price drops, increase of inventory, decrease of profit margin, and increase of losses. If this situation is allowed to continue, the root conflict of resource scarcity will worsen, the problem of structural imbalance will be aggravated, and enterprise bankruptcy as well as unemployment will significantly increase. These problems must be resolved.

Based on these judgments, the State Council in the Circular put forward eight key measures to promote the restructuring for industries with excess capacity: "Effectively preventing the resurgence of fixed asset investment", "strictly controlling newly initiated projects", "eliminating outdated production capacity", "promoting technological transformation", "accelerating mergers and restructuring", "strengthening the coordination between credit, land, construction, environmental protection, and security policies and industrial policies", "deepening the reform in such areas as administrative management, the investment system, pricing mechanisms, and mechanism for withdrawing from the market", and "improving the information disclosure system for industries".

It can be seen that excess capacity appeared before the RMB 4 trillion investment expansion plan.

So how do we view the RMB 4 trillion investment expansion plan today? What responsibility should it bear for the supply surplus after the implementation of this plan?

At that time, the RMB 4 trillion investment expansion plan was an emergency measure and a rescue plan. Its purpose was to save economic growth and employment, stabilize the economy and stabilize the society by vigorously expanding domestic demand.

Judging from the economic trend at that time, it is necessary to introduce the RMB 4 trillion investment expansion plan.

The subprime mortgage crisis in the United States and the subsequent international financial crisis first impacted China's exports, which made the growth of external demand in China's economy drop sharply and quickly fall into negative growth. China's gross export value had been growing in double digits monthly on a year-on-year basis until November 2008, with 21.5% and 19.2% growth in September and October 2008, respectively, but the export growth rate dropped sharply to −2.2% in November 2008, after which the negative export growth lasted for 13 consecutive months until November 2009. Specifically, the export growth rate dropped sharply to −26.4% in May 2009 (see Figure 2.1). In 2009, China's gross export and net export decreased by RMB 1,836.525 billion and

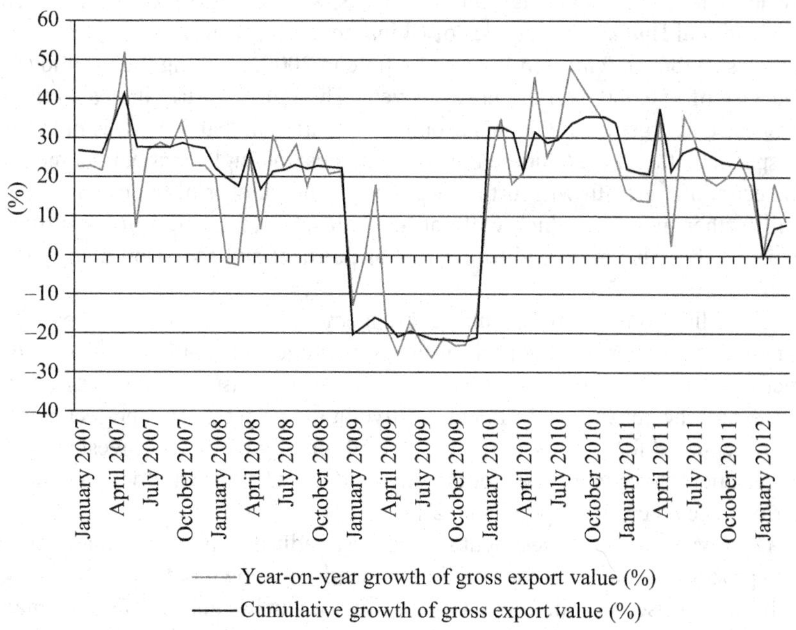

Figure 2.1 China's export growth (January 2007–March 2012)

Source: *China Statistical Yearbook* (2013) compiled by the National Bureau of Statistics of China

RMB 745.709 billion respectively compared with that in 2008, accounting for 5.26% and 2.14% of China's GDP in 2009 respectively. In 2009, China's exports decreased by more than the total of GDP of Shanghai and Gansu Province in that year![1] These goods that cannot be exported to the international market have to be returned to the domestic market for sale, thus greatly aggravating the excess production and the imbalance between AS and AD in China's domestic market.

The direct result of excess production is the decline in economic growth, because the surplus products cannot realize their value, and the rational response of profit-oriented enterprises is to reduce or even stop the production of such surplus products. The year-on-year growth of China's GDP dropped from a high of 15% in the second quarter of 2007 all the way down to 6.4% in the first quarter of 2009, a drop of 134.4%! This is the lowest growth rate since China established quarterly GDP accounting in 1992; the added value growth of the secondary industry was 15.6% in the second quarter of 2007 and fell to 5.8% in the first quarter of 2009, a drop of 169%! The growth of industrial added value decreased from 16% in the second quarter of 2007 to 4.6% in the first quarter of 2009, a drop of 247.8%!

As economic growth continues to decline, the number of unemployed people is increasing. According to the *Blue Book of China's Society* released by the Chinese Academy of Social Sciences on December 16, 2008, the urban unemployment rate in China has climbed to 9.4%. Although the State Council required state-owned enterprises not to lay off employees, according to the data released by the National Bureau of Statistics of China, the number of unemployed people in China still topped 9 million for the first time in 2009, reaching 9.21 million, a net increase of 350,000 over the previous year. These data clearly indicated the seriousness and urgency of China's economic situation at that time. It is not difficult to speculate that if the Chinese government does not implement bailout measures, the economic growth will further decline and the number of unemployed people will further increase, which will not only cause more idle resources and excess capacity, but also may lead to a series of political and social problems such as social unrest.

According to the initial planning arrangement for the RMB 4 trillion of government investment, it focused on the construction of major infrastructure, the recovery and reconstruction after the great flood disaster in southern China in 2008, and the construction of people's livelihood projects. This project construction accounted for 81.75% of the RMB 4 trillion of government investment. Such government investment was not directly made in what we call today sectors with serious excess capacity (see Table 2.1).

The RMB 4 trillion investment structure was adjusted in the actual implementation process, and its actual expenditure structure is shown in Figure 2.2.

It is easy to see that the RMB 4 trillion investment has not been directly made in industries with excess capacity. At the press conference held by the Third Session of the 11th National People's Congress on the morning of March 6, 2010, Zhang Ping, the then–Director of the National Development and Reform Commission, even said that not a penny of the RMB 4 trillion investment went to industries

Table 2.1 Key directions of the RMB 4 trillion investment

Key investment direction	*Capital calculation*
Low-rent housing, shantytowns transformation, and other indemnificatory housing	About RMB 400 billion
Rural water, electricity, roads, gas, housing, and other livelihood projects and infrastructure	About 370 billion
Railroad, highway, airport, water conservancy, and other major infrastructure construction and urban grid renovation	About RMB 1.5 trillion
Development of medical and health, education, culture, and other social undertakings	About RMB 150 billion
Energy conservation, emission reduction, and ecological projects	About RMB 210 billion
Independent innovation and structural adjustment	About 370 billion
Post-disaster recovery and reconstruction	About RMB 1 trillion

Source: Portal website of China's central government, www.gov.cn, March 6, 2009

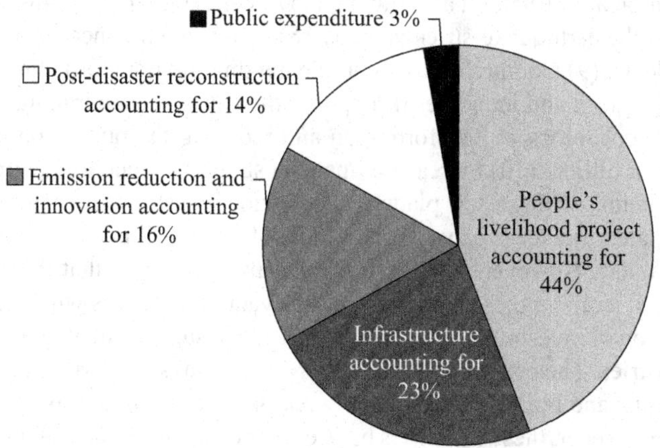

Figure 2.2 RMB 4 trillion investment structure

Source: Remarks by Zhang Ping, the then–Director of the National Development and Reform Commission, at the press conference held by the Third Session of the 11th National People's Congress on the morning of March 6, 2010

featuring high energy and resource consumption and serious pollution and with excess capacity, or went to investments such as real estate and land purchase.

So is there any relationship between the RMB 4 trillion investment and the subsequent excess capacity? Is there any problem with the RMB 4 trillion investment? The author's answers to the aforesaid two questions are affirmative.

In order to cope with the impact of the international financial crisis on China's economy, the Chinese government has not only introduced a plan for increasing the government investment by RMB 4 trillion, but also launched a "policy package" of which the RMB 4 trillion investment is only one element. The RMB

4 trillion investment expansion plan and the Ten Plans for Expanding Domestic Demand and the Plan for Invigorating Ten Key Industries issued by the Chinese government in 2009, together with loose fiscal and monetary policies, constitute the policy mix for the Chinese government to cope with the impact of the international financial crisis, ensure growth, expand domestic demand, adjust structure, and promote development. At that time, the main purpose of increasing government investment expenditure of RMB 4 trillion was to expand domestic demand and invigorate industries. Therefore, the RMB 4 trillion investment effect should be analyzed in combination with the implementation effect of the ten plans for expanding domestic demand and the plan for invigorating ten key industries.

The ten plans for expanding domestic demand include: (1) Accelerating the construction of government-subsidized housing projects. (2) Accelerating the construction of rural infrastructure. (3) Accelerating the construction of major infrastructure such as railways, highways, and airports. (4) Accelerating the development of medical, health, cultural and educational undertakings. (5) Strengthening ecological environment construction. (6) Accelerating independent innovation and structural adjustment. (7) Accelerating the post-disaster reconstruction in the earthquake-stricken areas. (8) Increasing the income of urban and rural residents. (9) Comprehensively implementing the transformation reform of VAT in all regions and industries throughout the country, encouraging enterprises to conduct technological transformation and reducing the burden on enterprises by RMB 120 billion. (10) Increasing financial support for economic growth.

The contents of these ten plans and relevant investment expansion are not directly related to excess capacity, and most of them still need to be vigorously promoted today. However, through further analysis, we find that the contents of items 1, 2, 3, and 7 in these ten plans and relevant investments will directly drive the expansion of investment and production scale in steel, cement, glass, coal, and other industries. The construction of railways, highways, airports, water conservancy projects, and houses will inevitably require a large amount of steel, cement and glass. However, these industries have excess capacity as early as around 2005. In addition, the expansion of production scale of these industries further drives the expansion of relevant industries. For example, the expansion of steel industry inevitably drives the expansion of electric power and coal industries, which may form the transmission effect and cumulative effect of excess capacity. Taking steel and electric power industries as examples, due to the international financial crisis, China's steel output experienced negative growth from September 2008 to January 2009, rebounded rapidly after the introduction of the RMB 4 trillion investment expansion plan, far exceeding the growth rate before the international financial crisis in 2008. The boost in steel output drove the growth rate of electric power to continue to climb (see Figure 2.3).

The plan for invigorating ten key industries refers to the adjustment made to the ten key industries such as steel, automobile, shipping, petrochemical, textile, non-ferrous metal, equipment manufacturing, electronic information, and logistics industries and light industry, so as to promote their revitalization and development.

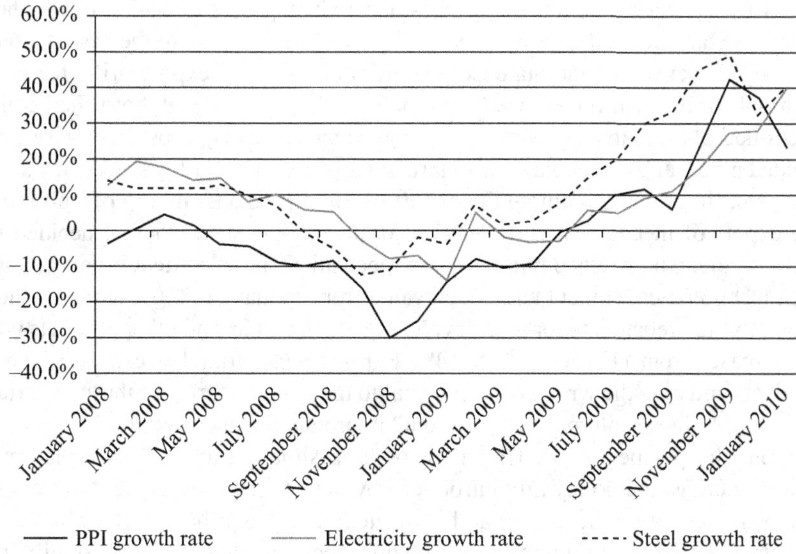

Figure 2.3 The RMB 4 trillion investment stimulus package in 2008 brought huge growth in steel and electric power industries

Source: *China Statistical Yearbook* (2010) compiled by the National Bureau of Statistics of China

It is easy to see that six of these ten key industries are industries with serious excess capacity at present.

The original intention of the plan for invigorating ten key industries is not to simply expand the scale and production capacity of these industries, but to combine the expansion of domestic demand, industrial revitalization and scientific and technological support, so as to improve the scientific and technological content and competitiveness of these industries, and strengthen and optimize these industries. For example, the executive meeting of the State Council held on February 14, 2009, when deliberating the plan for adjusting and invigorating the steel industry, emphasized that the total amount of steel should be strictly controlled, the outdated capacity should be eliminated, and the steel projects simply expanding capacity should be ceased to be initiated.

However, in the process of policy implementation, the intention of the central government has not been well implemented, and the plan for invigorating industries has turned into an impulse to expand the scale of production and expansion actions, because quantitative expansion is far easier to do than structural optimization and quality improvement, and quantitative expansion saves effort and cost, and has quick results. At that time, some supporting policy measures which were introduced to expand domestic demand also contributed to the expansion of production capacity by local governments and enterprises. For example, in order to expand exports, the business community and local governments in coastal areas at that time called for increasing corporate income and reducing the burden on enterprises by increasing export tax rebates and reducing or eliminating export tariffs. The State Council later adopted these recommendations: In the case of steel industry, for example, the State Council decided to cancel export tariffs for steel materials of 67 tariff lines since December 1, 2008, including all hot-rolled coils, hot-rolled plates, large sections (including heavy H-beams), most steel wires, all welded pipes, alloy steel plates with tariffs, narrow strips of alloy steel, alloy steel bars, etc., in order to promote the export of these products. In order to promote the export of mechanical and electrical products, the State Council decided to increase the export rebate rate for some mechanical and electrical products with high technological content and added value from January 1, 2009, among which the export tax rebate rate for motorcycle, sewing machine, and other products will be increased from 11% and 13% to 14%. Export rebates stimulate exports of these products and give the wrong market signal to the manufacturers of these exported products, so these enterprises "go all out" in production and investment.

From the perspective of China's economic situation after the international financial crisis, the policy mix introduced by the Chinese government to expand domestic demand is necessary and well intentioned, and has played a positive role in stabilizing employment, stabilizing economic growth, and stabilizing confidence and society. However, this policy mix has in fact aggravated or worsened the already existing excess capacity and exacerbated the already existing structural imbalance between AS and AD. The reasons therefor are now easy to sort out:

1. The expansionary policy brought about the expansion of domestic demand, which objectively provided a market for enterprises to expand production, thus stimulating them to expand investment and production capacity.
2. The central government's expansion plan triggered local governments to double their expansion. On November 21, 2008, a report with the title of "The RMB 4 Trillion Economic Stimulus Package of the Central Government Triggers an All-out Sprint by All Local Governments" was published on Xinhuanet.com. This report said "In the past ten days, in order to get benefit from the 'RMB 4 trillion' investment expansion plan, all local governments in China have been 'fighting night', and 'went into the capital and resorted to relevant state-level ministries (committees)'". "All hotels in Sanlihe where the building of the (national) development and reform commission was located were fully occupied". All local governments had the same mentality: the RMB 4 trillion investment plan was like a fragrant pot of rice, and fishing to their own bowl was their own, so everyone wanted to fish more quickly. On the second day after the State Council announced its "RMB 4 trillion" investment expansion plan for ensuring the growth, a vice governor of Henan Province led a team, of which members were chosen from the Development and Reform Commission, the Department of Construction, the Bureau of Land and Resources, the Environmental Protection Bureau, and other departments, to Beijing. They stayed at the Guohong Hotel ten minutes away from

the National Development and Reform Commission. And, on the same day, the government of Henan Province issued a document requiring all departments, cities and counties within the jurisdiction to submit materials to the provincial development and reform commission within three days. A director of the Zhengzhou Development and Reform Commission complained that the time was too tight. The director of Anhui Provincial Development and Reform Commission came to Beijing with a team of people and more than 200 projects, plus the projects declared previously, a total of 446 projects, requiring an investment of RMB 34.7 billion. On November 13, 2008, the then-secretary of Anhui Provincial Party Committee gave an instruction on the document of Latest Progress of Striving for National Projects and Funds in Our Province, stating that "it is good, and we should make more efforts and step up our work to gain more support". This instruction expressed the common voice of all local governments at that time. According to Xinhua News Agency, it was estimated that

> according to the data already published by various localities, the total investment in fixed assets that has been announced by all provinces, municipalities directly under the central government, and autonomous regions has exceeded RMB 10 trillion, far exceeding the target of the State Council to stimulate the local and social investment of RMB 4 trillion.

3. Since the RMB 4 trillion investment plan was introduced too quickly and too fast, the centralized approval and sudden approval of projects will inevitably reduce its rationality and scientificity, and some projects with repeated construction and wasting money will be inevitable. The executive meeting of the State Council held on November 5, 2008 called for "expanding investment to be fast and forceful" and "increasing support and speeding up the progress of the project, and simultaneously initiating a batch of new projects". Although this meeting also stressed that "measures should be accurate, and work should be put in place" and "it is imperative to highlight the key, make careful selection, strengthen management, and improve quality and efficiency", ultimately "giving absolute priority to urgent matters" and "quickly initiating new projects" became the mainstream at this meeting. As the saying goes, "quick work will be mixed up the false"; projects suddenly approved and quickly initiated are inevitable to play careless, fraudulent and shoddy. In the first half of 2009, when I gave a lecture on the causes and effects of the subprime mortgage crisis in the United States in a certain province in eastern China, the leader of a prefecture-level city proudly told me that a reservoir construction project in their city had received three state project funding grants in the recent five years, that is, the money for building three reservoirs were spent to build one reservoir. Another example is that, according to CCTV's Focus Report, a modern agricultural planting project in a certain northwestern province received RMB 50 million government investment during the approval of the RMB 4 trillion projects, but was abandoned because of lack of water after completion.

4. The expansion of scale of production in upstream and downstream industries indirectly driven by the RMB 4 trillion investment projects was not fully anticipated by the government expansion plan makers.
5. The increase in investment has dual effects: the increase in investment will not only expand the AD in the current period, but also increase the AS (capacity) in the future. The increase in investment will multiply the AD in the current period through multiplier effect, which is the short-term effect of investment. However, the increase in investment will increase capital formation (plant, equipment, and production lines) and capital stock, thus increasing future production capacity. This production capacity will continue throughout the life cycle of capital stock, which is the long-term effect of investment. The long-term effect of the massive increase in capacity brought about by the RMB 4 trillion investment expansion plan was not anticipated by the makers and implementers of this plan.

II. Slowdown of "troika of the economy factors"

In the process of substantial increase in capacity in many industries brought by the RMB 4 trillion investment, if AD can increase correspondingly, supply surplus will not appear. Unfortunately, China's economic growth in external demand and domestic demand suffered "Waterloo" before the expansion effect of the RMB 4 trillion investment was fully realized.

Stimulated by the expansionary policy, China's final consumption growth rate recovered from 9.84% in 2009 to 15.49% in 2010 and reached its highest growth rate of 21.41% in 2011 since the international financial crisis, but has been declining since then, falling to below 11% after 2013. Since 2014, China's consumption growth rate has dropped by nearly half from 19.39% in 2007, before the international financial crisis. Meanwhile, China's capital formation growth declined sharply from 21.48% in 2010 to 7.19%, 0.99%, and 6.84% respectively in 2014, 2015 and 2016, and the average growth rate of such three years was only one fifth of that (24.85%) (see Figure 2.4) in 2007.

Under the impact of the international financial crisis, the growth rate of China's net export showed sharp fluctuation and dropped sharply: China's net export growth rate was 63.13% and 40.64% respectively in 2006 and 2007, dropped to 3.4% in 2008, and further declined to −37.93% in 2009; the expansionary policy only boosted the net export growth to 0.13% in 2010, while the net export growth was −22.37% in 2011. Although there were large positive growth rates in 2012 and 2015, they were far from returning to the growth level before the financial crisis (see Figure 2.5). Therefore, the effect of expansionary policy mix on external demand growth is not obvious. This is because the financial crisis has led to shrinking demand in the international market and the resurgence of trade protectionism, which has severely hindered China's exports of goods and services.

The international financial crisis first caused a negative impact on the growth of China's external demand, and after the effect of the expansionary policy attenuated, the growth of China's domestic demand continued to decline. Moreover, there is also a mutual reinforcement effect in the slowdown of troika of the

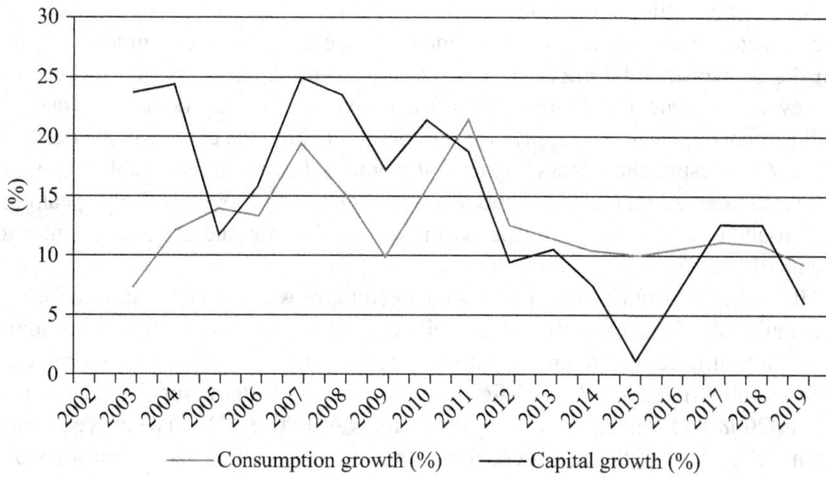

Figure 2.4 China's domestic demand (consumption and investment) growth (%) from 2003 to 2019

Source: *China Statistical Yearbook* (2021) compiled by the National Bureau of Statistics of China

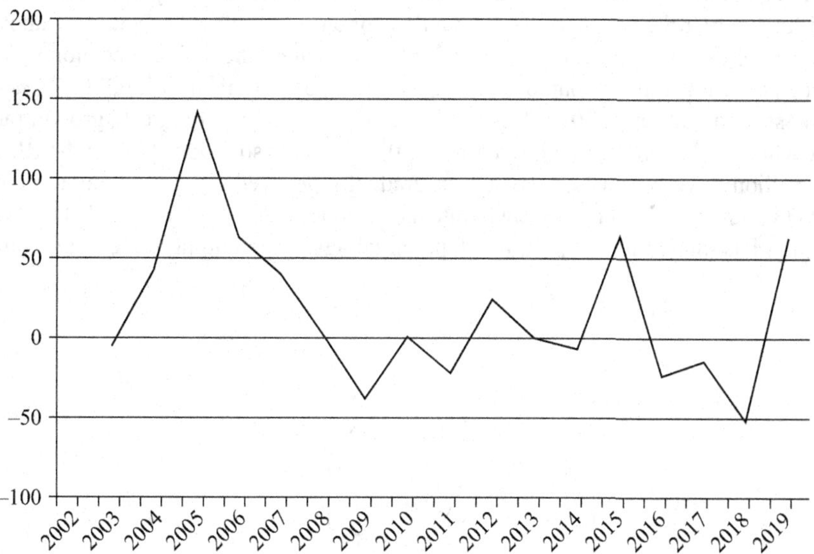

Figure 2.5 China's external demand (net exports) growth (%) from 2003 to 2019

Source: *China Statistical Yearbook* (2021) compiled by the National Bureau of Statistics of China

economy factors of AD: The slowdown in consumer demand growth directly leads to the increase in the inventory of enterprise products and excess production, and the investment of enterprises has to be reduced. According to estimates of the relationship between the structure of China's export goods and the growth of investment in several years after China's accession to the WTO, the impact of exports on Chinese investment is about 40%, so the slowdown in exports has depressed the growth rate of investment. In the process of continuous decline in the growth of total effective demand, due to the constraints of fixed capital renewal, investment direction selection, and investment and production cycle, the adjustments made to the supply side lags greatly behind the change in the demand side. As a result, the excess capacity in some industries is inevitably exposed, like a submerged reef after the ebb tide (see Figure 2.6). Comparatively speaking, this round of China's excess capacity mainly results from the decline in domestic demand growth.

If the equilibrium position of China's economy was E0 in Figure 2.6 before the outbreak of the international financial crisis, the capacity of China's economy was fully utilized, the actual output y = potential output y_f, and China's economy was running at a high double-digit growth rate. The international financial crisis in 2008 had a negative impact on China's AD. The AD curve moved down from AD_0 to AD_1, the macroeconomy equilibrium position moved down from E_0 to E_1, and the actual output decreased to y_1. In the fourth quarter of 2008, the Chinese government introduced the RMB 4 trillion investment expansion plan, which subsequently enabled the AD curve to shift to the upper right. Meanwhile, since the investment expansion increased the capital formation and expanded the economy's production capacity, the potential aggregate output curve moved from LS to LS_1, which caused China's economic growth to rebound to above 8% (8.2%) in the second quarter of 2009. Since then, the Chinese economy had been growing at more than 8% for 12 consecutive quarters until it fell to 7.6% in the second quarter of 2012. During this period, the highest quarterly growth rate reached 12.2% (in the first quarter of 2010). When the stimulus effect of the RMB 4 trillion government expansion plan gradually decayed after 2010, the scale of AD was increasing, but its growth rate had dropped greatly. Assuming that the AD curve has moved to AD_2, while the potential aggregate output curve at this time

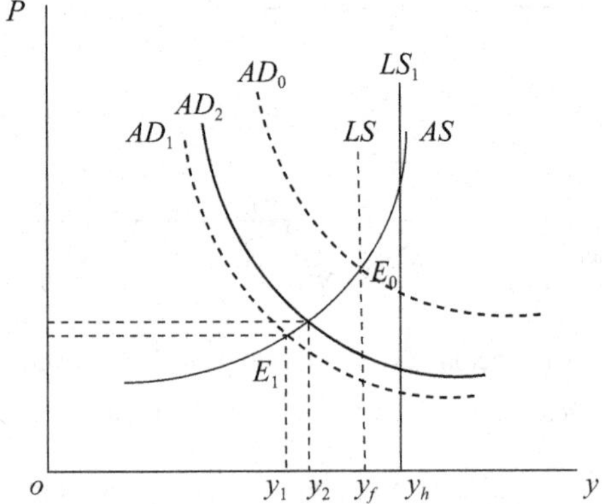

Figure 2.6 China's excess capacity: demand-side analysis

has moved to LS_1 through right shift, and, for the sake of simplification, assuming that the short-term AS curve remains unchanged, the gap between potential aggregate supply LS_1 and actual aggregate supply AS is $y_2y_h = y_h - y_2$, and y_2y_h is the scale of excess capacity caused by the decline in the growth rate of AD accompanied by capacity expansion.

It can be seen that although the scale of AD in China's economy is still increasing after 2010, its growth rate cannot keep up with the growth rate of potential output (capacity) (the distance between AD_1–AD_2 in Figure 2.6 is smaller than the distance between LS–LS_1), resulting in massive excess capacity.

Therefore, China's excess capacity after the international financial crisis is the result of the slow growth of effective demand and the substantial increase in production capacity caused by the expansion plan from 2009 to 2011, rather than a result of pure demand-side causes or pure supply-side causes.

III. Why the effects of the two rounds of expanding domestic demand are different

The stimulus package implemented by the Chinese government from 1998 to 2001 in response to the Southeast Asian financial crisis in 1998 did not cause serious excess capacity, while the expansion plan implemented from 2008 to 2010 caused serious excess capacity. Why are the effects of these two rounds of stimulus packages quite different?

The general tone of the 1998 expansion plan and the 2008 expansion plan is the same: that is to say, the government expands domestic demand by expanding government expenditure (investment) for the purpose of propping up economic growth, stopping the economic downturn, and stabilizing the economy and society.

Although the contents of the "policy package" of the 1998 expansion plan and the 2008 expansion plan are different, the main menu of the policy mix is similar: expanding AD mainly by expanding infrastructure investment. From 1998 to 2004, the Ministry of Finance issued RMB 910 billion of long-term treasury bonds for construction. By the end of 2004, RMB 864.3 billion of treasury bond project funds had been actually arranged in seven years, with the expenditure structure as shown in Figure 2.7.

From Figure 2.7, it can be calculated that in the RMB 864.3 billion investment expenditure, transportation and communication infrastructure construction and urban infrastructure construction together account for 35% in total. If agriculture, forestry, water conservancy and ecological construction as well as reconstruction of the rural power grid are also regarded as infrastructure construction, the aforesaid four expenditures account for 73% in total. Compared with the 2008 expansion plan (see Figure 2.2), a much larger proportion of investment expenditure in the 1998 expansion plan was spent on infrastructure.

According to the statistics of the Ministry of Finance of China, during the seven years from 1998 to 2004, the central government issued RMB 910 billion of long-term treasury bonds for construction, which stimulated the investment of local

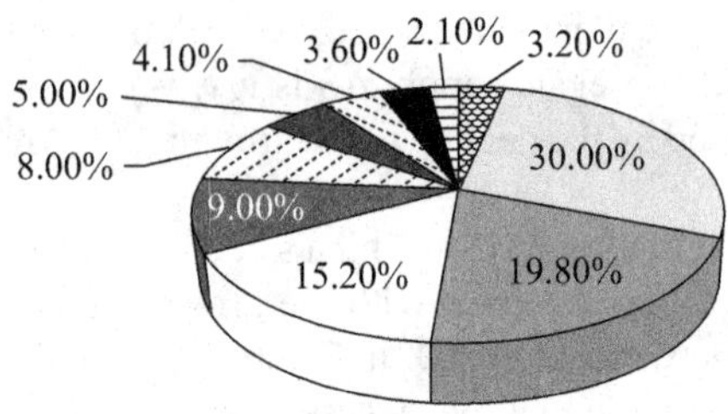

□ Agriculture, forestry, water conservancy, and ecological construction
▨ Urban infrastructure construction
□ Reconstruction of rural power grid
▨ Construction of grain depots directly under the central government
▨ Construction of facilities of public security bureau, procuratorate, court, and judicial bureau
■ Construction of transportation and communication infrastructure
▨ Technological progress and industrial upgrading
■ Construction of education, culture, health, and tourism infrastructure
▤ Investment in environmental protection
▩ Other

Figure 2.7 Expenditure structure of expansion plan from 1998 to 2004

Source: Jin Renqing (2006). *Science Development and Fiscal Policy in China*. Beijing: China Financial & Economic Publishing House, 82.

government matching funds, bank credit funds and enterprises' own funds, forming a total social investment scale of about RMB 4 trillion, with a cumulative investment of over RMB 3 trillion by the end of 2004.[2] This is much smaller than the scale of social investment driven by the RMB 4 trillion investment expansion plan in 2008. It is estimated that the accumulated scale of social investment driven by the RMB 4 trillion investment expansion plan was about RMB 20 trillion from 2008 to 2010.

The economic consequences of these two rounds of strong stimulus are different mainly due to the different economic environment and the different intensity of reform.

When the first round of strong stimulus was implemented, China's infrastructure represented by railways, highways, and airports was small and outdated, far from meeting the needs of rapid economic and social development. In 1997, the national railway mileage was 66,000 kilometers, the railway electrification mileage was only 12,000 kilometers, the highway mileage was 1,226,400 kilometers, and the expressway mileage was only 4,800 kilometers. China's automobile industry (especially sedan car production) began to develop on a large scale in 1990s. In 1997, the number of civilian cars and private cars in China was 12,190,900 and 3,583,600 respectively. The market-oriented development of real estate just started at the end of 1990s. The development of these industries such as "railways, highways, and airports", automobiles, and real estate has directly promoted the development of steel, cement, glass, coal, building materials, and other related industries, so there was not only great space and potential for government to expand investment, but also good investment results. In addition, China officially became a member of WTO in 2001, and its external demand has increased rapidly. The capacity growth of steel, cement, glass, coal, building materials, and other industrial products can be supported by a large increase in external demand, thus enabling investment and external demand to become the main forces supporting China's high economic growth.

But when the second round of strong stimulus was implemented in 2008, the economic environment has changed greatly: On the one hand, China's economy has experienced obvious structural imbalance and excess capacity around 2005; on the other hand, although the number of per capita ownership of some infrastructures is not high, the space of investment in infrastructure represented by "railways, highways, and airports" has been greatly reduced. In 2007, the national railway mileage has reached 78,000 kilometers, the railway electrification mileage has reached 24,000 kilometers, the highway mileage has reached 3,583,700 kilometers, and the expressway mileage has reached 53,900 kilometers. Moreover, China has become a big country in terms of automobile production and consumption. In 2007, the number of civilian car and private car ownership in China reached 43.5836 million units and 28.7622 million units respectively. The real estate market appeared a large number of bubbles, and the sales area of residential commercial houses nationwide has reached 701,358,800 square meters in 2007, which has greatly squeezed the development space of steel, cement, glass, coal, building materials, and other related industries. In addition, the outbreak of the international financial crisis has forced us to reduce our dependence on external demand. The two main carriages (investment and external demand) driving economic growth can now only rely mainly on investment. Meanwhile, without a support of moderate rate of technological progress, although the massive investment expansion through proactive fiscal policy could enable the economic growth to rally in a short term, with the slowdown of "troika of the economy factors", the excess capacity soon appeared, and the structural imbalance between AD and AS further worsened.

The better effect of the expansion plan in 1998 is also closely related to the three major market-oriented reforms of housing, education and medical care implemented at that time. The cessation of welfare house allocation and the introduction of housing monetization reform have directly given rise to a new industry or market, namely, the real estate industry or real estate market that has been booming for 20 years. The great prosperity and development of real estate industry and automobile industry have become the two pillar industries supporting the high growth in China's economy from the late 1990s to 2010. Although there are some controversies about the enrollment expansion of colleges, colleges charges, and the implementation of education industrialization since 1999, it is an indisputable fact that the reforms of education and medical care have expanded domestic demand.

Although the IT bubble burst in the United States in 2000, the development of Internet and IT in China was in the ascendant at that time. Internet and IT were two new industrial forces that boosted the high growth in China's economy from 1998 to 2004.

In 2001, China officially became a member of WTO, and its entry into WTO opened up a vast international market for Chinese products. On the one hand, the production capacity formed by the investment expansion by the Chinese government has a greater market demand support; on the other hand, the increase in investment and supply in China has been stimulated. In 2000, China's exports and net exports were RMB 2,063.44 billion and RMB 199.56 billion respectively, accounting for 20.6% and 2.0% of GDP in that year. From 2003 to 2008, China's exports increased by trillions of yuan every year, exceeding RMB 3 trillion (RMB 36,287.9 trillion), RMB 4 trillion (RMB 49,103.3 trillion), RMB 6 trillion (RMB 62,648.1 trillion), RMB 7 trillion (RMB 77,597.2 trillion), RMB 9 trillion (RMB 93,627.1 trillion), and RMB 10 trillion (RMB 100,394.94 trillion) (see Figure 2.8), accounting for 26.4%, 30.3%, 33.4%, 35.4%, 34.6%, and 31.4% of GDP in that year respectively. In 2005, the net exports exceeded RMB 800 billion, reaching RMB 837.44 billion. In 2006, they exceeded RMB 2 trillion, reaching RMB 2,033.02 billion, accounting for 9.3% of GDP in that year.[3] After China's entry into WTO, until 2008, the rate of contribution of net exports to China's GDP growth has generally been increasing. The data suggests that WTO accession is the main international factor for the success of China's first round of expansion plan.

However, the 2008 expansion plan was not so fortunate, with no opportunities for the housing and health care reforms nor for fast developments in automobile, IT, or Internet industries. This round of expansion not only failed to expand the international market through China's entry into WTO as it did in 2001. On the contrary, it suffered from the shrinking growth rate of external demand brought about by the international financial crisis and the prevalence of trade protectionism (see Figure 2.5), and the rate of contribution and pulling rate of external demand (net export) to China's GDP growth have been much lower than before. In particular, we have introduced and implemented few institutional reform measures with less efforts during the round of expansion that began in 2008.

Notes

1 In 2009, the GDP of Shanghai was RMB 1.4001 trillion, and that of Gansu Province was RMB 338 billion.

2 Jin, R. Q. (2006). *Science Development and Fiscal Policy in China*. Beijing: China Financial & Economic Publishing House, 97.

3 Compiled by the National Bureau of Statistics of China (2016), *China Statistical Yearbook* (2015), Beijing, China Statistics Press.

3 Cause of excess capacity

Supply analysis

Another important cause of excess capacity in China comes from the supply side, of which the cause can be divided into quantity cause—the supply quantity in excess of the demand quantity—and structural cause—the misalignment and mismatch between the supply structure and demand structure.

I. Rapid growth of the supply

As mentioned earlier, supply surplus is first manifested as excess production: the actual AS exceeds the effective demand. As mentioned in Chapter 1 hereof, China's economy has been transformed from a supply shortage to a relative surplus of supply in the late 1990s. In the 21st century, deepening reform and expanding opening up have further promoted an increase in the AS capacity, and a series of factors since the international financial crisis in 2008 have aggravated the supply surplus in China's economy.

Firstly, the construction project of China's socialist market economic system, which started in the mid-1990s, has greatly mobilized the enthusiasm of individuals, enterprises and local governments, and greatly improved the efficiency of resource allocation and economic vitality, thus greatly increasing the AS capacity of the economy. Secondly, after China became a member of WTO in 2001, China's external market expanded rapidly, thereby inducing Chinese enterprises to continuously expand employment scale and scale of production.

Thirdly, after China's entry into WTO, it is more convenient to introduce foreign capital, foreign advanced technology, foreign advanced machinery and equipment, and foreign technology and management talents, which helps to promote an increase of the AS capacity of China's economy. Finally, although the subprime mortgage crisis in the United States and the international financial crisis in 2007 to 2008 had a negative impact on China's economy, the impact of this shock was short lived due to the economic expansion package implemented by the Chinese government, and China's domestic demand and market recovered rapidly. The expansion of domestic demand boosted the growth of China's industrial, construction, and real estate industries, which are the three main pillars supporting China's high economic growth.[1]

DOI: 10.4324/9781003367000-5

Table 3.1 Output and growth of major industrial products in China

	1998	*2008*	*2015*	*An increase in 2008 over 1998*	*An increase in 2015 over 2008*	*An increase in 2015 over 1998*
Output of raw coal (100 million tons)	13.32	29.03	37.47	118%	29%	181%
Cement output (10,000 tons)	53600	142355.73	235918.83	166%	66%	340%
Output of flat glass (10,000 weight cases)	17194.03	59890.39	78651.63	248%	31%	357%
Output of pig iron (10,000 tons)	11863.67	47824.42	69141.3	303%	45%	483%
Output of crude steel (10,000 tons)	11559	50305.75	80382.5	335%	60%	595%
Steel output (10,000 tons)	10737.8	60460.29	112349.6	463%	86%	946%
Output of ten non-ferrous metals (10,000 tons)	615	2520.28	5155.82	310%	105%	738%
Output of primary aluminum (electrolytic aluminum) (10,000 tons)	233.57	1316.54	3141	464%	139%	1245%

Source: *China Statistical Yearbook* (2017) compiled by the National Bureau of Statistics of China

If we take the impact of the Southeast Asian financial crisis on China's economy in 1997 to 1998 as a starting point, by 2015, the output of China's main products increased by a minimum of 1.8 times (raw coal) and a maximum of 12.5 times (primary aluminum); during the ten years from the Southeast Asian financial crisis to the international financial crisis in 2008, the output of major industrial products in China increased by 1.2 times to 4.6 times; in the short seven years from 2008 to 2015, the output of major industrial products in China increased by 29% to 139%! (See Table 3.1).

II. Rising cost resulting in left shift of short-term AS curve

China's labor remuneration and other costs entering an upward cycle since 2004 and the wage growth rate exceeding that of labor productivity (see Figure 3.1) caused the transformation of China's economy from excess production to excess capacity; the continuous rise in the cost of production of enterprises resulted in the

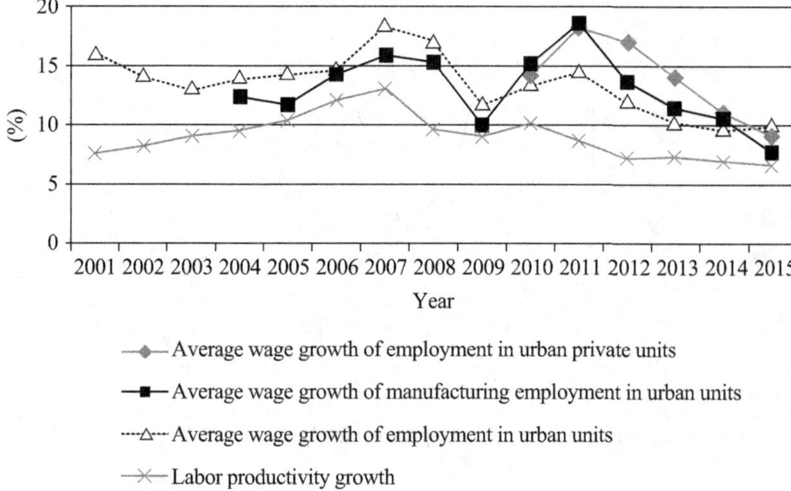

Figure 3.1 Wage growth and labor productivity growth in China

Source: Wage data from *China Statistical Yearbook* (2016) compiled by the National Bureau of Statistics of China, and labor productivity data from the International Labor Organization

short-term AS curve in macro economy moving to the upper left, thus widening the gap between actual AS and potential AS.

A significant change brought by the reform and opening up to China's economy is that a large number of agricultural surplus laborers have shifted from the agricultural sector and rural areas to the industrial sector and cities, becoming "migrant workers". At the beginning of the reform and opening up, China's agriculture was underdeveloped, and the annual income of farmers was generally low. Before 1983, the annual per capita net income of Chinese farmers was always lower than RMB 300. From 1978 to 1982, the annual per capita net income of Chinese farmers was RMB 133.6, RMB 160.2, RMB 191.3, RMB 223.4, and RMB 270.1, respectively. The average monthly wage of urban workers was less than RMB 100 before 1985, and increased to RMB 100 to RMB 170 from 1985 to 1989. Therefore, in 1980s, a per capita monthly wage of RMB 200 for migrant workers was a high wage. The monthly salary of migrant workers was RMB 300 to RMB 500 in the early 1990s, and rose to RMB 500 to RMB 700 in the middle and late 1990s and RMB 1,500 to RMB 1,700 in 2010. After 2008, the wage level of migrant workers has increased at an average annual rate of more than 20%. Figure 3.1 shows that wage growth of those employed in China's urban areas has been higher than labor productivity growth since the turn of the 21st century. Except for the impact of the international financial crisis in 2007 to 2009, the wage growth of employed people in China has also been higher than GDP growth and per capita GDP growth in other years.

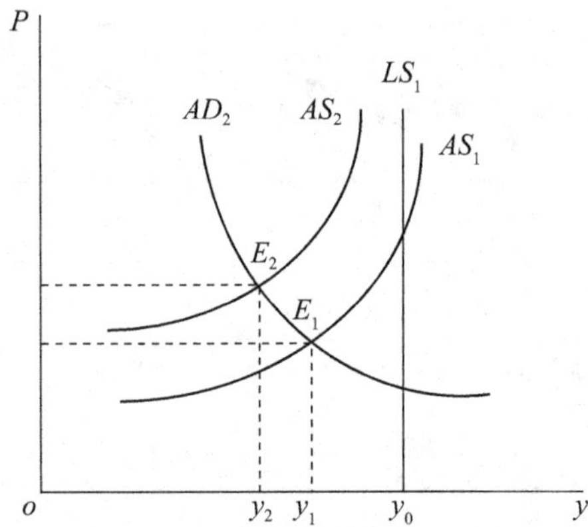

Figure 3.2 Excess capacity in China: supply-side analysis

In addition to the labor cost of enterprises, other costs also rise rapidly. In terms of energy costs, from 2004 to 2014, China's electricity consumption increased from USD 7 to USD 11 per kWh, while the cost of natural gas increased from USD 5.8 to USD 13.7 per million British thermal units. In terms of logistics cost, logistics cost accounts for about 30% of the production cost of China's current manufacturing industry, much higher than 10% to 15% in developed countries. At present, the ratio of total cost of social logistics to GDP in China is not only about twice as high as that in developed countries such as the United States, Japan and Germany, but also higher than that in other BRICS countries such as India and Brazil, and higher than the global average by about five percentage points. China is in the process of transitioning to a socialist market economy, and the friction between the old and new systems during the transition period is keeping the transaction cost or system cost high. In recent years, the price increase of resource products is another factor that leads to the rise in cost of production of enterprises.

These many factors previously mentioned keep pushing up the cost of production of enterprises, resulting in the short-term AS curve of China's economy moving to the upper left, and thus expanding excess capacity (see Figure 3.2).

In the analysis on Figure 2.6, we assume that the short-term AS curve remains unchanged. Now (see Figure 3.2), because the increase in labor remuneration, energy cost, logistics cost and system cost causes an increase in the cost of production of enterprises, the short-term AS curve moves from AS_1 to AS_2. If the AD is constant, the new equilibrium point is E_2 and the actual output is Y_2, causing the scale of excess capacity to be expanded from y_0y_1 to $y_0y_2 = y_0 - y_2$.

III. Slowdown in the TFP growth

The consensus among economists is that technological progress makes the AS curve move down to the bottom right, thus offsetting the pressure of the rise in overall price level and decrease in supply resulting from the rising cost of production; the TFP growth brought by technological progress will promote economic growth.

Unfortunately, in the process of continuous rise in cost of production in recent years, the rate of technological progress in China is slowing down, and the growth rate of TFP is declining. In the article "The Reason and Way out of Slowdown for China's Economy", we estimated the changes of China's TFP growth rate from 1988 to 2012 by using the generalized Solow Residual Value Method, and found that the TFP growth rate in China's economy has been declining continuously since 2008.[2] (See Table 3.2.)

According to the data in Table 3.2, the trend line of TFP growth rate in China is shown in Figure 3.3.

As can be seen from Table 3.2, the average annual growth rate of TFP in China from 1988 to 2012 was 6.82%. In particular, the growth rate from 1992 to 1993 was the highest, with an annual growth rate exceeding 12%; the TFP growth rate continued to decline after 2008, and was lower than its average annual growth rate from 1988 to 2013!

It is worth noting that TFP growth rate in China continued to decline in fluctuation after reaching the peak of 11.6735% in 2007, and significantly dropped to 3.8361% and 1.2673% in 2011 and 2012, respectively.

Table 3.2 TFP growth rate in China

Year	*TFP growth rate*
1988	8.1101
1989	1.8796
1990	−12.1182
1991	7.7491
1992	12.9513
1993	12.5943
1994	11.6564
1995	9.3997
1996	7.9373
1997	7.0943
1998	5.6469
1999	5.5121
2000	6.3715
2001	6.0755
2002	7.1964
2003	8.2315
2004	8.2073
2005	9.4277
2006	10.5294
2007	11.6735
2008	6.7776
2009	6.0614
2010	6.5653
2011	3.8361
2012	1.2673

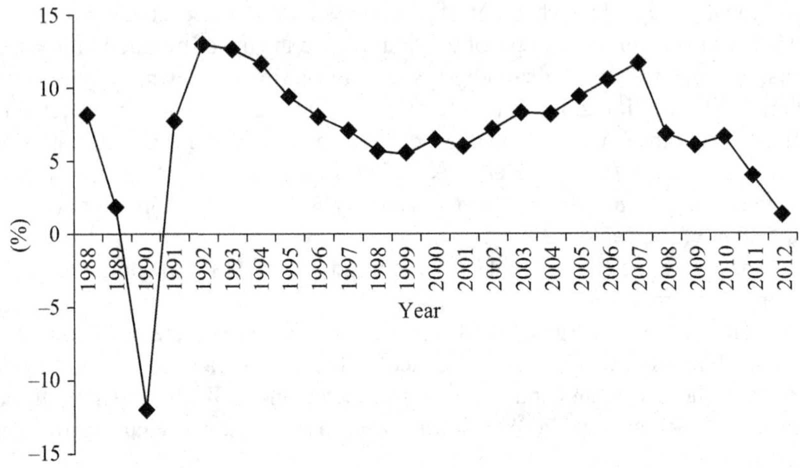

Figure 3.3 Estimation of the TFP growth rate in China from 1998 to 2012

According to research findings by Sheng Laiyun and others from the National Bureau of Statistics of China, China's TFP showed an overall downward trend with an average of 0.64% from 2008 to 2015. In particular, the average was 1.19% from 2010 to 2014; TFP rebounded from 2015 to 2017, with an average of 2.29%. However, the average of TFP in 1990–1992, 1993–2000, and 2001–200 were 5.25%, 2.45%, and 1.75%, respectively, with a high of 10.42% in 1992.[3] Although the TFP-related numerical values obtained from this research results are different from that obtained from our research, the downward trend of China's TFP they found since 2008 is generally consistent with our findings.

The supply side of China's economy is worsened in both directions by the slowdown in TFP due to rising cost of production and the slowdown in the rate of technological progress.

IV. Supply–demand structural imbalance

The supply surplus of China's economy is not only the relative surplus of AS quantity, but more importantly, the structure surplus: the misalignment and mismatch between AS structure and AD structure, with the coexistence of supply surplus and supply shortage. On the one hand, there is a considerable excess of some raw materials, such as coal, crude steel, and glass, and products with low technical content and quality; on the other hand, there is a considerable shortage of high-tech products, high-quality products, and products needed by middle- and high-income people and the elderly. Products at the low end of the industrial chain with low added value are relatively surplus, while products at the high end of the industrial chain with high added value are relatively short. Many industrial products are in surplus, while many services (such as high-quality education and medical services, industrial and agricultural productive services, household services, energy conservation and environmental protection services, leisure services, community services, etc.) are in short supply. Chinese consumers "sweep goods" overseas every year, such as snapping up face masks and cosmetics from South Korea, toilet seats and rice cookers from Japan, milk powder from New Zealand or Australia, bags from Europe and America, and health care products and iPhones from the United States. The reason for this is because the quality and function of these products are much better or (and) the prices thereof are lower than that of similar products in China. According to the Fortune Character Institute, the overseas luxury consumption by Chinese consumers in 2013 reached USD 74 billion, accounting for 47% of the global luxury consumption, while Chinese consumers consumed only USD 28 billion of domestically produced luxury goods. The amount spent by Chinese people on foreign luxury goods was more than 2.64 times that on domestic luxury goods. According to Xinhua News Agency, Gao Hucheng, Minister of Commerce of China, said at the press conference of the Third Session of the 12th National People's Congress on March 7, 2015 that the number of China's outbound visitors exceeded 100 million in 2014, and consumption abroad exceeded RMB 1 trillion, of which a considerable proportion was spent on purchasing foreign products. According to CCTV's March 15 Evening Party in 2016, the consumption by Chinese residents abroad reached RMB 1.5 trillion in 2015, up 50% from the previous year! Chinese consumers favor "foreign goods", which is related to some Chinese people's superstition of "foreign goods", but the main reason is that the quality and (or) price of these foreign goods are superior to those of similar Chinese goods. If the amount spent by Chinese residents abroad on foreign products every year is calculated at RMB 1 trillion, and the multiplier of consumption expenditure is calculated at 2, the annual outflow of Chinese domestic demand to foreign countries is RMB 2 trillion equivalent to the total GDP of Guizhou, Gansu, and Hainan provinces in 2015!

With the rapid development of the economy and the continuous improvement of per capita income, the demand structure of Chinese residents is constantly upgrading. Since the reform and opening up, the changes in the demand structure of Chinese residents have gone through five distinct stages:

The demand structure of the first stage mainly focuses on food and clothing. At the beginning of the reform and opening up, due to the low level of economic development and per capita income, there was an acute shortage of supply, and many Chinese people had not completely solved the problem of "feeding and clothing themselves". Therefore, the consumption structure of residents at this stage mainly focused on food and daily necessities consumption, and expenditure on food, clothing, and consumption was the bulk of consumption expenditure.

The demand structure of the second stage is represented by "a bicycle, a sewing machine, a watch, and a radio". From the 1980s to early 1990s, the demand structure of middle-income families in China shifted to bicycles, sewing machines, watches, and radios, which were the standard items for young people to get married and start a family at this stage.

The demand structure of the third stage is marked by three major household appliances: color TV sets, refrigerators, and washing machines.

The demand structure of the fourth stage is represented by housing and automobiles. Since the late 1990s, commercial housing and cars have become the focus of Chinese household consumption expenditure.

The demand structure of the fifth stage has entered the consumption period with the focus on high-level and high-quality education, medical care, elderly care, entertainment, tourism, and other services. Since the 21st century, Chinese residents have increasingly attached importance to the quality of their children's education, and paid attention to their on-the-job learning and improvement of education level. More and more people pay attention to fitness, health, and leisure, and join the tourist army.

The demand structure of more and more families among Chinese residents has entered the fourth and fifth stages. However, our production structure is still dominated by meeting the demand structure of the first, second, and third stages. The production to meet the demand structure of the fourth stage is developing. The insufficient and unequal allocation of education and medical resources and the insufficient supply of high-quality education and medical services, elderly care facilities, and elderly care services becomes a prominent problem at this stage. As a result, more and more people go abroad to study and seek medical treatment, and disputes over family old-age pension increase, even to the extent of filing a lawsuit.

There is also structure surplus in many industries in China's economy, such as the energy industry, the automobile industry, the real estate industry, the petrochemical industry, and so on. According to the survey and analysis of China's automobile capacity conducted by the National Development and Reform Commission, China Association of Automobile Manufacturers, and China Automotive Technology and Research Center, by the end of 2015, the capacity utilization rate of passenger vehicles in China's automobile industry was 81%, while that of commercial vehicles was only 52%.

The biggest imbalance between the AS structure and the AD structure of China's economy lies in the following: one the one hand, there is massive excess capacity and product inventory in China's economy, and many products are suffering from poor market; on the other hand, there are 600 million people whose monthly income is around RMB 1,000, and whose ability to pay is insufficient, resulting that many demands cannot be met.

Notes

1 Since the second half of 2010, China's economy has experienced moderate inflation, which can be regarded as a signal of market recovery and prosperity. In July 2010, China's CPI rose above the warning line of 3%, reaching 3.3%. Since then, prices have been rising slowly and continuously. From June to September 2011, it exceeded 6% for four consecutive months, reaching a maximum of 6.5%.

2 Fang, F. Q., & Ma, X. J. (2016). "The Reason and Way Out of Slowdown for China's Economy [J]", *Journal of Renmin University of China*, 6, 64–75.

3 Sheng, L. Y. et al. (2018). "Calculation of China's Total Factor Productivity and Forecast of Economic Growth Prospects", *Xi'an: Statistics and Information Forum*, 12, 3–11.

4 Cause of excess capacity

System analysis

The deeper and more important causes of the excess capacity and structural imbalance in China's economy are systems.

I. Semi-market economy system

After 1953, China gradually established a highly centralized planned economic system and a highly centralized political system. The economic management mode suitable for this system is that the central government directly controlled resource allocation and economic activities through directive plans, realized the comprehensive balance of the economy by means of planning, and coordinated major proportional relationships. Under this system, only the "control" was allowed for the resource allocation and economic operation, while the "adjustment" was not allowed. The basic economic issues of "what to produce", "how to produce", and "for whom to produce" were all controlled and solved by the government planning department. There was no basis and space for regulating the market mechanism. The market economy and its regulatory mechanism were excluded and denied.

The reform and opening up that started in 1979 initiated the process of market-oriented reform of China's economy. The process of China's reform and opening up is the process of transforming China's economic system from a highly centralized planned economic system to a market economic system, the process in which the government and the market play an alternate role in resource allocation, and the relationship between the government and the market is continually adjusted. The Decision on Several Issues concerning the Establishment of a Socialist Market Economic System adopted at the Third Plenary Session of the 14th Central Committee of the Communist Party of China (CPC) in November 1993 clarified that the goal of China's economic system reform was to establish a socialist market economic system. Since 1994, the Chinese government has further deepened reforms with respect to the pricing system, fiscal and taxation system, financial system, planning management system, investment system, system of ownership of the means of production, and state-owned enterprises. Through a series of reforms and adjustments, the commodity market and markets for various factors of production including the capital (financial) market have been gradually established,

DOI: 10.4324/9781003367000-6

and commodity prices and prices of factors of production have been gradually marketized and have reflected the scarcity of resources and the supply–demand relationship; enterprises (mainly state-owned enterprises) have gradually become microeconomic entities with well-defined power and responsibility, independent decision-making power, self-management power, and sole responsibility for their own profits and losses; the central banking system and the commercial banking system have been gradually established; the modern financial system and taxation system compatible with the market economic system began to take shape; a large number of laws and regulations, such as company law, contract law, patent law, copyright law, accounting law, and anti–unfair competition law, have been promulgated and implemented successively to protect the construction and development of the market economy, thus promoting the transition to the socialist market economic system. After more than 40 years of reform and construction, China has initially established a socialist market economic system, and the resource allocation and economic operation have gradually shifted to be regulated by the market mechanism. However, China's current market economy is generally still a "semi-market economy", not a "full market economy" or a mature and standardized market economy, and China's economic system is in the process of transition from a "semi-market economy" to a "full market economy".

Why is China's economy still a "semi-market economy"? The causes are as follows.

1. The consumer market in China's economy has basically achieved market pricing, but the markets for factors of production are still in the process of reform and cultivation.

In China's consumer market, the proportion of market-set prices has risen from less than 3% in 1978 to 97%, and the proportion of government-set prices and government-guided prices has dropped from 97% in 1978 to less than 3%; in the total purchase of agricultural and sideline products, the proportion of market-set prices increased from 5.6% in 1978 to 97%, and the proportion of government-set prices and government-guided prices decreased from 92.6% in 1978 to about 2%.

However, the marketization of the markets for factors of production in China's economy is not yet high, and the prices of factors of production are still subject to a "dual-track system" in which planned pricing and market pricing coexist. Factor prices have not been completely straightened out, and price distortion is still quite serious. Land in China is subject to a public ownership system (the rural land is collectively owned, and the urban land is owned by the state). What is the land used for—is it agricultural land, industrial land, commercial land, or land for education or real estate development? How much land is used for different purposes each year? What is the price of land for different purposes? Such a price is mainly decided by the government. In towns, the government has a complete monopoly or control over the primary land market. Rural land is now only partially tradable (transferable) in terms of the right to use, with quite low circulation (mobility) of the land, and there is actually no agricultural land market. According to systems and laws existing in China, individual urban and rural residents are not allowed to participate in land transactions, and it is difficult for land to be circulated or traded between individuals. At present, there is a huge difference of prices, subject to the dual-track price system, between the rural collective land and the urban state-owned land. Once the rural collective land is expropriated by the state and converted into the land for urban construction, industry, or real estate development, the land price will increase by dozens or even hundreds of times! However, this huge land premium has nothing to do with farmers.

China's natural resources, including minerals, rivers and lakes, forests, mountains, grasslands, wasteland, and tidal flats, are all owned by the state. These natural resources are not allowed to be used without the authorization by the state, and shall be priced by the state. As a result, the extravagant and distorted prices of electricity, coal, petroleum, natural gas, and other resource products in China are often criticized by the academic world and the public.

Officially, China currently recognizes only that labor has commodity attributes in theory, and does not recognize that labor is a commodity. China's labor price (wage) is not determined by and between the labor supply and demand parties through negotiation, but is dominated by the buyer (enterprise) or decided by the buyer. In the current labor market in China, workers are atomistic and scattered individuals who are unable to negotiate on wages with employers. Labor unions are quasi-government organizations parallel to the governmental hierarchy. They are not trade unions, and cannot represent workers in an industry to conduct collective bargaining. Moreover, existing laws, such as the Trade Union Law and the Labor Law, do not grant labor unions the power to negotiate with employers (enterprises) on labor conditions and wages.

China's financial market and capital market are still in the process of reform and construction. The deposit and loan interest rates in the financial market were not fully deregulated until 2015. At present, there is still an "interest rate corridor", and the degree of interest rate marketization is not high. Enterprises with different systems of ownership have different degrees of difficulty in obtaining bank loans. Banks grant credit selectively instead of treating them equally. Small and micro enterprises often find it difficult to obtain loans with high loan interest rate, and credit rationing is common. On the one hand, the capital market is manipulated by a few large capitals, and, on the other hand, improper intervention and inadequate regulation by the government coexist; excessive speculation, insider trading, unequal competition, opaque information, and blockage of information dissemination are still quite common in the financial market and capital market.

2. The market competition in China's economy is insufficient, and some industries or markets have a high degree of monopoly, or even complete monopoly.

Since the reform and opening up, China's consumer market and markets for factors of production have gradually opened up to foreign-funded enterprises and non-state-owned enterprises in China. The diversification of market players has greatly improved the degree of market competition. At present, the competition in markets of a majority of consumer goods in China is sufficient. At the same time, some markets in China are still highly monopolized, and some markets are closed to potential competitors. In addition to some natural monopoly industries such as water supply and natural gas supply, some industries are still controlled by the state or monopolized by state-owned enterprises, such as arms, petroleum, tobacco, electricity, communications, civil aviation, and railways. At present, China's financial market and insurance market are mainly dominated by state-owned commercial banks and state-owned insurance companies and their holding companies.

China's important service industries, such as medical care, education, culture, publishing, newspapers, radio, film, television, and other industries, are still highly administratively monopolized by the government.

3. The labor market, especially the talent market, has strong rigidity—there are many system obstacles, policy obstacles, and artificial obstacles to the mobility of the labor force between urban and rural areas, between regions, between industries, and between state-owned enterprises and non-state-owned enterprises, with low free mobility and degree of competition. China has not yet formed a manager market or a market in which only entrepreneurs are allowed to trade.

In the mid-1990s, China loosened restrictions on the influx of rural labor into cities, and a large "demographic dividend" brought about rapid growth of China's economy. However, China's labor market was still relatively rigid, with insufficient free mobility: the mobility of rural labor to cities was still constrained by housing, children's schooling, social security, and medical care. The urban–rural separation caused by the household registration system has just broken the ice. Due to the large urban–rural gap and system restrictions, the current urban–rural labor mobility in China was still unidirectional: a large number of rural labor flowed to cities, while urban labor, especially scientific and technical personnel and entrepreneurs, were unwilling or unable to flow to rural areas. The mobility of talents between different units, enterprises with different systems of ownership, and different regions was not only hindered by local protectionism and unit protectionism, but also constrained by the personnel system. The obstacles to the vertical mobility of talents in China are particularly prominent. A person's family background directly affects his or her educational conditions, employment options, and even labor compensation from kindergarten to university. Even if the child of a farmer or an ordinary worker is very talented and works hard, it is still difficult for him/her to enter the middle or upper class of society, or he or she has to work several times or even dozens of times harder than those with a good background.

4. The government controls too many resources and powers, and too much government intervention and improper intervention still exist from time to time.

From 2002 to 2012, the State Council of China abolished the administrative examination and approval power for 1,992 projects in six batches, and nearly 439 projects were changed from the approval system to the filing system or decentralized to the management level. By March 2013, when Li Keqiang took office as the new Premier of the State Council, there were still more than 1,700 projects to be examined and approved by the government. Premier Li Keqiang made it clear that the current government was determined to step up efforts to streamline administration and delegate power to the lower levels, and to cut projects to be examined and approved by more than one third. In May 2015, the State Council officially implemented the reform of the "streamlining administration, delegating power and strengthening regulation, and upgrading services". From March 2013 to February 2017, the State Council reviewed and approved the cancellation of 491 examination and approval powers in nine batches, and delegated 127 administrative examination and approval powers. The reduction in examination and approval power means that more power of resource allocation is handed back to the market.

However, many examination and approval powers in China are still controlled by governments at all levels or by quasi-governments (such as industry associations or XX centers under government departments), and the role of market mechanisms is still limited by government powers. For example, the scale of investment in fixed assets, the pricing of petroleum, natural gas, water supply, coal for power generation, and pharmaceuticals, the examination and approval of major projects, and the arrangement for special funds are still controlled by the National Development and Reform Commission; more than 80 projects in 13 categories of agriculture, forestry, water conservancy, energy, transportation, information industry, raw materials, machinery manufacturing, light industry and tobacco, high-tech, urban construction, social undertakings, finance, foreign investment, and overseas investment must be approved by the National Development and Reform Commission; many professional qualification certificates are still examined, approved, and issued by different industry associations; running a business, initiating a project, and launching a new product also need to be examined and approved by many government departments with their official seals. Governments at all levels also guide or constrain corporate behavior through various excellence selection and awarding activities and administrative penalty measures.

More importantly, some government departments and government officials still have relatively large discretionary powers: deciding on whether some matters can be done or not, whether they can be done quickly or slowly or even not be done; to whom a project is granted; who should receive the subsidy and how much—things like these are often decided by the responsible officials, causing some officials to act willfully, and even to refuse handling matters before giving benefits.

Among the previously mentioned matters, some examinations and approvals are necessary, because some projects and production involve national security and economic security, as well as environmental, sanitation, and health standards. However, some examinations and approvals do inhibit the role of the market mechanism, not conducive to the development of the market economy, and need to be cancelled and liberalized gradually. For example, a few years ago, an enterprise in Beijing developed a kind of environmentally friendly and ultra-thin building insulation materials, whose price was comparable with that of similar products. Because the relevant government departments did not approve these insulation materials to be incorporated into the government procurement catalog, these new insulation materials produced by the enterprise could not open the market.

Some empirical research results also show that China's socialist market economic system is still under construction, and the level of marketization needs to be further improved. According to the 2005 China Market Economy Development Report provided by the Institute of Economics and Resource Management of Beijing Normal University, the degree of marketization of China's economy in 2003 was 73.8%. According to the research finding by Chen Dandan and Ren Baoping, the marketization index of China's economy in 2006 was 78.2%.[1] According to the 2018 Index of Economic Freedom released by the Heritage Foundation and the *Wall Street Journal*, the index of economic freedom in China in 2016 was 57.8, 5.3 percentage points higher than that in 2014 and 0.4 percentage points higher than that in 2015.[2] This shows that the degree of freedom or marketization of China's economy is constantly developing.

II. Market economy with Chinese characteristics

Unlike the market economy with European characteristics represented by the United Kingdom, China's market economy has many of its own characteristics, two of which are the most distinctive and important, namely, different system origins and different system foundations.

1. Different system origins

Different from the European market economy countries represented by the United Kingdom, China's market economy originated not from a feudal economy but a planned economy.

The establishment process of the British market economy system from the second half of the 17th century to the 19th century, which was led by the bourgeois revolution in the 1640s and the overthrow of the feudal autocratic monarchy, was a process of constantly destroying the feudal economic system and economic structure while establishing the capitalist private ownership and free market system. The establishment of this market economy system eventually replaced various privileges, monopolies, and guild systems in feudal society with capital freedom and self-discipline, contract freedom and constraint, and replaced government intervention and mercantilist policies with free competition and free trade. Since its formal establishment, this market economy system has taken laissez faire as its ideology, with the market mechanism determining the resource allocation and the government merely serving as the "night watchman" as its principal character. Although the capitalist market economy changed from free competition to monopoly in the late 19th century and early 20th century, and government intervention prevailed after the "Keynesian Revolution", the main mechanism for allocating resources and regulating economic operation was the market.

The construction of China's market economy system actually began with the reform and opening up in 1979. The construction process of China's market economy system is a process of constant reform and transition of the mode of resource allocation: after the founding of the People's Republic of China in 1949, a highly centralized planned-economy system was established, then was transitioned to a planned commodity economy system in the 1980s, and last was transitioned to a socialist market economy system after the mid-1990s, which was the transition process of the mode of resource allocation under the socialist system structure. Therefore, the process of establishing China's market economy is a process of independent reform and transition, rather than a revolutionary process in which one system overthrows another.

From the perspective of the mode of resource allocation or allocation mechanism, the establishment process of the capitalist market economy represented by the United Kingdom is a process of alternation between the market regulation and government (feudal country) intervention—in the growth process of the market economy, the power of capital constantly removes various obstacles to its free development. The establishment process of China's socialist market economy is a process of alternation between the government intervention (planned-economy control) and market regulation. Through continuous and deepening economic system reform, the government's power to control resources and intervene in economic activities has been continuously reduced and liberalized, thus freeing up more and more space for the market to allocate resources and regulate economic activities.

In the process of the market economy construction with British characteristics, the growth and expansion of market forces is offensive, and the growth process of the market economy is a blistering revolutionary process. In the process of the market economy construction with Chinese characteristics, the growth and expansion of market forces is a combination of offense and defense, and the growth process of the market economy is a gradual process of gradually getting rid of the shackles of the old system. The force of the old system is reluctant to withdraw from the economic stage easily, and tries its best to keep its territory, which forces the force of the new system (market) to attack and defend at the same time, and the fight for forces between the old and new systems is a seesaw and sometimes in a stalemate. The growth rate of the market economy with Chinese characteristics depends on the intensity of reforms and the speed of the government's "delegation" or "conceding" of powers to the market. Under the old system, the government controlled resources and resource allocation, as well as economic activities. If the government did not "delegate" or "concede" these powers to the market, market forces could not grow. Therefore, we often see the authority and the media's formulation of "delegating powers to invigorate the market", that is to say, only when the government delegates the powers to the market can the market be invigorated—the government "delegates" or "concedes" certain powers to the market, which is a reform. In fact, the correct statement should be to "return" the resource allocation power to the market. Since it is to establish a socialist market economic system, the market should have the final say on how to allocate resources.

2. Different system foundations

So far, only China's market economy is established based on the socialist system, while the market economy of other modes are established based on the capitalist system. Although both the capitalist economic system and socialist economic system in the world today belong to a public-private hybrid system, and pure capitalist private ownership and pure socialist public ownership are hard to find, China's current market economy system is still dominated by the socialist public ownership, while the capitalist market economy system of western countries is still dominated by the private ownership. Unlike the market economy established based on capitalist private ownership, under China's socialist market economic system, the government and state-owned enterprises control key economic resources and the country's economic lifeline. The government also participates in resource allocation and even dominates resource allocation in some fields and industries. Local governments still dominate the economic development of their respective region. Local governments, enterprises (producers), and consumers (laborers) are the three main bodies driving China's economic development, while enterprises and consumers serve as the dual bodies driving the economic development in western market economic countries.

In the future Chinese socialist market economy, the status and role of the government cannot revert to that of a "night watchman". To establish a socialist market economy, it is inseparable from public ownership, state-owned enterprises, fair distribution, common prosperity, government planning, and government regulation. Therefore, the function and role of the government in economic activities are certainly much greater than those of the government in the western market economy. The degree of freedom and competition in economic activities is correspondingly lower than that in the western market economy.

The previous two characteristics make China's market economy unique in the development of the human market economy, and simultaneously make the relationship between the market and the government and the functional orientation of the government have China's own characteristics. And, because the construction time of China's socialist market economic system is still very short, and the process of the government "delegating" or "conceding" powers to the market is still in progress, the growth and development of the market mechanism is not perfect. The current market mechanism is like bamboo shoots in spring. It grows fast but has not yet been formed and become strong, and the strength and hardness of its regulation are insufficient. As a result, the role of the market mechanism in regulating resource allocation is not fully played.

III. Rigidity and weakness of market mechanism

The market economy naturally has a self-regulation capacity, which is the main difference between the market economy system and other modes of resource allocation or economic system. The self-regulation capacity of the market economy originates from the function of the market mechanism. Milton Friedman summarized the functions of the market (price) mechanism into three types in the article "Market Mechanism and Central Economic Planning": (1) Conveying information—to convey information about preferences, resource availability, and production possibilities via prices. (2) Providing incentives—to get people to adopt the lowest cost production methods and to use the available resources for the highest value purposes. (3) Distributing income—to decide who gets what and how much. The price provides incentives to people only because it is used to distribute income; people's income is linked to their contribution, which naturally motivates people to pay attention to the message conveyed by price, and motivates people to work hard to reduce costs.[3] However, Friedman's generalization omitted another significant function of the market mechanism, which is the function of "automatic removal, automatic adjustment, and self-rehabilitation". From a microeconomic perspective, when there is excess production of a product or service, its price must fall, and if other conditions remain unchanged, the profits of the enterprise producing such product will be reduced, and those enterprises with high production costs or weak competitiveness will certainly have to be the first to exit the market due to losses, which removes some excess products and excess capacity. In this removal process, the economic proportional relationship or structure is adjusted and optimized, and the imbalance between supply and demand is repaired. This suggests that the market economy itself has a set of endogenous exit mechanisms for excess products and excess capacity.

From the perspective of macroeconomics, in the economic operation, when the economy deviates from its equilibrium path (steady state) due to the shock of the AD or AS, there are three mechanisms that play a regulating role, restoring the balance between AD and AS. The three mechanisms include the quantity regulatory mechanism, the price regulatory mechanism, and the mixed mechanism of quantity and price regulation.

Since the aggregate expenditure (AE) of an economy is equal to the aggregate demand (AD) plus the unintended inventory investment (IU), that is, AE = AD + IU; in equilibrium, aggregate output (Y) is equal to AE and equal to AD, that is, Y = AE = AD, that is, in equilibrium, IU = 0, or, the economy is out of balance if IU ≠ 0.

When Y > AD and IU > 0, it indicates that the aggregate output is greater than AD. At this time, there will be excess product inventory (excess production) in the economy, and product prices will drop; in this case, profit-maximizing manufacturers will reduce production and inventory until output and AD return to equilibrium.

When Y < AD and IU < 0, it indicates that the aggregate output is less than AD. At this time, the product inventory in the economy is less than the normal level (supply shortage), and the shortage of some products will lead to an increase in product prices; in this case, manufacturers, as economic people, will expand production and increase investment in inventories until output and AD return to equilibrium. Therefore, IU becomes a mechanism to adjust the macroeconomy to achieve equilibrium.

There is also a price regulatory mechanism for macroeconomic equilibrium—to achieve an equilibrium between aggregate output and AD by regulating money wage rates, interest rates, or expected prices. If the money wage rate is elastic, when the supply exceeds the demand in the labor market, i.e., a surplus of labor supply, the money wage rate will decrease, thereby causing a decrease in the labor supply and an increase in the demand for labor, which eventually restore the labor market to equilibrium. When the labor market is in short supply, i.e., a shortage of labor supply, the money wage rate will increase, thereby stimulating an increase in the labor supply and a decrease in the demand for labor, which eventually also restore the labor market to equilibrium. If the interest rate is elastic, when the demand for investment in the capital market exceeds the supply of savings, the interest rate will rise, which will stimulate an increase in savings and a decrease in investment, thus restoring the equilibrium of supply and demand in the capital market. When there is too much saving or too little investment, interest rates will fall, which will stimulate an increase in investment and a decrease in savings, ultimately leading to an equilibrium of supply and demand in the capital market.

If money wage rates, interest rates, and prices in the economy are rigid or sticky, once AS and AD are out of balance, the macroeconomy will gradually restore equilibrium after a long or short cycle through the slow adjustment of money wages and prices.

There is a third regulatory mechanism for macroeconomic operation, namely, a mixed mechanism of quantity and price regulation in the IS-LM model.

According to the IS-LM model, when the product market and the money market are out of balance at the same time, that is, when the total investment I and the total savings S are unbalanced ($I \neq S$) and the money demand L and the money supply M are unbalanced ($L \neq M$) at the same time, $I > S$ will cause an increase in aggregate output Y, because $I > S$ implies an unexpected reduction in enterprises' inventories, which will cause a rise in inventory prices, thereby stimulating enterprises to expand output; while $I < S$ will cause a decrease in aggregate output Y. The changes in Y will cause the changes in the money demand L_1 of transaction and prudence motive. Under the condition that the quantity of money M in the economy remains unchanged, the quantity of money used to satisfy the money demand L_2 of speculative motive will decrease or increase accordingly, thus affecting the interest rate r in the money market. $L > M$ will lead to a rise in r, and when other conditions remain unchanged, a rise in r will discourage the private (enterprise) investment I, thereby inhibiting the increase in employment N and output Y; while $L < M$ will reduce r, which will expand employment and output by stimulating investment. Through the automatic regulation of the mechanisms for the product market and the money market, the macroeconomy will move from imbalance to general equilibrium. The process of the economy from imbalance to restoration of equilibrium is a gradual elimination process of supply surplus or supply shortage.

The market mechanism cannot completely remove excess products and excess capacity, as evidenced by the financial and economic crises that erupt from time to time. When the economy is out of balance, the market mechanism is not always able to adjust the economy to the level of full employment (Keynes, 1936). However, the function of automatic adjustment, automatic removal, and automatic optimization (regarding economic structure and economic proportional relationship) and the function of self-stabilization of the market mechanism exist objectively and functioning.

In the current Chinese economy, the market mechanism has both a rigid side and a weak side. This may seem like an oxymoron, but this is the reality of China's economy. This also shows the complexity of China's economic problems and reforms. At the present stage, the degree of rigidity of the interest rates of deposits and loans in China's economy, the prices of some government-controlled products, services, factors of production, and resource products, the wages of state-owned enterprises, and the prices of products or services of monopoly enterprises are still relatively high. These prices cannot fluctuate along with the changes in the supply–demand relationship, and they are actually rigid rather than elastic. On the other hand, due to the following causes, the regulatory function of the current market mechanism in China is weak, which is manifested in that once supply and demand are out of balance, or once supply is excessive, the regulation capacity of the market mechanism is insufficient, the regulatory function is difficult to fully exert, and the regulation results are often difficult to be in place.

1. Since the market mechanism is not fully developed, the prices of some products and services are still distorted, and some prices are still artificially set. These prices cannot truly and promptly reflect the changes in the supply–demand relationship and the scarcity of resources.
2. Some market entities are insensitive to changes in price signals and react sluggishly. For example, state-owned enterprises are less responsive to changes in interest rates than private enterprises, and monopoly enterprises are less concerned about changes in market prices; local governments and state-owned enterprises are far more responsive to changes in central government policies than to changes in market prices.
3. On the whole, the market competition in China's economy is not sufficient. The degree of competition in some markets (industries) is not high, and the free mobility of resources is low. Resource misallocation is often difficult to be corrected through automatic regulation by the market mechanism, and resource allocation has difficulty in achieving "Pareto improvement".
4. The regulatory function of the market mechanism is also restricted by multiple factors such as the force of the old system and government intervention. In view of factors such as politics, political achievements, and social stability, local governments have consciously protected or implicitly guaranteed some excess products, loss-making enterprises, and excess capacity that should

have been removed according to the cost–benefit accounting principle, so that they can survive. Government intervention and protection cause the failure of the market competition mechanism of selecting the superior and eliminating the inferior, and they cause the failure of exit mechanism of excess capacity.

The previous causes make the market mechanism unable to effectively exert its regulatory and removal functions, causing the following consequences: there is persistent and long-run supply surplus of some products; "zombie enterprises" are stuck in the market; the excess product or capacity and otherwise that should be eliminated fail to be eliminated; and the imbalances of the economic structure are slow to be adjusted, making it more difficult to optimize and upgrade.

Establishing a relatively perfect market economy system is a long process and cannot be completed in the short run. If the construction period of China's socialist market economic system is counted from the time when the Decision on Several Issues concerning the Establishment of a Socialist Market Economic System adopted at the Third Plenary Session of the 14th CPC Central Committee in November 1993, it is less than 30 years; even when such period is counted from the reform and opening up in 1979, it is only 43 years. The construction of the market economy in the United Kingdom, the United States, and continental European countries took at least one or two hundred years. What's more, China's economic system transition adopts a gradual approach rather than "shock therapy". The path China has taken to construct a socialist market economic system is exploratory, with Chinese style or characteristics, rather than imitative and replicative. The gradual approach and the exploratory path naturally take a relatively long time. Even if China's "catch-up" speed is taken into account, we cannot expect that the market system and market mechanism will be perfected and functioning properly through 30 or 40 years of reform and construction. The establishment and improvement of a new system cannot be achieved quickly, and the system established with "fast-food style" must be undernourished and underdeveloped. We should do a good job of long-run reform and construction of new systems, and reform and opening up must be done generation after generation in succession.

IV. Catch-up strategy, official system, and policy leverage

As a great and powerful country in history and one of the four ancient civilizations in the world, China slowly fell behind from the 1820s until the first half of the 20th century, when it became the object of aggression and partition by the world powers. When the People's Republic of China was established in 1949, China was the largest poor and developing country in the world, so it has always been the Chinese dream to "catch up" with the developed countries in the world in terms of economic development, scientific and technological development, and military power, and to "revitalize the Chinese nation".

To realize the "catch-up" strategy, the first-generation leaders of the CPC put forward the goal of "catching up with and surpassing the United Kingdom and the United States in 60 years".[4] The second-generation leaders put forward that it would take about 100 years to catch up with developed countries and realize modernization, and to catch up with middle-developed countries in per capita GDP in the mid-21st century; to achieve this catch-up goal, the Chinese government has formulated a development strategy of "quadrupling per capita income via the three-step strategy".[5] The current generation of leaders, with Comrade Xi Jinping at the core, has put forward the "Two Centenary Goals and Three Stages": The first stage is to build a moderately prosperous society in all respects in 20 years by the centenary of the CPC (founded in 1921); the second stage is to realize the socialist modernization with Chinese characteristics in all aspects in another 30 years by the centenary of the People's Republic of China (founded in 1949); and the third stage is to realize the great rejuvenation of the Chinese nation step by step throughout the 21st century. The report to the 19th CPC National Congress also put forward the "two-stage goal of modernization": in the first stage, from 2020 to 2035, we will build on the foundation of the moderately prosperous society with 15 more years of hard work to see that socialist modernization is basically achieved; in the second stage, from 2035 to the middle of the 21st century, having achieved basic modernization, we will work hard for 15 more years and develop China into a great modern socialist country.[6]

Under China's current political system and government administration system, this "catch-up strategy" must be implemented and realized through local governments at all levels. Since GDP and per capita GDP are the most important indicators of economic development and the easiest to measure and compare, local governments at all levels take GDP growth as their primary target. In order to clarify the economic growth tasks and responsibilities of local governments, the CPC Central Committee and the State Council propose the annual economic growth target every year. In order to achieve or exceed this growth target, and to mobilize the enthusiasm of local governments, each level of government from the central to the local level will formulate a set of systems for evaluating officials' political achievements with GDP growth as the core for the next level of government. Such a set of systems will serve as the main basis for the promotion of officials at all levels—whoever in charge of the local economy that grows faster will have good political achievements and be promoted quickly, resulting in the integration of the pursuit of high GDP growth and officials' pursuit of personal political future.[7]

Since the reform and opening up, especially since the central government and local governments implemented the tax-sharing system in 1995, local governments have been granted independent authority over administrative affairs and financial affairs. The tax revenue of the place where the economy develops well and rapidly will naturally go up. As the saying goes, "money makes the world go round", and "the more money you have, the more things you can do". The local government with high tax revenue can control more resources and accomplish many things that the leader of the local government wants to do, including many "overblown vanity projects" and "achievement projects", such as urban demolition for reconstruction, road repairing, construction of development zones with government subsidies and the realization of "four completions" (completion of infrastructure of water, electricity, and gas supply, and roads), building of luxury office buildings and government hotels, increase of employment opportunities with enough financial resources, improvement of people's livelihood and maintaining of local stability, etc.; the completion of these things by the local government not only promotes the growth of local GDP and tax revenue, but also adds a lot of points to the image (political achievements) of the local leader. Under this fiscal decentralization system, the local government (in fact, the main officials of the local government) has strong and independent economic interests, which are closely linked with the speed of local economic development, making local governments have the characteristics of "economic man" and become one of the market entities of economic development. It is not difficult to find that in places where China's economy is developing rapidly and well, local government leaders have outstanding talents in organizing and allocating resources.

Therefore, we found that the behavior of Chinese local governments (officials) at the present stage is driven by dual incentives: on the one hand, there is the political incentive for official career promotion; on the other hand, there is the economic incentive for more local tax revenue to control more resources. The system for evaluating officials' political achievements integrates these two incentives for mutual reinforcement. In addition, many local government officials have a sense of mission and responsibility, which has created a strong driving force for local governments to promote economic development.[8] Therefore, we often see that many local government officials have more entrepreneur characteristics than general entrepreneurs—government officials have more incentive than entrepreneurs to increase aggregate output.

Under the background of weak economic foundation and shortage of capital in China, the most convenient way to increase GDP growth rate is to expand investment, introduce foreign capital, and initiate more construction projects, especially large projects and extra-large projects. Therefore, we can see that the enthusiasm of local governments to "attract investment" is very high; many local governments not only engage in attracting investment in China, but also often organize groups to attract investment around the world. The competition under the market economy is supposed to be the market competition among enterprises, but at the present stage in China, besides the competition among enterprises, there is also the competition among local governments, and the competition among local governments to pursue the maximization of their own interests has evolved into the competition to pursue the growth of local aggregate output. All local governments pursue investment growth, initiation of projects, and economic growth in their respective region, which inevitably lead to excessive investment and repeated construction, as well as environmental and ecological damage. More importantly, in order to pursue their political goals of promotion, local government officials often ignore costs, distortions of the market mechanism, misallocation of resources, and even the fair distribution and sharing of economic reform and development achievements. Because, for an official, promotion is the main goal he or she pursues, and "he or she who doesn't want to be a general isn't a good soldier", the economic interests he/she pursues serve his/her political interests, and his/her economic goals lay the foundation for his/her political goals; moreover, for local government officials, repeated investment, investment failure, waste of resources, and price distortion are all external costs, which are borne by society rather than by himself/herself. Therefore, China's economic development has formed such a situation: economic growth and development at the national level are planned—"catch-up strategy" is a long-run plan, and the five-year plan is a medium-run plan. The Central Economic Working Conference at the end of each year gives an annual (short-run) plan. An overall plan is made for the allocation of resources across the nation, but the investment and economic growth between local governments are out of balance, disorderly, and out of proportion, and go on their own way. Each local government pursues investment growth, initiation of projects, resource utilization, and economic growth only from local conditions, local needs, and local interests. Even if he/she wants to make investment decisions and resource allocation from the overall perspective of the whole country, he/she can't do it objectively, because he/she lacks information on supply and demand, economic structure, resource scarcity, and price outside his/her region. Such information is an indispensable basis for him/her to make scientific and reasonable economic decisions; moreover, it is not within the duty and authority of local governments or local officials to seek the proportional relationship coordination and balanced development of the national economy. As a result, this disorderly competition caused by local government officials in pursuit of GDP growth (and also in pursuit of their own promotion) leads to repeated construction, wasteful or inefficient or even ineffective investment, excess capacity, and imbalance of economic structure. In recent years, we often see a phenomenon: a local government official has been promoted to other places, but left behind a large pile of "mess" and government debts related to construction projects; the project built by the predecessor was reinvented by the successor.

In order to achieve the government's development goals, pursue high economic growth, and turn the government's development intentions into reality, the central government often issues corresponding fiscal policies, monetary policies, and industrial policies. However, in order to create their own achievements and improve their promotion competitiveness, and to fulfill their duties and missions as a big official, every local government will maximize and competitively use policy leverage to promote local economic growth, while the tenure system and exchange position system of officials aggravate the short-run behavior of local government officials. Therefore, "striving for more preferential policies" and "taking full advantage of the central policies" have become the public slogans of local government officials. How many preferential policies they have strived for, how to take full advantage of the central policies, and what is the degree of taking full advantage of the central policies reflect the administrative skills and abilities of local government officials. Obviously, "taking full advantage of the policy" does not mean that the policy is effectively implemented or a scientific decision-making is made.

This motivation and behavior of local government officials cause enterprises to often decide on "what to produce" and "how much to produce" not based on market price signals, and make investment decisions and production and business decisions around the preferential policies introduced by the government, which in turn makes the enterprise and the local government form a relationship of interest-related party.

The policy leverages often used by the central and local governments mainly include:

1. Industrial policy

In order to guide and encourage certain industries to give priority to development or key construction, the central government often issues some industrial policies, including the list of industries with priority development or key construction, the development goals of these industries, various preferential policies and measures given by the government, etc. Such industrial policies are not only a strong signal to guide local governments and enterprises in terms of the direction of investment and "what to produce", but also an effective incentive mechanism for local governments and enterprises to "act according to the central government's policy guideline". Actively implementing these industrial policies will not only be politically manifested as "aligning with the central government", but will also be economically rewarded with many preferences and benefits, such as access to more financial subsidies, tax incentives, and bank credit incline, thereby increasing local GDP, per capita GDP, local government revenues, and employment opportunities. This is not only beneficial to the promotion of local government officials, but also brings tangible economic benefits to this region and enterprises. Why not do such a thing of "killing two birds with one stone"?

In 2009, the ten key industries to be invigorated and developed in a focused manner set forth in the Plan for Invigorating Ten Key Industries issued by the Chinese government enjoyed preferential policies, such as financial subsidy, tax relief, or low-cost allocation of construction land. Therefore, these industries were the objects of competition for the initiation of projects and development by various local governments. As a result, six key industries among them became the industries with serious excess capacity, which became the key reform and adjustment objects in the supply-side structural reform.

2. Financial subsidy

Financial subsidy is the main policy tool of the Chinese government to support industrial development. In order to encourage and promote the development of certain industries, the central government often directly uses the financial subsidy to support these industries in expanding investment and production scale and carrying out transformation and upgrading. For example, in order to promote the development of photovoltaic industry, the central government has given up to 70% investment subsidies to photovoltaic projects. On August 30, 2013, the National Development and Reform Commission issued a document, stipulating that distributed photovoltaic power generation shall be subsidized according to the power generation capacity, with the subsidy standard of RMB 0.42 per kWh, while the photovoltaic electricity price stipulated by the state was RMB 0.9, RMB 0.95, and RMB 1 per kWh, that is, the state subsidies accounted for 46.7%–42% of the electricity price respectively. In addition, all local governments have added some financial subsidies. For example, Zhejiang Province stipulated that additional RMB 0.1 would be subsidized for distributed photovoltaic power generation per kWh on the basis of state subsidies. These subsidies have triggered a photovoltaic investment boom all over China. All localities only see that photovoltaic investment is economical and profitable, but can't see how big the market capacity of photovoltaic is. The competition of local governments leads to the rapid development of photovoltaic investment. As a result, photovoltaic, a new industry, has become one of the industries with excess capacity in China shortly after its development.

3. Bank credit

For industries supported by industrial policies, the State Council usually requires bank credit funds to focus on these industries, and local governments to provide financial support through financing methods such as the loan with discounted interest and extension of loan repayment period, or directly through local government investment and financing platforms, so as to guide and encourage enterprises to invest in these industries.

4. Other preferential policies

These preferential policies can be described as diverse, including the supply of cheap or even free construction land for investment projects, or subsidies by the local government for enterprises to purchase land for project construction, subsidies for enterprises' electricity and water consumption, allocation of a specific amount of resource development rights to enterprises, tax relief for enterprises or tax exemptions for a number of years after the start of the project, free construction of office buildings and villas for investors, solutions for investors to settle in the city where the project is located and for their children to attend the best local primary and secondary schools, etc.[9]

In addition, in order to accelerate the development of the local economy and industries, some local governments have intentionally lowered the access standards of environmental protection, health, and safety for enterprises to enter certain industries, and tacitly allow or even connive at the failure of enterprises to comply with these access standards. For example, some steel, cement, electrolytic aluminum, and flat glass projects, and even photovoltaic projects, are often projects with heavy energy consumption and emission and serious pollution. In order to encourage enterprises to invest in production, some local governments set no restrictions on these projects featuring heavy energy consumption and emission and serious pollution, and turned a blind eye to the environmental pollution and ecological damage caused by enterprise production, and even when the central inspection team found the problem in the inspection, the local government intentionally covered for enterprises to absolve them of liability.

These government policy leverages are much more powerful and effective than the market price mechanism regarding guiding the enterprises' investment direction and stimulating enterprises' investment intensity under China's current system and economic environment; the investment and production decisions of enterprises (including foreign-funded enterprises in China) are often guided by government policies, rather than by market demand and price signals.

From the subjective wishes of policy makers, the government's industrial policy orientation is to keep consistent with market demand, to act according to economic laws, and to promote and accelerate industrial and economic development through industrial policies, especially to support, cultivate, and develop some emerging industries and leading industries through industrial policies. However, with hindsight, the implementation of industrial policies often produced the following results, some of which were consistent with, and some of which were contrary to, the planning or policy objectives.

1. Some industrial policy orientations were consistent with the market demand and market orientation, and the implementation effect of these policies was relatively good. For example, from 1979 to 1984, in order to solve the serious shortage of supply in the consumer market at that time, the Chinese government implemented the principle of "six priorities" for the development of light industry, which greatly promoted the development of consumer goods production and gradually eased the supply shortage. By around 1990, China's consumer market basically achieved a balance between supply and demand.[10]
2. Although some industrial policy orientations were consistent with the market demand and market orientation, the economic situation and objective conditions changed in the process of policy implementation, or the local government "distorted" or "watered down" the policies in the implementation process, such as level-by-level upgrading of the preferential policies and the repeated relaxation of environmental protection standards, resulting in the failure to achieve the expected policy effect, and even causing many sequelae, which backfired, such as the Chinese government's support policy for photovoltaic industry mentioned earlier.
3. Some industrial policy orientations deviated from the market demand and market orientation, which not only did not promote economic structure optimization or economic development, but aggravated the imbalance of the economic structure, excess production, and excess capacity. The serious excess capacity caused by the implementation of the Plan for Invigorating Ten Key Industries by the Chinese government in 2009 was an example. As we said earlier, around 2005, China's economy had experienced serious imbalance of economic structure, and some industries had excess capacity to varying degrees. In 2009, in order to cope with the international financial crisis, the Chinese government issued the Plan for Invigorating Ten Key

Industries, which further aggravated the imbalance of economic structure and excess capacity.

The government's industrial policies sometimes fail, causing the consequence of "good intention, bad result". The reason for this is mainly that market demand information, economic structure change information, information on economic development situation, expectation and behavior change information of economic entities, especially the potential technological innovation information and the development information of emerging industry caused by technological innovation, cannot be controlled by policy makers, which may lead to the policy intention being unrelated with the objective market needs, or policy objectives and the implementation results being poles apart.

Judging from the economic performance in recent years, the regulation capacity of the market mechanism in China is weak and insufficient.

In the current international financial crisis, China's economy suffered a negative impact about one year later than the American economy, and then the macroeconomic situation turned from sunny to cloudy. The federal government of the United States introduced a total of USD 1.633 trillion stimulus package three times from February 2008 to February 2009, while the Chinese central government introduced a RMB 4 trillion stimulus package in November 2008, with the scale of stimulus of China and the United States accounting for 11.59% and 11.45% of their respective GDP (in 2009). It can be said that the intensity of stimulus in China and the United States is roughly equivalent. However, the American economy has been improving and recovering since 2013, with economic data such as unemployment rate, industrial production index, PMI, growth of total retail sales of consumer goods, business inventories, CPI, and PPI continuing to improve. The Federal Reserve ended quantitative easing policy in October 2014 and entered the interest rate hike cycle in December 2015, which indicated that the American economy had come out of its slump and entered the recovery. Despite the twists and turns of the recovery process, the American economy came out of the bottom of this economic cycle, and the general trend of continuous improvement of the economic situation was certain. However, after China's economy recovered in 2009, its economic growth rate continued to decline from the second quarter of 2010, dropping from 12.2% in the first quarter of 2010 to 6.7% in 2016, a drop of 45.1%. More importantly, the downward pressure on China's economy still exists, and it is still unknown when the economy will hit bottom and where the bottom of the current economic cycle is located. The economic structural adjustment in China has been conducted for more than ten years, but the adjustment has not been properly implemented for a long time, and the imbalance of economic structure is still quite serious in many aspects.[11]

Even more noteworthy is the competition of local governments chasing economic indicators. In order to "maintain stability", local governments protected enterprises on the verge of bankruptcy and protected excess capacity and outdated capacity, which had a significant inhibiting effect on the supply surplus in China's economy, economic structural adjustment, and transformation of economic development mode in the international financial crisis. The local government's excessive concern with short-run economic growth goals conflicts with the central government's medium- and long-run development goals, causing the following consequences: The industrial structure and economic structure that should have been adjusted were deformed and were watered-down; the "automatic regulation" and "automatic removal" functions of the market mechanism have been destroyed and weakened in many aspects, and low-end capacity and capacity with pollution are difficult to be removed to varying degrees. The massively cumulative local debts incurred by local governments for pursuing their own short-run goals (political achievements) has undoubtedly formed another important obstacle to the transformation and upgrading of the economic structure in China.

The sharp contrast in the economic performance between China and the United States, in addition to the fact that the United States may have done better in macroeconomic control than has China, may be mainly due to the differences in the effect strength of the market mechanism and regulation capacity in the Chinese and American economies and the differences in the roles of the market and government in resource allocation between China and the United States. These differences show that the market-oriented reform of China's economy has a long way to go.

Notes

1 Chen, D. D., & Ren, B. P. (2009). "Performance Analysis of China's Economic Transformation: 1992–2006 [J]", *Finance and Economics*, 5, 80–88.

2 Miller, T. et al. (2018). "The Heritage Foundation". *2018 Index of Economic Freedom*, 5 & 140.

3 Friedman, M. (2001). *The Essential of Friedman*. Vol. 1. Chinese 1st Ed. Beijing: Capital University of Economics and Business Press, 28–29.

4 *Collected Works of Mao Zedong*. Vol. 6. Beijing: People's Publishing House, 1999, 500. *Collected Works of Mao Zedong*. Vol. 7. Beijing: People's Publishing House, 1999, 89.

5 According to Deng Xiaoping's vision at that time, the first step was to double China's per capita income in the 1980s, with per capita GDP reaching USD 500; the second step was to double per capita income again, to USD 1,000 by the end of the 20th century; the third step was to quadruple per capita income again, to about USD 4,000 by the 2030s to the 2050s.

6 Xi, J. P. (2017). *Securing a Decisive Victory in Building a Moderately Prosperous Society in All Respects, and Striving for the Great Success of Socialism with Chinese Characteristics for a New Era—Report to the 19th CPC National Congress*. Beijing: People's Publishing House, 28.

7 Since the 18th CPC National Congress, the central government has reformed and improved the assessment system and assessment indicators for officials, emphasizing that

> we must assess the overall work, the actual results of economic, political, cultural, social, and ecological civilization construction and party building of officials, and the results of resolving prominent contradictions and problems in the self-development of officials. Only regional GDP and growth rate should not be used as the main indicators for assessing political achievements of officials, and regional GDP and growth rate rankings should not be carried out.

Since then, the motivation of local governments to pursue growth and compete for quantity has weakened. However, in the new assessment indicator system, economic growth and economic performance are still important indicators.

8 In my opinion, it is an incomplete explanation to explain the behavioral motivation of local government officials in China by using "official carrer promotion competition".

9 For example, the government of Inner Mongolia Autonomous Region issued a policy in 2011, stipulating that, for projects related to coal conversion and comprehensive utilization, coal resources shall be allocated according to the actual coal consumption by the ratio of 1:2 in the effective production period of the projects; for equipment manufacturing projects and high-tech projects, 100 million tons of coal resources shall be allocated for every RMB 2 billion of investment in fixed assets, and the maximum amount of coal resources allocated for a project subject shall not exceed 1 billion tons. In 2011, the profit per ton of coal in Inner Mongolia was about RMB 300. Allocating more rights to exploit coal resources means providing more risk-free profits for the project.

10 The principle of "six priorities" to support the development of light industry cover: priority to the supply of raw materials, fuels, and electricity; priority to tapping of the production potential of enterprises, technological innovation, and reformation measures; priority to capital construction; priority to bank loans; priority to foreign exchange and introduction of advanced technology; priority to transportation.

11 According to the data from the Department of Labor and the Ministry of Commerce of the United States, the unemployment rate in the United States has dropped below 5% since April 2016, and further dropped below 4.5% since March 2017, the lowest unemployment rate in 16 years. The industrial production index began to break 100 (at 100.4) in September 2013, and has been rising since then. In September 2016, the manufacturing PMI exceeded 50% (at 51.5%), and has been climbing ever since, rising to 58.8% in August 2017; non-manufacturing PMI has been between 51.4% and 57.6% since 2015. Business inventory growth has been declining since reaching a high of 5.9% in July 2014, falling to below 3% since March 2015. The year-on-year growth of total retail sales of consumer goods rebounded from a trough (1%) in September 2016 (1%) to a peak of 5.6% in February 2017, and has since been at around 4%. Since 2015, the year-on-year growth rates of CPI and core CPI have been below 2.8% and 2.4% respectively, and the year-on-year growth rate of PPI has turned from negative to positive since August 2016, and has since been below 2.6%.

Part II

General plan and results

This part focuses on answering the following questions: How to carry out a supply-side structural reform? How to choose the path of supply-side structural reform? How to effectively handle the relationship between the government and the market, short-run adjustment and long-run development, and AS and AD in the supply-side structural reform?

DOI: 10.4324/9781003367000-7

5 Effective handling of two relationships

I. Supply reform with laying equal emphasis on the demand

The Chinese government began to implement the proactive fiscal policies aimed at expanding domestic demand in 1998, and launched a supply-side structural reform in November 2015. These great changes in the reform and policies caused a great discussion on "which is more important between the (aggregate) demand and the (aggregate) supply" in Chinese academic circles and a debate on "which is correct between Say's Law and Keynes' Law" among economists.[1] Some Chinese scholars believe that the theoretical source of supply-side structural reform is Say's Law, and the theoretical basis thereof is supply-side economics or Reaganomics, appearing in the United States in the late 1970s and 1980s, while scholars believe that Keynes' economic theory is a wrong analytical framework, and the "troika of the economy factors" theory and policies are "deceptive tricks"; meanwhile, some scholars advocate "abandoning Keynes' theory and returning to Hayek's theory".

In my opinion, these views are one-sided and make an "either–or" mistake; "which is important between the (aggregate) demand and the (aggregate) supply" is a false proposition. According to the analysis we made in the part of "a basic analytical framework", macroeconomic variables of an economy such as aggregate output, employment quantity, and overall price level are determined when AD and AS depend on and influence each other, and finally reach an equilibrium state. Neither AD nor AS can determine the balanced or actual output, employment, and price alone. If there is market demand, the output will be sold; it is a simple economic principle that the demand can be realized only in case of production results. Marx pointed out: "Production mediates consumption; it creates the latter's material; without it, consumption would lack an object". "Products only become realistic products in consumption", and "consumption creates new production demand, that is, it creates the conceptual intrinsic motivation of production, which is the premise of production".[2]

Say's Law emphasizes the importance of the supply and holds that the supply determines the demand, while Keynes' Law emphasizes the importance of the demand and holds that the demand determines the supply. These two laws seem to be completely opposite and incompatible, as if only one of them can be selected.

DOI: 10.4324/9781003367000-8

In fact, both Say's Law and Keynes' Law hold conditionally; they do not hold under all conditions. From the perspective of the AD-AS analysis framework, both Say's Law and Keynes' Law are correct and one-sided.

Say's Law implies the following preconditions: (1) The market price mechanisms are fully elastic, and their automatic regulation can ensure that various markets are cleared in a timely manner. (2) The automatic regulation of interest rate can ensure that all the part of current income (savings) that is not used for consumption can be converted into investment, which is based on the assumption that the interest is the return on savings and the cost of investment, and that interest rates have complete elasticity. (3) Money is neutral, and is only a medium of transaction. The changes in quantity of money only affect nominal variables in the economy, but not real variables. (4) The distribution system in the economic society can ensure that the aggregate output and the corresponding total income are converted into an equal amount of effective demand.

Say's Law holds that, in the relationship between the supply and the demand, the supply is decisive and comes first, and it will create demand. If system factors are put aside, this idea is correct in the long run—because, in the long run, AS is the main decisive factor for the growth of aggregate output (economic growth). Generally speaking, in the long run, from the perspective of macroeconomics, the available resources and technologies are certain, and thus the potential aggregate output is certain (the long-run AS curve is vertical), but the price and money wages can be freely and fully adjusted, so the effective demand can adapt to the AS capacity, and the potential aggregate output can be produced under the condition of full employment; in the long run, the supply not only creates the object of demand (consumption), but also creates income, that is, the capacity to pay; people's income that they don't spend in the current period will always be used for future consumption.

However, Say's Law is one-sided: (1) In the long run, the AS capacity of an economy can adapt to the aggregate purchasing capacity, but it may not be so in the short run; the short-run AD can be less than or greater than AS. Therefore, an economy may have underemployment or actual aggregate output less than the natural rate level of aggregate output in the short run, or may appear the overheated economy or inflation. (2) In an economy with supply shortage or strong demand, in the early stage of economic development, increasing supply or expanding production is undoubtedly the first, and the importance of the supply is higher than that of demand; while in an economy with supply surplus, or in an economy with highly developed production or supply capacity, AD does not necessarily increase in proportion to the increase in AS. (3) If the distribution system and wealth possession in the economic society are unreasonable, and the gap between the rich and the poor is too large, the aggregate output and the corresponding total income cannot be converted into an equal amount of effective demand, and thus the balance between AD and AS cannot be realized.

Keynes' Law implies the following preconditions: (1) The production capacity of the economy is highly developed, and the potential aggregate output level is very high. (2) The price mechanisms including money wage rate, price of goods, and interest rate are sticky or rigid. (3) Money is non-neutral. (4) The marginal propensity to consume (MPC) is between 0 and 1, and decreases with the increase in income. (5) The marginal efficiency of capital (the expected profit rate of investment) fluctuates in the short run and decreases in the long run. (6) There is unfair distribution of income and wealth in the economic society. When these conditions are met, the effective demand becomes the main determinant of short-run employment quantity and aggregate output.

Keynes' Law is also one-sided: (1) Under the condition of certain AS capacity of the economy, the scale and growth of effective demand determine the realization degree of the AS capacity, but the demand cannot determine the supply capacity and its growth. (2) The equilibrium between AD and AS in quantity does not mean that they are matched and consistent in structure. It is possible for an economy to simultaneously have a supply surplus of one part of its products and an undersupply of another part of its products in a given period. (3) In the long run, production (supply) plays a decisive role. Without production, there is no object of distribution, exchange, or consumption. "Certain production determines certain consumption, distribution, exchange, and certain relationships between these different factors".[3]

From the perspective of analysis, Say's Law is a conclusion concluded from the perspective of long-run or very-long-run analysis, while Keynes' Law is a judgment made from the perspective of short-run analysis; in the long run or very long run, the supply plays a decisive role in the actual aggregate output level; in the short run, the demand is the decisive factor for the actual aggregate output level. Therefore, there is no "either–or" question that is correct between Say's Law and Keynes' Law.

From the history of economics, mainstream economics emphasized the importance of the supply in the period of classical school, the importance of the demand at the time of the popularity of Keynesianism, and the importance of the supply at the time of the popularity of supply school, and economists seemed to be not "loyal" to supply or demand. After further study, it is not difficult to find that whether economists attached importance to supply or demand is related to the economic development stage and the economic environment they were in at that time, and their views are "changing when they see different things". The "different" mentioned here refers to the change in economic conditions, the difference in economic environment, and the change in the comparative relationship between AD and AS. Both Say's Law and Keynes' Law hold conditionally, so when the economic conditions have changed, the original applicable theory is no longer applicable, and a new theory is needed.

Classical economics came into being during the rise of the capitalist market economy and the establishment of the capitalist system, and in the transition period from workshop handicraft industry to machine industry. In this great transition period and the era of great change, the development of the capital and commodity economy objectively needs to: (1) Remove the shackles of feudal autocracy and mercantilism policies on the development of emerging market economy, and theoretically deny the preaching of mercantilism that "wealth comes from circulation (trade)". (2) Promote the increase in supply by vigorously developing productivity to lay a material foundation for the capitalist system. It is against this background that "labor creates wealth" has become an idea generally recognized by classical economists. William Petty, the founder of classical political economy, put forward the famous motto that "labor is the father of wealth, and land is the mother of wealth". Adam Smith, the founder of the system of classical political economy, devoted himself to exploring the source of a country's national wealth and the causes of its growth. In his view, labor is the source of national wealth, and the growth of a country's wealth depends on the development speed of division of labor and the amount of capital accumulated. This is so because, in his view, there are only two ways to increase national wealth: one is to improve labor productivity, and the other is to increase the number of useful laborers; and the development of division of labor, the use of machinery, and the improvement of labor allocation will promote the improvement of labor productivity, and the increase of capital accumulation will increase the number of useful laborers employed. The classical school's idea of attaching importance to supply reached its peak in the early 19th century when Say proposed the proposition that "aggregate output necessarily creates an equal amount of AD".

Unlike classical economists who lived in the adolescence period of the capitalist market economy, Keynes was in the middle-age period of the capitalist market economy. On the basis of the industrial revolution, the capitalist system was finally established and the market economy developed rapidly. In 1700 and 1801 before and after Adam Smith published the Wealth of Nations, British GDP was 10.709 billion international dollars and 25.426 billion international dollars respectively, and British per capita GDP was 1,250 international dollars and 1,579 international dollars respectively. By 1913 before the outbreak of the First World War, British GDP and per capita GDP had reached 224.618 billion international dollars and 4,921 international dollars respectively.[4] Different from the adolescence period, capitalism in the middle-age period had many ailments, among which the most prominent ailment on economy was that excess production or insufficient effective demand, unfair distribution of income and wealth, and underemployment became the normal state of the economy. At the beginning of Chapter 24 of the General Theory, Keynes wrote: "The remarkable disadvantages of the economic society in which we live include: Firstly, it cannot provide full employment; and secondly, it distributes wealth and income in an unprincipled and unfair way".[5] It was against this economic backdrop that Keynes denied Say's Law, founded the effective demand theory, and put forward the idea of demand management. The idea of "demand is important" replaced the idea of "supply is important". This idea of Keynes quickly formed a consensus in mainstream economics in the United States and the United Kingdom, and became the theoretical basis for formulating macroeconomic policies in market economy countries such as the United States and the United Kingdom.

In the 1970s, under the impact of the two oil crises in 1973 and 1979–1980, the cost of production in the American economy rose sharply, and the short-run AS curve moved to the upper left (Figure 5.1, from AS_1 to AS_2). At the same time, due

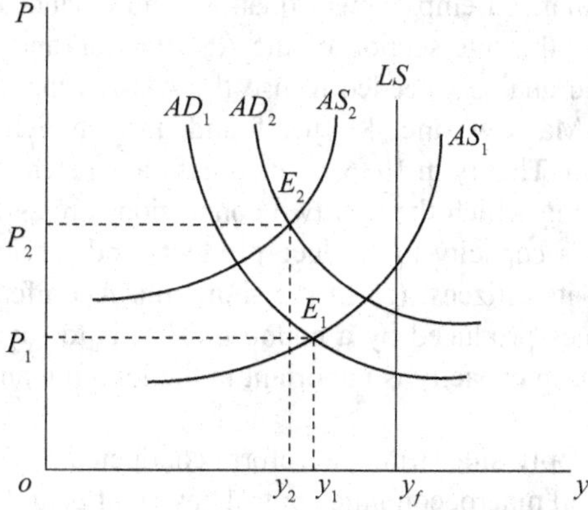

Figure 5.1 Explaining the stagflation of the American economy with AD-AS Model

to the government's long-run implementation of the policy of Keynesianism stimulating AD, the AD curve moved to the upper right (from AD_1 to AD_2), and the interaction between AS and AD eventually evolved into "stagflation". In Figure 5.1, the overall price level P_2 at the equilibrium point E_2 of the economy is higher than P_1 at E_1, while the aggregate output Y_2 at E_2 is lower than Y_1 at E_1. The second scientific and technological revolution, which arose after the end of the Second World War and was marked by the electrification of modes of production, greatly promoted the development of productivity and economic growth, and simultaneously caused great changes in production structure and economic structure. Because the adjustment of AD structure lagged behind, the economic structure was out of balance. One of the signs of the imbalance of the economic structure was the structural unemployment in the American economy and the coexistence of job vacancies and unemployment in the labor market. Under this economic background, supply-side economics rose by taking advantage of the momentum, and the Reagan Administration's economic policy focused on adjusting the structure and stimulating supply. As a result, the balance of mainstream economic theory and government policies tipped towards the AS.

It is important to note that although mainstream economics and government policies sometimes favor the supply side and sometimes the demand side as the economic environment changes and the stage of economic development varies, this bias still does not depart from the AD-AS analysis framework: economists do not ignore the demand when emphasizing the importance of supply, nor do they ignore the supply when emphasizing the importance of demand. In the General Theory, Keynes wrote: "In analyzing the economic behavior of such a system (the economic system of money–initiator), the method we use remains the interaction between supply and demand".[6] In his view, "the balanced employment quantity is determined by: (1) The AS function; (2) the propensity to consume; and (3) the amount of investment. This is the gist of the general theory of employment".[7]

As can be seen, although Keynes believed that demand was important, he still believed that the balanced employment quantity and balanced aggregate output were determined by the intersection of the AS function and AD function, and that macroeconomic analysis needed to use the AD-AS theoretical framework. According to N.G. Mankiw, since Keynes founded the modern macroeconomics system in the General Theory in 1936, economists have reached four consensuses or conclusions, among which the first two conclusions are as follows: (1) In the long run, a country's capacity to produce products and services determines the living standards of its citizens. (2) In the short run, AD affects the quantity of products and services produced by a country.[8] That is to say, most economists believe that production capacity is important in the long run and AD is important in the short run.

For the current supply-side structural reform conducted by China, although the focuses of reform and macroeconomic control have shifted to the supply side and its structure, we still cannot ignore AD in theory and concept, and cannot abandon AD management in policy practice. We should promote the moderate growth of AD and optimization of AD structure on the basis of stabilizing AD, which is not only the need of stabilizing growth and promoting employment, but also the need of guaranteeing the smooth progress of supply-side structural reform. Without a moderate growth of AD, excess capacity will become more serious, because past and present investments are still forming capital stocks and increasing production capacity; without the adjustment and optimization of the AD structure, the structural reform of AS will have no frame of reference, thus losing its direction. This is so because we carry out the supply-side structural reform and even the socialist market economy production for the purpose of better meeting the growing material and cultural needs of the people and continuously improving the quality of life and welfare of the people. To make the AS structure better match with and adapt to the AD structure, the adjustment of the supply structure must be aimed at adapting to the demand structure and must be guided by the demand structure. The improvement of AS capacity must be guided by the scale and growth of AD, and the improvement of AS quality must be based on the AD structure. If the production capacity is improved, but the demand cannot keep up, new excess capacity will be formed; the quality of supply has improved, but if the supply structure does not match the demand structure, this "quality" cannot be recognized by the market.

A few Chinese scholars have dismissed the "troika of the economy factors", namely, China's AD regulation mode, and its relevant theory as "deceptive tricks", arguing that China's macroeconomic control in recent years has been guided by the wrong theoretical framework of the "troika of the economy factors". The basis they hold is that the "troika of the economy factors" theory runs counter to the modern economic growth theory; the medium- and long-run economic growth problem is not a demand problem, but a supply problem and a problem on a country's production capacity. According to the modern economic growth theory (neoclassical growth theory) of Robert Merton Solow and others, there are only two engines of economic growth: one is the growth of per capita capital (including material capital and human capital), and the other is the improvement of TFP. Neither of these engines has anything to do with the "troika of the economy factors". Therefore, the "troika of the economy factors" theory goes against the common sense of economics, misjudges the real causes for China's economic growth over the past 30 years, and misleads the choice of China's economic policy orientation.

There is some basis for these scholars' views, because the determinants of medium- to long-run economic growth do lie on the AS side, which I have elaborated earlier in this monograph. However, this view has certain one-sidedness: The supply-side factors (per capita capital and TFP) determine the potential economic growth rate, not the actually achieved economic growth rate. Under the condition that the AS capacity (production capacity) or potential growth rate is certain, the effective demand and its growth determine the actual economic growth rate and the utilization degree of the AS capacity; although the hypothesis of economic growth theory (especially the Solow Growth Model) is that factors of production and technologies are fully utilized, it is a hypothesis of very-long-run analysis after all. The real economic growth is not always realized under the condition of full employment (full utilization), especially the short- and medium-run economic growth. Therefore, it is unlikely that the actual economic growth rate achieved by a country in a given period is unrelated to the "troika of the economy factors".

In 2010, China's GDP growth rates in the four quarters were 12.2%, 10.8%, 9.9%, and 9.9% respectively. Meanwhile, commodity prices were basically stable without any obvious inflation, indicating that the AS capacity of China's economy could support the economic growth at about 10% around 2010; however, at present, the growth rate of China's economy has dropped below 7%, and there is a continuous large-scale excess capacity at the same time. The actual economic growth rate has dropped rapidly in recent years, which cannot be said to be unrelated to the continuous decline in domestic and external demand growth of China's economy.

Although the macroeconomic relationship is very complex, the basic relationship in macroeconomy is the relationship between AD and AS, which includes the quantity equilibrium relationship and structural matching relationship between AD and AS. Only when AD and AS are coordinated in quantity and structure can the economy be stable and grow. Economic analysis and policy choice should pay attention to both the supply side and the demand side, and pay attention to the interaction between supply and demand. We should pay attention to both long-run economic growth and short-run economic stability, so as to achieve stable and sustainable economic growth; the long run cannot be separated from the short run, because the long run consists of several short runs. If we only emphasize the supply side but neglect the demand side, only pay attention to the supply-side reform but neglect the demand stability and adjustment, and only focus on the long run but ignore the short run, this may not be the correct approach for economists and policy makers, and may bring negative effects in practice.

China's economy has experienced high growth for about 40 years, and successfully passed the economic take-off stage. At present, it has entered the sprint stage of crossing the "middle-income trap"; an economy at different stages of its growth or development has different requirements for the structure, quality, and dynamics of AS, just as an aircraft flying at subsonic speed has different requirements for aircraft engine, quality, and structure than one flying at supersonic speed. Therefore, we now emphasize the supply-side structural reform, the transformation and upgrading of economic structure or supply structure, the optimization of the economic structure, the coordinated and sustainable development of economy, society, and environment, and the seeking of new impetus for economic development. It is undoubtedly the right choice to shift the focus of economic work and macroeconomic control to the supply side. However, the transformation and upgrading of supply is a medium- and long-run process, which is accompanied by major changes in production technology, technological innovation, and economic structural adjustment in many aspects, and depends on the further reform of the economic system and even the political system, and thus this process cannot be completed in a short run. Even for "Reaganomics", which is regarded by some Chinese scholars as a successful example of supply reform, the supply reform took effect in terms of the economic structure and economic performance only in the second tenure of the Reagan Administration. Therefore, in order to maintain the steady development and smooth progress of transformation and upgrading of China's economy, the demand analysis and demand management cannot be abandoned.

After more than 40 years of reform and opening up, China's productivity and AS capacity have been greatly improved. The supply shortage that has plagued us for a long time since the founding of New China has become history, and China's economy has changed from a shortage economy to a relatively demand-deficient economy at the end of 1990s. In the future, insufficient effective demand will be the normal state of China's economy and the background of China's economic operation and development. From this point of view, we cannot only emphasize AS and ignore AD.

Through the previous analysis of Figure 2.6, we find that the excess capacity in China's economy is the result of the combined effects of slowdown of growth of effective demand and the substantial increase in production capacity caused by the expansion plan in 2009–2011, rather than a result of pure demand-side causes or pure supply-side causes. Therefore, to solve the problem of excess capacity, it is necessary to take into account the stability and growth of AD in the process of supply-side structural reform, instead of ignoring AD.

We have noted that Comrade Xi Jinping first proposed the supply-side structural reform at the 11th meeting of the Central Leading Group on Financial and Economic Affairs on November 10, 2015. He proposed that

> efforts should be made to strengthen supply-side structural reform, focus on improving the quality and efficiency of the supply system, enhance the momentum of sustained economic growth, and promote China's social productivity level to achieve an overall leap, while moderately expanding AD.[9]

This passage gives attention to both supply and demand. In 2020, the Central Economic Work Conference put forward: "We must firmly grasp the main line of supply-side structural reform, pay attention to demand-side management, . . . and form a higher level of dynamic balance between demand pulling supply and supply creating demand".[10] This idea actually emphasizes the interdependence and interaction relationships between supply and demand.

II. Structural adjustment and growth promotion

The relationship between economic structure and economic growth is like the relationship between car condition and speed. If the car is in good condition, it will run steadily and quickly; if the car is in poor condition, it will run unsteadily and slowly, and even stall. To achieve long-run stability and sustainable development of the economy, the economic structure must be constantly adjusted and optimized.

In recent years, the supply surplus in China's economy is the manifestation of the imbalance of economic structure, which not only drags down the economic growth rate, but also reduces the quality and efficiency of economic growth. Large inventory of products and under-utilization of capacity are themselves a waste of resources, increasing the cost of economic development.

Economic structural adjustment and economic growth are contradictory in the short run. To some extent, they are the relationship between the fish and the bear's paw, and we cannot have both. Adjusting the economic structure by cutting overcapacity, reducing excess inventory, and deleveraging will inevitably reduce the production of some products or even destroy some products, shut down some enterprises, and compress some investment, which will directly reduce the increase in output. However, in the medium and long run, an effective adjustment of economic structure is conducive to stabilizing and promoting economic growth. Therefore, structural adjustment and economic growth are like the relationship between "sharpening the axe" and "cutting wood"; in the long run, "sharpening your axe will not delay your job of cutting wood", but in the short run, "sharpening your axe" will inevitably delay "your job of cutting wood".

Structural reform and structural adjustment are two problems with not exactly the same connotation but intertwined contents. Structural adjustment is mainly to correct and reposition the unbalanced economic structure, eliminate excess capacity, and ease the burden on economic growth. Structural reform is to rebuild, optimize, and upgrade the economic structure, and realize the kinetic energy upgrading of economic growth. If structural reform is a big topic, the structural adjustment is a sub-topic thereunder. Supply-side structural reform is far more ambitious and important than structural adjustment.

To achieve the objective of supply-side structural reform, we must effectively handle the relationship between structural adjustment and growth stability (or growth promotion). If the relationship between structural adjustment and growth stability fails to be effectively handled, the process of supply-side structural reform will inevitably be delayed and the effectiveness of supply-side structural reform will be reduced.

From the perspective of China's economic work and policy practice since the 21st century, it seems that we have not effectively handled the relationship between structural adjustment and growth stability. The central government and local governments have a long-standing preference of "giving priority to growth", giving priority to stabilizing or promoting economic growth, and will not operate on the unbalanced economic structure unless there is no other way—when the serious imbalance of the economic structure hinders the normal operation and growth of the economy. Once the economic growth drops too much and too fast, or the structural imbalance is alleviated, growth stability replaces structural adjustment as the primary goal of the economic policy, and structural adjustment is slowed down or retreated to a secondary position.

See the changes in the main tasks of China's economic work and the objectives of economic policies (macroeconomic control) since 2008 (see Table 5.1). China's annual tasks of economic work and policy objectives were determined by the Central Economic Work Conference in December last year. Table 5.1 is compiled according to the decisions made at the Central Economic Work Conference every year since 2008.

From Table 5.1, we can see that since 2008, we have put price stability (control) first in tasks of economic work and policy objectives in two years (2008 and 2011), put structural adjustment or economic growth quality first in two years (2010 and 2012), and put growth stability first in the remaining ten years. It can be seen that the Chinese government attaches much more importance to economic growth than to economic structural adjustment.

The main reasons why the central government has formed the preference of "giving priority to growth" are as follows: (1) The "catch-up" strategy dominates short-run economic work and economic policies. To achieve the long-run catch-up goal, we must ensure the realization of short- and medium-run economic growth goals. (2) Political requirements for maintaining stability. In the era of reform, and in the period of system transition, there will inevitably be some political and social instability factors, because the vested interests of some people will be damaged due to the adjustment and redistribution of interests brought about by reform, or their interests will be promoted unevenly. The government's idea is that with a certain economic growth rate, the economic cake is getting bigger and bigger, which can provide material guarantee for social stability and political stability, and alleviate or even shield some social contradictions. (3) For a leader of local government, growth promotion and his political achievements and promotion are consistent, and are integrated into one. (4) Comparatively speaking, growth promotion has less risks, fewer obstacles, and is easy to achieve; however, structural adjustment has risks and great resistance, and is not easy to produce the desired result in the short run, because structural adjustment requires shutting down enterprises, cutting employees, and reducing GDP and tax revenue. Growth promotion means giving producers and consumers "sugar", while structural adjustment means giving producers and consumers "medicine". Growth promotion can be effective in the same year as sowing, while structural adjustment is like one man sows and another reaps. From the perspective of risk avoidance or

Table 5.1 Main tasks of China's economic work and policy objectives (2008–2021)

Year	*Main tasks of economic work and policy objectives*
2021	Focus on stabilizing the macroeconomic market, keeping the economy running in a reasonable range, and maintaining the overall social stability
2020	Strive to keep the economy running in a reasonable range, adhere to the strategy of expanding domestic demand, strengthen the support of science and technology strategy, and expand high-level opening up
2019	Stabilize growth, promote reform, adjust structure, benefit people's livelihood, prevent risks, ensure stability, and keep the economy running in a reasonable range
2018	Stabilize growth, promote reform, adjust structure, benefit people's livelihood, and prevent risks
2017	Stabilize growth, promote reform, adjust structure, benefit people's livelihood, and prevent risks
2016	Stabilize growth, promote reform, adjust structure, benefit people's livelihood, and prevent risks
2015	Stabilize growth, adjust structure, benefit people's livelihood, and prevent risks
2014	Keep the economy running in a reasonable range, put the mode change and structural adjustment in a more important position, pay close attention to reform, highlight innovation drive, strengthen risk prevention and control, and strengthen the safeguard of people's livelihood
2013	Make overall planning for stabilizing growth, adjusting structure, and promoting reform, and keep the economic growth rate running smoothly in a reasonable range
2012	With the focus on improving the quality and efficiency of economic growth, further deepen reform and opening up, further strengthen innovation drive, actively expand domestic demand, intensify strategic adjustment of economic structure, target our efforts on safeguarding and improving people's livelihood, enhance endogenous vitality and impetus of economic development, keep the overall commodity price level basically stable, and achieve sustained and healthy economic development and harmonious and stable society.
2011	Stabilize commodity prices, guarantee growth, and adjust structure
2010	Adjust structure, guarantee growth, and prevent inflation
2009	Expand domestic demand, guarantee growth, change mode, and adjust structure
2008	Control the total amount, stabilize commodity prices, adjust structure, and promote balance

risk aversion, the government and officials also prefer "growth promotion" over "structural adjustment".

Correctly understanding and effectively handling the relationship between structural adjustment and growth promotion is an important part of promoting supply-side structural reform. Whether from the perspective of the current supply surplus and the seriousness of the imbalance of economic structure in China, or from the perspective of changing the mode of economic development and realizing long-run sustainable development, it is necessary to sacrifice some output and economic growth rate in the short run. Such sacrifice is the price that must be paid for adjusting the structure and changing the mode. From the law of economic fluctuations, the turning point for the economy to reverse upward from the downside is when excess capacity and excess inventory of enterprises are removed. Only at this time will market demand turn booming, fixed assets be updated on a large scale, and new investment grow steadily; in the economic downward (or recession) stage, the slower excess capacity is removed, the slower the structural adjustment is; the longer the economy takes to consolidate in the trough, the slower the economic recovery is. Moreover, the longer supply surplus and imbalance of the economic structure are delayed, the greater the damage to economic health and long-run growth is. We would rather endure the short-run pain of structural adjustment than the long-run pain of structural imbalance. As pointed out at the Central Economic Work Conference in December 2016, structural excess capacity was a "historical barrier that cannot be bypassed", and we cannot avoid it. The best policy is to solve such problem and pass the barrier.

In order to effectively handle the relationship between short-run growth stability and medium- and long-run structural adjustment, I suggest that

1. Unless major external shocks (such as the international financial crisis that broke out in 2008 and the global epidemic since 2020) require special emphasis on stabilizing growth, supply reform and structural adjustment should be given priority in economic work, with supply-side structural reform as the main line of economic work.
2. The target range of China's economic growth at this stage should be adjusted to 6%–8%, and the quarterly economic growth rate can fluctuate at around 7%. Setting such a target range can reserve more leeway for the government to deal with the relationship between structural adjustment and growth promotion, which is not only conducive to reducing the pressure on the government to stabilize growth, and avoiding frequent policy switching between growth stability and structural adjustment, but also conducive to stabilizing the confidence and expectations of enterprises and consumers.
3. Realizing the employment stability through stabilizing growth should be adjusted to realizing the growth stability through stabilizing employment; that is, employment stability should be put in a prominent position. Judging from China's current industrial structure and production technology used by enterprises, growth stability does not necessarily lead to employment stability, but employment stability often leads to growth stability. Moreover, in case of the steady growth of employment, it will bring the following benefits: the income growth of urban and rural residents will be guaranteed; people's livelihood will be improved; society will be stable; and economic structural adjustment and long-run sustainable development will be guaranteed.
4. By deepening reform, we should further dilute the quantitative indicator assessment of local governments, and increase the assessment of its structural indicators and quality indicators. For example, the progress of removing enterprises featuring heavy energy consumption and emission and serious pollution, the degree of improving water quality, soil quality, air quality, and environmental quality, the bankruptcy, reorganization, or conversion rate of "zombie" enterprises with high inventory and continuous losses for many

years, food safety, and the increase or decrease in counterfeit and shoddy products can be listed as indicators for assessing local governments.

5. The investment expansion, initiation of projects, and structural adjustment are combined.

Under the situation of increase in excess capacity and excess inventory, it seems inappropriate to re-expand government investment. In fact, that is not the case. At present, the increase in excess capacity and excess inventory in China mainly appear in the secondary industry, especially the industrial manufacturing industry. The primary and tertiary industries still have great space and potential for expanding investment. As far as infrastructure investment is concerned, there is still a lot of room and even a lot of debts in the vast rural and western regions. Land leveling and transformation in rural and western regions, water and land pollution control, water conservancy projects, power grid construction and transformation, road and railway construction, promotion of network and home computer, teaching instruments in primary and secondary schools, books and sports equipment, rural medical facilities, rural cultural projects, and garbage disposal can be regarded as the object of expanding investment. China's education (including vocational training), medical care, science and technology, and military industry are still areas with great investment potential. As long as there is demand, investment will not lead to excess production and excess capacity; and such investment is also an effective way to digest the existing excess capacity. For example, a large amount of cement is needed to repair water conservancy and roads in rural areas, and a large amount of steel is needed to repair railways, which helps to digest and absorb the excess capacity in the cement industry and metallurgical industry. Therefore, the expansion of government investment mentioned here should be selective, differentiated, and targeted. The principle of this choice is that expanded government investment should be simultaneously conducive to stimulating domestic demand, digesting excess capacity, adjusting and optimizing the economic structure, and enhancing the stamina of economic development. The investment chosen according to this principle will promote the optimization and upgrading of economic structure in the process of stimulating economic growth.

The "cutting overcapacity, reducing excess inventory, and deleveraging" in the "cutting overcapacity, reducing excess inventory, deleveraging, lowering costs, and strengthening areas of weakness" implemented currently refers to structural adjustment in terms of the stock, and the selective investment I mentioned here can be regarded as an initiative to adjust the structure in terms of the increment. Structural adjustment should be made with the focus on adjusting the structure in terms of both the stock and the increment.

In the long run, structural adjustment is mainly to depend on the market mechanism, relying on the automatic regulation (resource allocation), automatic removal (excess capacity and excess inventory), and self-rehabilitation (proportional relationship between supply and demand) functions of the market mechanism. Chapter 7 will further discuss this issue.

Notes

1 Say's Law: Supply creates its own demand; Keynes's Law: Demand creates its own supply.
2 Marx, K. (2012). *Marx & Engels Selected Works*. Vol. 2. Beijing: People's Publishing House, 691.
3 Marx, K. (2012). *A Contribution to the Critique of Political Economy. Marx & Engels Selected Works*. Vol. 2. Beijing: People's Publishing House, 699.
4 [Britain] Maddison, A. (2003). *The World Economy: A Millennial Perspective*, translated by Wu Xiaoying, etc. Beijing: Peking University Press, 244.
5 [Britain] Keynes, J. M. (1999). *The General Theory of Employment Interest and Money*, retranslated by Gao Hongye. Beijing: The Commercial Press, 386.
6 [Britain] Keynes, J. M. (1999). *The General Theory of Employment Interest and Money*, retranslated by Gao Hongye. Beijing: The Commercial Press, 3.
7 [Britain] Keynes, J. M. (1999). *The General Theory of Employment Interest and Money*, retranslated by Gao Hongye. Beijing: The Commercial Press, 34.
8 [America] Mankiw, N. G. (2016). *Macroeconomics*. 9th Ed., translated by Lu Yuanzhu. Beijing: China Renmin University Press: 459–460.
9 Quoted from the *People's Daily*, November 11, 2015, 1st Edition.
10 Quoted from the *People's Daily*, December 19, 2020, 1st Edition.

6 Three-step strategy of supply-side reform (1)

Symptomatic treatment

China's supply-side structural reform is a series of major topics related to the present and future development of China's economy, and involving economic structural adjustment, the generation of new supply impetus, the improvement of supply quality, the transformation of development pattern, and the further reform of the economic system. It is a great reform or revolution, not a simple adjustment of supply structure or economic structure, nor a simple elimination of supply surplus. Therefore, the supply-side structural reform cannot be completed in a short run or quickly completed by doing a quick and sudden job. It will be a long-run, arduous, and complex project. How to choose the path of this reform and how to conduct this reform concern the effectiveness and destiny of this reform.

In my opinion, to guarantee the success and substantial results of the supply-side structural reform and achieve the expected goals of the supply-side structural reform, the supply-side structural reform needs to adopt a three-step strategy. The first step is to conduct the symptomatic treatment through taking the main measures of "cutting overcapacity, reducing excess inventory, deleveraging, lowering costs, and strengthening areas of weakness"; the second step is to conduct the consolidation treatment—the main plan is to adjust, optimize and upgrade the economic structure—and the third step is to conduct the radical treatment mainly by system reform, construction, and innovation.

This three-step strategy is subject to the principles of cross-implementation, ladder-like improvement, and progressive deepening, rather than the principle of complete separation. Overall, "cutting overcapacity, reducing excess inventory, deleveraging, lowering costs, and strengthening areas of weakness" is the premise of effectively taking the second and third steps, and is the necessary preparation for the second and third steps, sweeping away the obstacles for the development of the last two steps; the second step "structural adjustment" is the key content of supply-side structural reform; the third step "system reform" is the finale and foothold of supply-side structural reform.

However, this three-step strategy should not be conducted through complete separation, and is not conducted in the manner of completing the latter step after completing the former step, but is conducted in the manner of cross-advancement and mutual penetration; "cutting overcapacity, reducing excess inventory, deleveraging, lowering costs, and strengthening areas of weakness" mainly focuses on

DOI: 10.4324/9781003367000-9

solving the supply surplus, but it also contains the content of structural adjustment; to implement the second-step strategy, it is necessary to continuously lower costs and strengthen areas of weakness. It is particularly important that system reform, construction, and innovation should run through the whole process of supply-side structural reform. Without the system reform, "cutting overcapacity, reducing excess inventory, deleveraging, lowering costs, and strengthening areas of weakness" and structural adjustment cannot be effectively carried out, and deepening system reform is the fundamental way to do a good job of "cutting overcapacity, reducing excess inventory, deleveraging, lowering costs, and strengthening areas of weakness" and structural adjustment. I designed the path of supply-side structural reform as a three-step strategy for the purpose of highlighting the focus of each step of strategy, emphasizing the depth and hierarchy of reform, and highlighting the criticality and importance of system reform.

This chapter discusses the first step in the three-step strategy, followed by the second and third steps in Chapters 7 and 8, respectively.

I. Urgency of "cutting overcapacity, reducing excess inventory, deleveraging, lowering costs, and strengthening areas of weakness"

In recent years, the prominent problems in China's economy are that enterprises have excessive excess inventory and many products are unsalable; capacity is excess, and capacity utilization rate is excessive low; leverage ratio is too high, and financial risks accumulate; and the cost of production of enterprises rises too fast, and the unreasonable cost burden is too much; meanwhile, there are still many shortcomings and deficiencies in China's economic development, that is, there are many shortcomings, such as lagging agricultural and rural development, insufficient scientific and technological innovation capability, insufficient accumulation of knowledge and human capital, and large but not strong manufacturing industry, and so on.

According to the estimation of Mao Deshu, executive vice president and secretary general of the National Inventory of Merchandise Discount Professional Committee, the inventory of overstocked materials in China has exceeded RMB 3 trillion in October 2015. The amount of inventory overstocked is equivalent to 4.7% of China's GDP in 2014, which is almost equal to the GDP of Sichuan Province in 2015. According to the National Bureau of Statistics, from 2007 to 2014, the inventory of industrial enterprises above designated size in China's mining and washing of coal industry increased from RMB 70.822 billion to RMB 246.771 billion, an increase of 2.48 times in seven years. According to the *China Real Estate Data Yearbook* (2017), in 2016, there were 35,334 completed residential buildings for sale in China, with a building area of 8,402.04 million square meters. 13,813 buildings have been started or are for sale, with a building area of 1,658.46 million square meters; there were 5,512 unsold buildings, with a building area of 523.8 million square meters. In case of the calculation on the basis of 30 square meters per capita, these residence areas on sale and unsold can meet the living needs of 353 million people. Due to the rapid growth of real estate investment in recent years, the inventory area of commercial housing continues to grow.

Excess production and large-scale continuous excess capacity causes many industries to fall into the situation of continuously decreasing profits or even losing money, which makes enterprises in these industries have to reduce production or even production with losing money. According to the National Bureau of Statistics, from 2011 to 2015, the numbers of loss-making industrial enterprises above designated size in China were 30,456, 39,664, 41,711, 43,452, and 48,248 respectively, accounting for 9.35%, 11.54%, 11.28%, 11.50%, and 12.59% of the total number of industrial enterprises above designated size in that year. Not only is the number of loss-making enterprises increasing year by year, but also the scale of losses is constantly expanding.

Enterprise inventory exceeds the normal or desirable level, which, on the one hand, hinders the increase in enterprises' investment in fixed assets, and which, on the other hand, occupies extra working capital, and which will lead to the break of the enterprise capital chain in case the circumstance is serious. In this situation, enterprises have neither the incentive nor the capacity for increasing the investment. As a result, many enterprises, especially industrial enterprises and real estate development enterprises, have to be in the dormant or even necrotic state as the cells of macroeconomy.

The deterioration of the financial condition of enterprises leads to an increase in bad and doubtful debts of banks and a decrease in the government tax revenue and fiscal revenue, thus causing an increase in financial risks and a rise in the government deficit ratio and debt ratio.[1] According to the calculation by the National Institution for Finance & Development of the Chinese Academy of Social Sciences, the debt ratio of Chinese financial enterprises increased rapidly from 2010 to 2015. At the end of 2015, the debt ratio of Chinese financial enterprises rose to 131%, and the result calculated by the Bank for International Settlements was 170.8%; according to the statistics by the National Institution for Finance & Development of the Chinese Academy of Social Sciences, the overall leverage ratio of China's non-financial sector at the end of 2015 was 249%, and the overall debt ratio of China announced by the Bank for International Settlements was 254.8%; at the end of 2015, China's government debt ratio was about 41.5%, and the leverage ratio of China's household sector was about 40%.

The excessive burden on enterprises and the rapid rise in the cost of production have been a common concern of Chinese entrepreneurs and economists over the years. According to the enterprise cost survey conducted by Chinese Academy of Fiscal Sciences in 12 provinces of China from April to June 2016, the total costs (main business costs + sales expenses + administrative expenses + financial expenses + business tax and surcharges) of sample enterprises accounted for 109%, 103.6%, and 138% of income respectively from 2013 to 2015, and the sample enterprises were generally in a loss state. From the six major components of enterprise cost—enterprise tax burden, labor cost (including "five social insurance and one housing fund"), energy cost, logistics cost, financing cost, and institutional transaction cost—except for the steady decline in tax burden, the remaining five major costs are on the rise.[23] Some scholars and government officials believe that the manufacturing cost in China is already higher than that in Southeast Asian, South Asian, and Eastern European countries, and is about 90% of the manufacturing cost in the United States. Specifically, the cost of production of enterprises in the Pearl River Delta and Yangtze River Delta has reached 95% of the manufacturing cost in the United States, and even a few Chinese enterprises have transferred textile mills and glass factories to the United States, in order to save costs.

As mentioned earlier, there are many shortcomings in China's economic development, which hinder the steady growth and efficiency improvement of China's economy, and among which the biggest shortcoming may be the lack of independent innovation capability.

The technological progress of an economy mainly comes by two ways: independent innovation and technology introduction. In different countries or the same country at different stages of development, the promoting effect or importance of independent innovation and technology introduction to technological progress is different. For developed countries, independent innovation and technology introduction serve as the main and secondary sources of their technological progress, while for developing countries, technology introduction and independent innovation serve as the main and secondary sources of their technological progress, because these countries are relatively backward in science and technology as well as innovation. When an economy transforms from underdeveloped state to developed state, a remarkable sign is that independent innovation has become the main source of technological progress instead of technology introduction.

For a long time after the reform and opening up, China has greatly improved the speed of technological progress and the technical level of economic activities by vigorously introducing foreign capital, foreign equipment, foreign technology, and foreign management methods, coupled with our continuous study, imitation, and transformation, and improved China's economic growth rate by significantly increasing TFP growth rate; China's economy has achieved a high annual average growth rate of nearly 10% for more than 30 consecutive years, which benefited from the vitality of individuals and enterprises stimulated by continuously pushing forward the reform, coupled with the large-scale "demographic dividend".

Generally speaking, technology imported from abroad can be divided into two categories: conventional technology and high technology (high-tech). Through introduction, digestion, absorption, and independent research and development over the past 40 years of reform and opening up, China's conventional technology level has approached the level of developed countries, and some have exceeded the level of developed countries. Therefore, the number of conventional technology imported has naturally decreased and the speed of introduction has naturally slowed down. Since 2008, the speed of technology introduction to China has been declining in fluctuation. First, the speed of conventional technology introduction has declined, and then the speed of high-tech introduction has slowed down. Figure 6.1 shows that due to the impact of the international financial crisis, the import of high-tech products in China recorded negative growth in 2009, with a

Figure 6.1 Growth rate of China's high-tech imports from 2003 to 2020 (%)

Source: *China Statistical Yearbook* (2021) compiled by the National Bureau of Statistics of China

growth rate of −9.35%, and a recovery growth rate of 33.18% in 2010; excluding the sharp drop and rise in the past two years, it is easy to see that the growth rate of China's high-tech product imports has generally shown a trend of substantial decline since 2003 (see Figure 6.1).

In the process of slowing down the speed of technology introduction, if the speed of independent innovation increases and can offset the slowdown of technology introduction, the speed of technological progress in China will remain unchanged or even increase. But unfortunately, since the speed of China's technology introduction began to decline in 2004, the speed of independent innovation has not accelerated, but declined, causing China to be unable to effectively replace technology import through independent technological innovation. Figure 6.2 shows that if independent innovation is measured by the number of invention patents granted, the annual growth rate of invention patents granted in China reached the highest in 2008–2009, with an annual growth rate exceeding 37%, but then it declined in fluctuations, and only rebounded sharply in 2015, reaching 54.06%.

According to the report of the World Intellectual Property Organization (WIPO), the number of international patent applications in China has maintained double-digit growth since 2002. In 2014, China became the fastest growing country in the world in terms of patent applications, with a growth rate of 18.7%, and the only country that reached double-digit growth; in 2015, the number of international

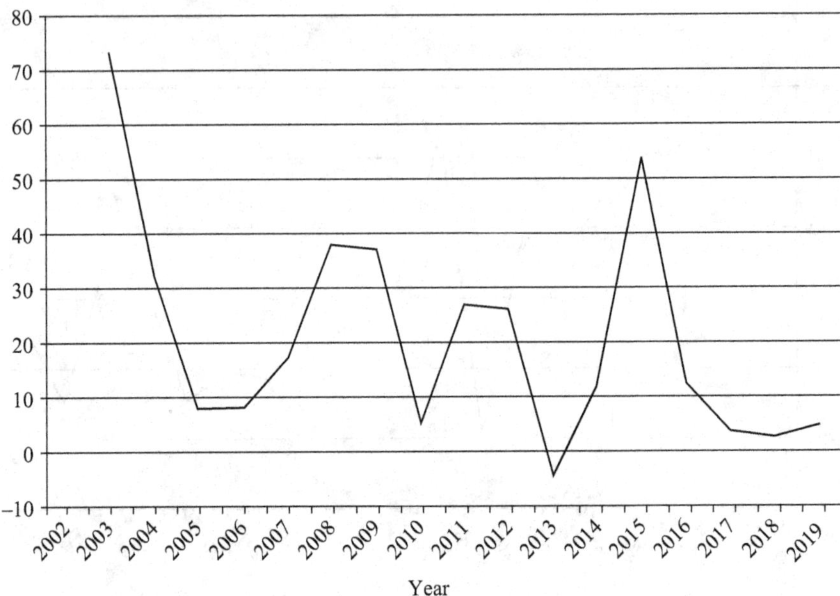

Figure 6.2 Growth rate (%) of patents for invention (the number of granted patents) in China from 2003 to 2019

Source: *China Statistical Yearbook* (2021) compiled by the National Bureau of Statistics of China

patent applications increased by 1.7% over the previous year, and the number of international patent applications in China (29,800) increased by 16.8%, ranking first in the world in terms of growth rate; in 2016, the number of international patent applications increased by 7.3% on year-on-year basis, while the number of international patent applications in China (43,000) increased by 44.7%! However, among the patents applied for in China and patents granted by WIPO, the proportion of utility patents is on the high side, while the proportion of invention patents is low. Moreover, most of the patents applied for by Chinese enterprises are "micro-innovations" based on mature technologies, and the innovation achievements in major-frontier scientific and technological fields are insufficient. According to the division of technological innovation by Dewar, R. D. and Dutton, J. E., most of China's technological innovation is "incremental innovation", and "subversive innovation or radical innovation" accounts for a low proportion.[4]

After 2009, the speed of both high-tech introduction and independent innovation declined, which led to the slowdown of China's technological progress and the decline in TFP growth rate (see Table 3.2).

These problems lead to an increase in hidden dangers and risks in China's economy, which hinders the normal operation and healthy development of China's economy. In particular, the superposition of these problems has further intensified these hidden dangers and risks. Faced with this economic situation, the CPC Central Committee and the State Council put forward that the key point of supply-side structural reform is to effectively implement the five major tasks of "cutting overcapacity, reducing excess inventory, deleveraging, lowering costs, and strengthening areas of weakness" in concrete work. In my opinion, "cutting overcapacity, reducing excess inventory, deleveraging, lowering costs, and strengthening areas of weakness" is the symptomatic treatment, emergency treatment, and the first step necessary for the supply-side structural reform. "Cutting overcapacity and reducing excess inventory" is to reduce swelling and remove the sludge in the economy, and "deleveraging" is to reduce economic risks, all of which are aimed at making the economy move forward lightly, safely, and revitalize; "lowering costs" is to reduce the burden on the economy, and "strengthening areas of weakness" is to coordinate the industrial chain and economic structure, both of which have the nature of economic structural adjustment.

II. How to promote the implementation of "cutting overcapacity, reducing excess inventory, deleveraging, lowering costs, and strengthening areas of weakness"

At the Central Economic Work Conference in December 2015, the effective implementation of cutting overcapacity, reducing excess inventory, deleveraging, lowering costs, and strengthening areas of weakness was identified as the five major tasks of China's supply-side structural reform in 2016. For "cutting overcapacity, reducing excess inventory, deleveraging, lowering costs, and strengthening areas of weakness", its main direction is to reduce ineffective supply, increase effective supply, reduce economic operation costs and risks, solve the imbalance of total amount of supply and demand and structural imbalance as soon as possible, and improve the adaptability between supply structure and demand structure; its purpose is to improve the quality of supply and economic development, enabling the supply capacity to better meet the growing material and cultural needs of the people.

In the past few years, reducing excess inventory and deleveraging focused on curbing excessive speculation and real estate bubbles and resolving the debt burden on local governments; in the long run, the debt burden on enterprises can be fundamentally resolved only by improving their production and operation environment, enhancing their innovation ability, and allowing the debt interest rate to exceed the rate of return on capital by improving the latter.

Lowering costs is mainly to cut taxes and fees, with the focus on fee cut. The logistics costs, financing costs, and institutional transaction costs are reduced through reform and policy adjustment. We can consider temporarily slowing down the speed and frequency of wage increase, in order to avoid the excessive increase in labor costs, and keep the speed of wage increase in line with the speed of improvement in labor productivity as far as possible. Expressway toll is a major cause of the high logistics cost. The toll standard for expressway can be reduced by extending the toll years. For the expressway that has recovered its investment, the toll should be cancelled or the toll standard should be greatly lowered, and it should not be regarded as a "cash cow" for a long time.

The key fields requiring strengthening the areas of weakness include people's livelihood security, public services, how to develop the economy and prevent returning to poverty after the rural areas are lifted out of poverty as a whole, the construction and improvement of agricultural infrastructure, environmental and ecological construction, and scientific and technological innovation. The task of strengthening areas of weakness is more to be completed in the second and third steps of supply-side structural reform.

To further promote the implementation of "cutting overcapacity, reducing excess inventory, deleveraging, lowering costs, and strengthening areas of weakness", we should pay attention to the following issues.

1. The five major tasks of "cutting overcapacity, reducing excess inventory, deleveraging, lowering costs, and strengthening areas of weakness" are a systematic project, which must be comprehensively considered and promoted as a whole.

Each task of "cutting overcapacity, reducing excess inventory, deleveraging, lowering costs, and strengthening areas of weakness" has its own emphasis and is very important. The tasks are interdependent and mutually influential, with strong correlation and complementarity. For example, reducing excess inventory should be combined with cutting overcapacity. If cutting overcapacity fails to be effectively implemented, the old excessive inventory will be removed, and new excess inventory will appear again; if the high leverage ratio does not fall, not only will the systemic risks be too large, but the real economy will be difficult to develop and lowering costs will be difficult to work; if the unreasonable tax burden cannot be reduced and the cost of enterprises cannot be reduced, enterprises will have no way to live, and the revitalization of the real economy is empty talk; if the areas of weakness in the system and economy are not strengthened, excess capacity, excess inventory, and excessive leverage will come back soon and appear periodically even if they are removed this time. Therefore, the "cutting overcapacity, reducing excess inventory, deleveraging, lowering costs, and strengthening areas of weakness" should be comprehensively considered and promoted as a whole, and should not catch one and lose another.

Relatively speaking, cutting overcapacity and reducing excess inventory are relatively easy to do and achieve results quickly, while deleveraging, lowering costs, and strengthening areas of weakness are not easy to achieve obvious results in the short run, because these three tasks involve deeper system problems and development problems, and need to be completed by implementing the strategies of the second and third steps. Therefore, we can not equate the progress of cutting overcapacity and reducing excess inventory with the overall progress of "cutting overcapacity, reducing excess inventory, deleveraging, lowering costs, and strengthening areas of weakness", assuming their basic completions are synchronous.

2. "Cutting overcapacity" cannot be across the board, and should allow "cutting" and "retaining".

As we said earlier, excess capacity includes absolute excess capacity and relative excess capacity. We can neither regard all the current excess capacity as absolute excess capacity and eliminate it, nor regard all the current excess capacity as outdated capacity. It is necessary to keep the relative excess capacity until the market demand recovers and turns booming. To deal with "zombie enterprises" and outdated capacity, we should be cruel and pack a punch, and should not be soft-hearted. However, we should not excessively "cut overcapacity", cutting the relative excess capacity and advanced capacity at the same time. China's steel price rose in the second half of 2016, coal price rose in two rounds respectively in 2016 and 2021, and cement price rose in the fourth quarter of 2019, which was largely related to the excessive cut of overcapacity in these industries.

3. "Cutting overcapacity" should be treated dialectically, and should not be "across the board".

The causes and conditions of supply surplus in different industries and enterprises are different, and the standards for excess capacity are different. To cut overcapacity, according to industry characteristics, the severity of excess capacity in different industries and enterprises, and the market space and market demand potential of different enterprises in different industries, differentiated policies and measures should be implemented for classified governance, and it is not allowed to be "across the board" or require the capacity utilization rate of all industries and enterprises to meet the unified standard.

4. "Cutting overcapacity" should be handled fairly without any discrimination on ownership.

In the actual operation of cutting overcapacity in previous years, some local governments first aimed at private enterprises and middle- and small-sized enterprises when cutting overcapacity, and the indicators of cutting overcapacity were preferentially apportioned to these enterprises. In order to survive, these enterprises dare not be angry or speak out about this practice of local governments, so they have to submit to humiliation. This practice is actually unfair. In cutting overcapacity, the principle of fair competition should also be pursued: Whether for a state-owned enterprise or a non-state-owned enterprise, or for a large enterprise or a middle- or small-sized enterprise, it should be included in the list of elimination, provided that it really has excess capacity measured according to the efficiency principle and technical standards, and its excess capacity should be eliminated according to the same proportion and standards, without any discrimination. We should not favor some enterprises and be prejudiced against the others.

5. "Cutting overcapacity" should lay the equal emphasis on both stable output and stable employment.

Cutting overcapacity is a means, not an end. Cutting overcapacity is to reduce swelling and remove the sludge in the economy, adjust and optimize the structure, and achieve sustainable growth of output, employment, and economic benefits. In the process of cutting overcapacity, we should stabilize and increase output by stabilizing employment and improving labor productivity and resource utilization efficiency. Therefore, "cutting overcapacity" cannot only passively eliminate capacity, blindly pursuing the quantity of bankruptcy liquidation to reach the standard. It should pay attention to proper merging and reorganization, joint ventures, and cooperation, minimize unemployment, make full use of idle capacity, and digest excess capacity as far as possible.

6. To complete the five major tasks of "cutting overcapacity, reducing excess inventory, deleveraging, lowering costs, and strengthening areas of weakness", we must do a good job of both subtraction and addition.

In the process of "cutting overcapacity, reducing excess inventory, deleveraging, lowering costs, and strengthening areas of weakness", the first four do subtraction, while the last one does addition. On the one hand, China's economy has bubbles, risks, and excess, so it needs "cutting" and "lowering" for "slimming". On the other hand, China's economy has many shortcomings and deficiencies, and even some aspects are stunted, such as market mechanism and independent innovation. Therefore, China's economy needs to "keep fit", and, through reform and adjustment, improve internal strength, expand effective supply, and improve supply quality. In terms of regional economic development, the development of western China is a weakness; in terms of industrial development, China's agricultural development is a weakness; in terms of industrial development, China's manufacturing industry is big but not strong, which is a weakness; in terms of urban and rural population, farmers' low income, slow income growth, and too many poor people are weaknesses; in terms of the relationship between the real economy and the virtual economy, the slow and inadequate development of the real economy is a weakness; in terms of the impetus of sustainable economic development, the lack of independent innovation is a weakness; and so on. These weaknesses require us to do a good job of addition.

7. The completion of the five major tasks of "cutting overcapacity, reducing excess inventory, deleveraging, lowering costs, and strengthening areas of weakness" does not mean the completion of the task of supply-side structural reform.

If the supply-side structural reform is a lasting battle, "cutting overcapacity, reducing excess inventory, deleveraging, lowering costs, and strengthening areas of weakness" is only the first stage or hierarchy of this battle. "Cutting overcapacity, reducing excess inventory, deleveraging, lowering costs, and strengthening areas of weakness" is mainly to solve the problems of excess production and excess capacity. At most, it is only a process of adjusting industrial structure and economic structure. Although this process also involves structural reform, "cutting overcapacity, reducing excess inventory, deleveraging, lowering costs, and strengthening areas of weakness" itself is not a structural reform. "Cutting overcapacity, reducing excess inventory, deleveraging, lowering costs, and strengthening areas of weakness" is the outpost battle and peripheral battle of structural reform, which sweep away obstacles and lay the foundation for structural reform. The core task of supply-side structural reform is "structural reform", including transformation and upgrading of economic structure, reforms of the economic system and political system, and remodeling and repositioning of the relationship between government and market, among which system reform is the core and key.

8. Attention should be paid to establishing a long-effect mechanism for solving supply surplus.

At present, the government mainly plays a leading role in "cutting overcapacity, reducing excess inventory, deleveraging, lowering costs, and strengthening areas of weakness". The government solves excess capacity and imbalance of economic structure through adopting some administrative means, laws, and policy measures. For example, the central government issues the indicators, tasks, and deadlines related to "cutting overcapacity" to local governments, industry associations, and large enterprises, assesses the completion of the tasks of "cutting overcapacity", and imposes administrative accountability and economic penalties on the units and their principal responsible persons failing to complete the tasks on time and as required. This is an emergency solution, and one that works faster under China's current system. However, in "cutting overcapacity, reducing excess inventory, deleveraging, lowering costs, and strengthening areas of weakness", we should give full play to the role of the market mechanism and make more use of market methods. We should not go back to the old road of economic rectification by means of a planned economy, turn "cutting overcapacity, reducing excess inventory, deleveraging, lowering costs, and strengthening areas of weakness" into "closure, suspension, merger, or shifting of the enterprise" led by the government, or regard "cutting overcapacity, reducing excess inventory, deleveraging, lowering costs, and strengthening areas of weakness" as an opportunity for government control and "reset" of a planned economy. There are nearly 30 million enterprises of various types in China. There are great differences in regions and industries, and supply and demand are dynamically changing. It is difficult for the government to accurately identify and define which industries and enterprises have absolute supply surplus and relative supply surplus, to judge the condition of excess capacity and financial leverage ratio in a certain industry or enterprise, and to find out the specific causes of the high cost of an enterprise. The government is also unable to know the "weaknesses" of each enterprise in detail. Therefore, the government's capacity for "cutting overcapacity, reducing excess inventory, deleveraging, lowering costs, and strengthening areas of weakness" is limited, and the effect arising therefrom is limited. In the long run, to solve excess capacity, we not only need to rely more on market mechanism, but also need to eliminate the system mechanism for generating and accumulating excess capacity from the source, instead of excessively relying on administrative orders and administrative penalties for a long time. To solve supply surplus, a mechanism for dynamic adjustment and optimization of economic structure is required to be established through system reform and innovation, replacing government dominance with market dominance. Market mechanism is the long-effect mechanism for solving supply surplus and dynamically optimizing economic structure. The next two chapters hereof will discuss this topic more.

Notes

1 According to the National Bureau of Statistics of China, the growth rates of China's fiscal revenue from 2011 to 2015 were 25%, 12.9%, 10.2%, 8.6%, and 5.8% respectively, and the growth rate dropped rapidly.
2 As to whether the tax burden on Chinese enterprises is too heavy, there are great differences between Chinese fiscal and taxation authorities and their research institutions and other researchers: the former researchers believe that the tax burden on Chinese enterprises is lower than the international average, while the latter researchers believe that it is much higher than the international average. See the article "How Heavy Is the Corporate Tax Burden?" published on hexun.com on January 24, 2017, the article "Survey of Manufacturing Tax Burden: How Heavy Is the Corporate Tax Burden?" published on caijingz.com (Beijing) on January 26, 2017, and the article "How Heavy Is the Tax Burden on Chinese Enterprises?" published on wallstreetcn.com on March 1, 2017.
3 Quoted from the article "How Heavy Is the Corporate Tax Burden?" published on hexun.com on January 24, 2017.
4 Dewar, R. D., & Dutton, J. E. (1986). "The Adoption of Radical and Incremental Innovations: An Empirical Analysis", *Management Science*, 1422–1433.

7 Three-step strategy of supply-side reform (2)

Consolidation treatment

"Cutting overcapacity, reducing excess inventory, deleveraging, lowering costs, and strengthening areas of weakness" aims at excess production, excess capacity and economic structural imbalance. To consolidate the achievements of "cutting overcapacity, reducing excess inventory, deleveraging, lowering costs, and strengthening areas of weakness" and prevent the rebound of supply surplus and structural imbalance, it is required to promote the supply-side structural reform to the second stage (the second step), which is to consolidate and treat supply surplus and structural imbalance. The so-called consolidation treatment is to adjust, optimize, and upgrade the economic structure, thereby curbing the rebound of excess production and excess capacity and making the economy strong and healthy.

Excess production and excess capacity are the representation of economic structural imbalance, and economic structural imbalance is manifested in excess production and excess capacity. Therefore, the adjustment, optimization, and upgrading of the economic structure are required for consolidating the effectiveness of controlling excess production and excess capacity.

I. Perspectives on the structural imbalance of China's economy

The economic structure is rich in contents and broad in meanings, including AS structure and AD structure, industrial structure, regional structure, urban–rural structure, composition of real economy and virtual economy, ownership structure, market structure, etc. The structural imbalance of China's economy is the imbalance of AS and AD in quantity and structure. As mentioned earlier, in terms of aggregate, since the late 1990s, China's economy has been in an unbalanced state of AS exceeding AD or relative excess production capacity; on the other hand, from the perspective of structure, the AD structure of China's economy is not coordinated and mismatched with the AS structure, and supply surplus and supply shortage coexist. In the past, the production and supply system of China's economy was mainly to solve the problem of insufficient production and high shortage of supply, as well as the problem of food and clothing for the majority of urban and rural residents. The new Chinese economy was developed on a poor foundation, and the production technology and equipment of most products were still relatively backward; therefore, in the aggregate output,

DOI: 10.4324/9781003367000-10

there were more popular products and fewer personalized products, more homogeneous products and less differentiated products, more low-grade products in mass production and less medium- and high-grade products with high quality; more products in the middle and low end of the value chain and less products in the high end of the value chain, and so on. With the rapid development of China's economy after the reform and opening up, the continuous improvement of per capita income level, the continuous expansion of middle-income groups, and the upgrading of residents' demand structure to medium and high grades, some low-grade consumer goods and investment goods have become surplus products, and the corresponding production capacity has become excess capacity. At the same time, due to the growth of income and the upgrading of the demand structure, residents' demand for medium- and high-grade products continues to expand, while the production and supply system of China's economy has not been transformed and upgraded in time to meet the needs of this upgrading of demand structure, which leads some Chinese residents to go abroad to buy American health care products, Japanese rice cookers and toilet seats, Korean cosmetics, Italian shoes, French perfume and bags, German iron pots, New Zealander milk powder, etc., resulting in part of China's effective demand draining abroad.[1]

In order to achieve the economic goal of "catching up and surpassing", China has been implementing the strategy of unbalanced development for a long time. For example, China implemented the strategy of prioritizing heavy industry and urban industry in the 1950s and 1960s, and the strategy of prioritizing the development of eastern regions, coastal or special zones and the strategy of export-oriented development etc. since the reform and opening up. To realize such a strategy of unbalanced development, in terms of development concept, more emphasis was placed on investment over consumption, total quantity over structure, output over efficiency, growth over quality, urban over rural areas, and industry over agriculture. In terms of development means, the policy or system of low prices (including artificially lowering the prices of resources and factors through planned pricing), low wages and low welfare, and the strategy of high savings (high accumulation) and high investment were implemented to provide primitive accumulation for urban development and industrialization. The successful implementation of these strategies of unbalanced development enabled China's economy to achieve leapfrog development, making China leap from a poor and backward economy to the world's second largest economy 61 years after the establishment of the People's Republic of China.[2] However, the long-term implementation of the strategy of unbalanced development and the solidification of this development strategy also led to the structural imbalances in many aspects of the Chinese economy. Seen from the AD-AS analysis framework, these imbalances mainly involve the AD structure, the industrial structure on the AS side, the regional economic structure, the urban and rural development, and the relationship between real economy and virtual economy.

1. Imbalance of AD structure

Both before and after the reform and opening up, China's economic growth has been investment-driven, which is reflected in the rising capital formation rate and declining final consumption rate in the AD structure (see Figure 7.1); the growth rate of fixed asset investment is much higher than that of final consumption (see Figure 7.2), thus causing an imbalance in the proportional relationship between investment and consumption.

Figure 7.1 shows that China's final consumption rate and capital formation rate were 63.2% and 37.3%, respectively, in 1979, and 51.8% and 44.7%, respectively, in 2015, with the proportions of these two gradually approaching, and in 2010 the proportions of these two were even almost equal, with the final consumption rate and capital formation rate being 48.5% and 47.9%, respectively.

Figure 7.2 shows that in the 40 years (1981–2019) after the reform and opening up, the growth rate of social fixed asset investment was lower than that of final consumption in only 14 years,[3] and in the remaining 26 years, the growth rate of fixed asset investment was higher than that of final consumption, and in some years the growth rate of fixed asset investment was 2–3.2 times that of final consumption!

This model of supporting high economic growth through long-term high investment inevitably leads to extensive investment growth and extensive economic growth, and thus resulting in a rapid increase in the accumulation of low-technology capital, a sharp increase in low-grade production capacity, and poor investment efficiency and economic growth quality.

2. Imbalance of industrial structure

When New China was established, it was an agricultural country with a low level of science and technology and a low level of economic development. In 1952, the added value of China's primary, secondary, and tertiary industries

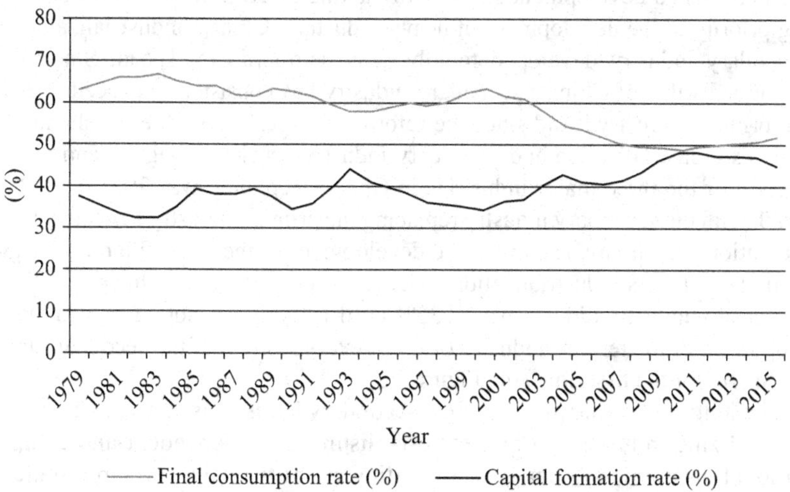

Figure 7.1 China's final consumption rate and capital formation rate

Source: *China Statistical Yearbook* (2016) compiled by the National Bureau of Statistics of China

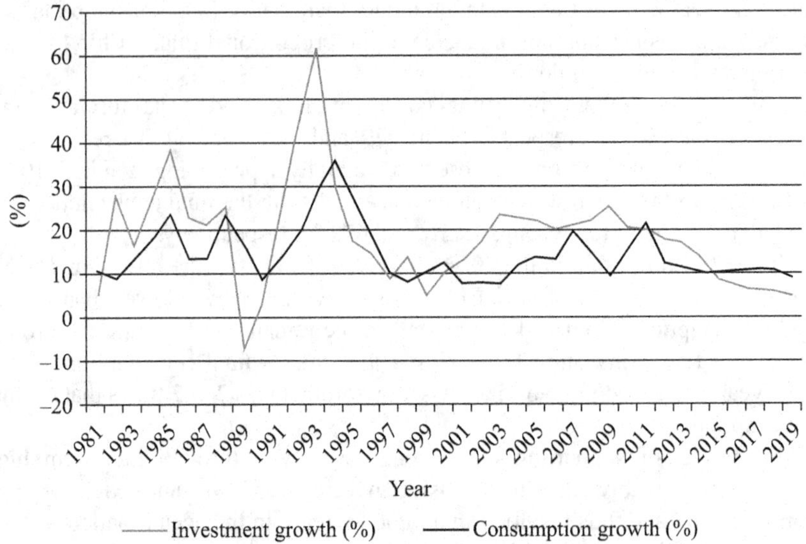

Figure 7.2 Growth of China's final consumption and growth of investment in social fixed assets

Source: "National Data 1979–2021", published by the National Bureau of Statistics of China

accounted for 45.9%, 23.2%, and 30.9% of GDP respectively, and the primary industry accounted for almost half of the national economy. By implementing the unbalanced development strategy of "taking steel as the key link" and "giving priority to the development of heavy industry", China's industrialization and secondary industry developed rapidly at an extraordinary speed. Since 1970, the added value of China's secondary industry has consistently exceeded that of the primary industry.[4] And since the reform and opening up, the development of China's industrialization and secondary industry accelerated again, and the proportion of the three major industries in China's economy was 29.6:48.1:22.3 in 1980, with the secondary industry replacing the primary industry to occupy half of the national economy. However, the development of the tertiary industry lagged behind in China's industrialization process for a long time, and the proportion of the tertiary industry did not exceed 35% until 1998; it was not until 2013 that the proportion of the tertiary industry (46.7%) exceeded that of the secondary industry (44%) for the first time (see Figure 7.3).

The long-term rapid growth of the secondary industry is of great significance for realizing industrialization, for establishing an independent and complete national economic system, and for getting rid of the backward appearance of the economy, but the one-way breakthrough of the secondary industry and the lagging development of the primary and tertiary industries inevitably lead to an imbalance in the industrial structure. After all, the development of

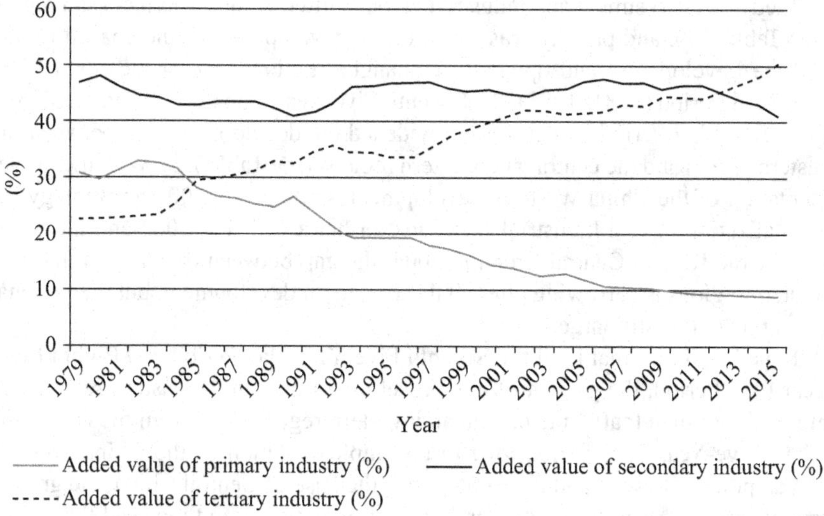

Figure 7.3 Changes in the structure of China's three industries (1979–2015)

Source: *China Statistical Yearbook* (2016), compiled by the National Bureau of Statistics of China

the secondary industry needs the corresponding development of the primary and tertiary industries to provide support and market. Some people simply regard the declining proportion of primary industry, mainly agriculture, in the national economy as an indicator of the upgrading and optimization of China's industrial structure. In fact, in the process of declining proportion of agriculture, the level of production technology and the productivity of China's agriculture have not improved significantly, and the degree of modernization of agriculture is still relatively low, and small-scale production based on household contract is still the main form of organization of agricultural production, which has limited development potential. Moreover, in the process of excessively rapid development of the secondary industry, due to the lagging technological progress and innovation and the poor operation of the mechanism for the replacement of old and new production equipment and capacity, a large number of low-grade or even obsolete production equipment and capacity that should be eliminated were precipitated, leading to the serious excess capacity in the future. This can explain to some extent why excess production and excess capacity have been mainly concentrated in the secondary industry over the years.

3. Imbalance of regional economic structure

Since modern times, China's eastern region has been more economically developed; in addition, due to the implementation of the strategy of "giving priority to the development of the eastern region" since the reform and opening up, the focus of fixed asset investment and industrial layout shifted to the eastern coastal region (see Table 7.1), and priority was given to the development of the coastal region and the development and opening of Shanghai Pudong during the Sixth Five-Year Plan Period (1981–1985), the Seventh Five-Year Plan Period, and the Eighth Five-Year Plan Period, which further widened the development gap between the eastern region and the central and western regions (see Table 7.2). With the implementation of the China Western Development Strategy in 2000, the Strategy for Revitalization of Old Industrial Bases in Northeast China in 2003 and the Strategy for the Rise of Central China in 2004, the gap between eastern, central, and western regions is narrowing after all these years of development, but the regional economic gap is still large.

Table 7.1 shows that until the Seventh Five-Year Plan Period and Eighth Five-Year Plan Period, the growth of fixed asset investment in the eastern region was much higher than that in the central and western regions, and from the end of the Ninth Five-Year Plan Period, due to the implementation of the China Western Development Strategy and the Strategy for the Rise of Central China, the growth rate of investment in the central and western regions began to exceed that in the eastern region.

This long-term difference in the regional investment structure will inevitably make the infrastructure, capital stock, and supply capacity of the central and western regions lag far behind that of the eastern region, as shown by some major economic indicators (see Table 7.2 and Table 7.3).

As can be seen from Table 7.2, until the beginning of the 21st century, the major macroeconomic indicators of the central and western regions lagged significantly behind those of the eastern region.

From Table 7.3, we find that in 1978, before the reform and opening up, the GDP per capita in the central and western regions was 64.4% and 52.8% of that in the eastern region, while by 2015, after 36 years of reform and development, the GDP per capita in the central and western regions was 57.9% and 42.6% of that in the eastern region, and the economic development gap between the eastern, central, and western regions has widened instead of narrowing!

4. Imbalance between urban and rural development

China used to be a large agricultural country and has been implementing the unbalanced development strategy favoring urban development and industrial development. The government systematically suppressed the prices of agricultural products, requisitioned grain from farmers and then supplied them to the industrial sector and urban residents at low prices, and restricted the movement of farmers to cities through the household registration system and policies. Until the early 1990s, we still regarded the farmers entering the cities to work as "vagrants" and restricted and cracked down on such behaviors, thus solidifying the dual structure of urban and rural areas, resulting in the coexistence of developed cities and backward rural areas, and modern industry and agriculture. Since the reform

Table 7.1 Investment growth in eastern, central, and western China in different periods

Region	*The Seventh Five-Year Plan Period*		*The Eighth Five-Year Plan Period*		*The Ninth Five-Year Plan Period*		*The Tenth Five-Year Plan Period*		*The Eleventh Five-Year Plan Period*	
	Total amount (RMB'00,000,000)	*Average annual growth rate %*	*Total amount (RMB'00,000,000)*	*Average annual growth rate %*	*Total amount (RMB'00,000,000)*	*Average annual growth rate %*	*Total amount (RMB'00,000,000)*	*Average annual growth rate %*	*Total amount (RMB'00,000,000)*	*Average annual growth rate %*
Eastern Region	10051	21.0	35477	40.8	75700	9.3	154941	19.7	408767	20.1
Central Region	3705	11.9	9846	32.1	23566	14.1	52145	21.5	198084	31.6
Western Region	3506	12.2	10182	33.6	24312	16.0	24117	22.2	197758	28.2

Source: *China Statistical Yearbook* of relevant years compiled by the National Bureau of Statistics of China

Table 7.2 Proportion of major economic indicators in the eastern, central, and western regions of China (%)

	Eastern Region		*Central Region*		*Western Region*	
Year *Indicator*	*1978*	*2001*	*1978*	*2001*	*1978*	*2001*
Total population at the end of the year	40.9	41.3	35.6	35.1	23.1	22.9
GDP	50.2	66.3	29.4	29.9	16.0	15.1
Primary industry	40.9	49.8	37.1	36.7	21.2	19.9
Secondary industry	60.1	62.5	28.3	26.8	14.7	12.3
Tertiary industry	41.1	79.6	26.0	31.4	12.7	17.2
Total imports and exports	32.0	92.6	2.7	4.9	1.2	2.6
Gross industrial output value	60.1	71.6	27.0	19.1	13.2	9.3
Total retail sales of consumer goods	54.8	62.5	40.6	28.5	20.0	13.6

Source: *The Statistical Yearbook of the Xinjiang Production and Construction Corps* (2003), edited by Shen Weizhen (China Statistics Press, May 2003)

Table 7.3 GDP per capita in eastern, central, and western regions of China (unit: RMB)

	1978	*1985*	*1990*	*1995*	*2005*	*2010*	*2015*
Nationwide	379	853	1634	4854	14368	30876	50251
Eastern Region	483	1113	2080	7104	23303	46034	70587
Central Region	311	716	1268	3691	11108	24979	40901
Western Region	255	565	1060	3029	8720	22476	39053

Source: *China Statistical Yearbook* (2016), compiled by the National Bureau of Statistics of China

and opening up, through the implementation of the contract responsibility system based on the household with remuneration linked to output in rural areas and the reform of the rural governance system (e.g., abolishing people's communes, abolishing districts, and merging townships), the situation of agriculture, rural areas, and farmers has changed greatly, and the income and living standards of farmers have improved substantially. However, due to some historical, institutional, and policy reasons, China's agriculture, rural areas, and farmers are still generally an antonomasia of backwardness and poverty, and the development gap between China's urban and rural areas is still relatively large, judging from some data.

In the first 10 years of the 21st century, the per capita income ratio between urban and rural areas in China has been maintained at 3:1, and the per capita consumption ratio between urban and rural areas has been maintained at 3.4:1; i.e. in this period, the per capita income of urban residents was three times that of rural residents, and the per capita consumption of urban residents was 3.4 times that of rural residents. Since the 18th National Congress of the Communist Party of China, the per capita income ratio and per capita consumption ratio of urban and rural areas have both gone down due to the implementation of the development strategy of rural revitalization, vigorous construction and improvement of institutional mechanisms for the integration of urban and rural development, steady progress in poverty eradication and building a moderately prosperous society in all aspects, and obvious results in the integrated development of urban and rural areas. According to the calculation under the new statistic specifications adopted by the National Bureau of Statistics of China in 2013, the urban–rural per capita income ratio decreased from 2.81:1 in 2013 to 2.64:1 in 2019, and the urban–rural per capita consumption ratio decreased from 2.47:1 in 2013 to 2.11:1 in 2019, and the gap between urban and rural income and consumption has narrowed significantly.

5. Imbalanced relationship between real economy and virtual economy

A landmark difference between a market economy (or commodity economy) and a physical economy is that a market economy must have financial markets (including monetary markets and capital markets) with leverage effect, speculation, and arbitrage, which will cause the price of commodities (including financial products) to deviate from their value, thus creating bubbles and virtualizing the economy. Therefore, speculation, arbitrage, leverage, and bubbles are normal and inevitable components of a market economy. However, the development of everything must have a "degree" beyond which it will become abnormal. An important aspect of the structural imbalance of China's economy in recent years is the excessive expansion of the virtual economy, the excessive fanaticism in speculation and arbitrage activities, and the excessive leverage and the excessive bubbles in the economy. This is mainly manifested in the imbalance between the financial sector and the real economy, and the imbalance between the real estate sector and the real economy. Chinese scholars regard the former imbalance as monetary or financial, "moving away from the real economy to the virtual economy", and the latter imbalance as the "bubbling of the real estate market".

The imbalance between China's financial sector and the real economy is manifested in the following aspects.

First, the M2-to-GDP ratio is too high.

China's M2-to-GDP ratio exceeded 1 (1.064) for the first time in 1996 and exceeded 2 (2.012) in 2015. This ratio greatly exceeds both the developed market economies of Europe and the United States, as well as other BRIC countries such as India, Brazil, and Russia.

China's money stock accounts for a disproportionate share of GDP, and the growth rate of the money supply far exceeds that of GDP (see Figure 7.4).

According to Milton Friedman, the commodity prices in a country can be maintained stable only when the growth rate of its money supply = the real economic growth rate. Figure 7.4 shows that during the 26 years from 1994–2019, the growth rate of China's M2 has been higher than that of the GDP, with the difference between these two growth rates reaching a maximum of 21.5 percentage points (1994), the next highest difference being 19.1 percentage points (2009), and the lowest difference being 1.2 percentage points (2017).

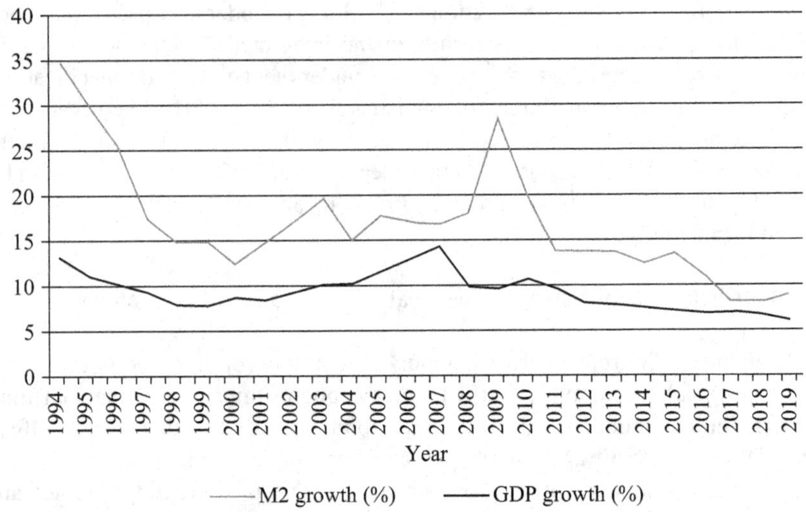

Figure 7.4 Comparison between M2 growth and GDP growth in China

Source: *China Statistical Yearbook* (2021) compiled by the National Bureau of Statistics of China

The money stock is twice the size of GDP and the growth rate of money supply is much higher than that of the economic growth, which is certainly related to China's economic development and financial deepening, and to the fact that China's economic activities are dominated by indirect financing rather than direct financing, but it is undeniable that there exists super currency in the process of China's economic development.

According to the quantity theory of money or Milton Friedman's new quantity theory of money, the increase rate of price in a country = the growth rate of the money supply − the growth rate of real economy if the velocity of money circulation is constant. Confusingly, this formula cannot explain the relationship between the change rate of commodity prices (CPI), the M2 growth rate, and the GDP growth rate in China. From 1994 to 2019, except for 1994, 2006, 2007, and 2017–2019, China's M2 growth rate was significantly higher than the sum of the GDP growth rate and the CPI growth rate in the remaining 20 years (see Figure 7.5), which suggests that part of the M2 growth was not used to drive either economic growth or price increases, but rather "lurked" in the economic system, which was called "The Mystery of the Missing Money in China" by Chinese scholars. This "mystery" is actually the existence of a "bubble" in the China's economy, but this bubble has not yet broken.

Second, a large amount of funds flow into the virtual economy sector, and the proportion of funds flowing into the real economy sector is too low.

According to data provided by Li Yizhong, former Minister of the Ministry of Industry and Information Technology, the new loans in China's banking industry

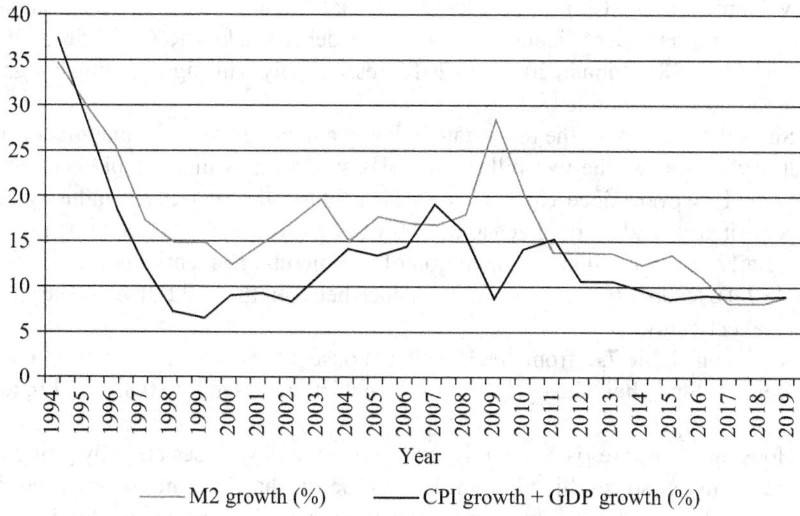

Figure 7.5 The Mystery of the Missing Money in China

Source: *China Statistical Year7book* (2021) compiled by the National Bureau of Statistics of China

reached RMB 12.65 trillion in 2016, of which the real estate loans accounted for 44.8%, nearly half. The total loan balance was RMB 106.6 trillion, with real estate loans accounting for 25.03% and industrial loans accounting for only 17%–18%. Funds flowed excessively to the stock market, bond market, housing market, and futures market, which were used by speculation to obtain high profits; there is also a large amount of funds circulating in the financial system through financial derivatives such as wealth management, or circulating outside the financial system.

Third, the debt ratio and the leverage ratio are too high.

How high are China's debt ratio and leverage ratio? At present, there seems to be no authoritative data. According to information provided by the State Council Information Office on June 23, 2016, as of the end of 2015, the debt of China's central government was RMB 26.66 trillion, accounting for 39.4% of GDP. By the end of 2015, the balance of debt for which local governments at all levels in China have direct repayment responsibility was RMB 15.4 trillion, and the debt for which the government has guarantee responsibility and may assume certain bailout responsibility was RMB 8.6 trillion, totaling RMB 24 trillion, accounting for 35.1% of GNI and 34.8% of GDP, respectively. In 2016, the debt balance of China's central and local governments was about RMB 27.33 trillion with a debt ratio of about 36.7%, including the debt of RMB 17.18 trillion for which the local governments have repayment responsibility. Data from China's Ministry of Finance show that the debt-to-GDP ratio of Chinese state-owned enterprises rose to about 115% in 2015 from less than 100% in 2012.

According to the data provided by the National Institution for Finance & Development of the Chinese Academy of Social Sciences, the balance of China's local government debt (including contingent debt) reached RMB 27.56 trillion and RMB 30.28 trillion in 2013 and 2014, respectively. This figure is much higher than the official data released.

Since the late 1990s, the real estate industry and the automobile manufacturing industry have been the two pillar industries supporting China's rapid economic growth. However, since entering the 21st century, the real estate industry has become increasingly virtualized and bubbly due to profiteering and soaring prices, especially the production and operation of commercial residential properties (see Table 7.4), leading to a significant imbalance between the real estate industry and the real economy.

As seen in Table 7.4, from 2003 to 2016, house prices in China's first-tier cities of Beijing, Shanghai, Guangzhou, and Shenzhen increased by 10.8, 9.2, 4.9, and 6.5 times, respectively.

Housing prices are rising rapidly, and in many cities, prices are only going up without falling, so reselling commercial properties has become the most profitable speculative activity. Through the development of real estate and buying and selling of second-hand houses, it can make more money in a shorter time than any real economic activity, and the high temperature of the real estate market has ripened a group of tycoons in Chinese mainland; the real estate industry not only makes houses fast, but also makes Chinese tycoons even faster, and the real estate industry is the fastest producer of tycoons among all industries in China (see Table 7.5).

The continued overheating of the real estate market has led to a large number of resources being misallocated to the real estate industry, and the real economy has been left out in the cold.

If a country's capital and talent flood into the virtual economy, while there is a shortage of funds and talents in its real economy, the country's economy will be inevitably "hollowed", the relationship between the real economy and the virtual economy will be out of balance, and the economy will be naturally "virtual but not real".

Because of its easy use of debt leverage, the virtual economy sector may provide services that generate (monetary) income and may even generate higher

Table 7.4 Average price change of commercial residential properties in Beijing, Shanghai, Guangzhou, and Shenzhen (RMB/m_2)

Year *City*	*2003*	*2006*	*2009*	*2012*	*2015*	*2016*
Beijing	4737	8080	13799	20700	36373	55779
Shanghai	4670	6085	10735	13870	28343	47625
Guangzhou	3888	6315	10189	14044	18637	22752
Shenzhen	5879	9190	14858	18847	24136	44114

Source: *China Real Estate Data Yearbook* (2017)

Table 7.5 Five industries with the highest proportion (%) of tycoons in the Chinese mainland

Year *Industry*	*2013*	*2014*	*2015*	*2016*
Other manufacturing industries	20.3	23.1	28.1	26.2
Real estate	23.5	19.8	16.1	15.4
IT	9.6	10.1	11.2	11.8
Finance and investment	7.0	7.8	9.1	10.8
Medical industry	6.6	6.9	6.8	6.6

Source: (Rupert Hoogewerf) Rich List of Chinese Mainland in related years.

income than the real economy sector. However, creating income is not the same as creating physical goods and real wealth. Real wealth is the accumulation of physical goods, while money is only a symbol of real wealth. The physical goods and real wealth of a society are mainly created by the real economy sector. Opening banks or speculating in houses and stocks can make money and increase monetary income, but these activities themselves cannot directly produce physical products and real wealth. The moderate and appropriate development of these virtual economy activities can improve the convenience of services and promote the production of physical goods and real wealth, but these activities are not themselves activities that produce physical goods and real wealth. It is just like the role of a midwife, whose labor contributes to the successful birth of a baby, but she is not the woman who gives birth, and the child is not produced by her. If all women in a society are eager to be midwives and unwilling to be parturients, even if the technology of midwifery is very advanced and developed, the child can still not be produced.

If virtual economic activities do not facilitate and promote the production of physical products and the creation of real wealth, but become “bloodsuckers” and “parasites” of the real economy, the real economy will not be able to grow healthily and will become a sick economy.

II. Entry point and focus point of economic structural adjustment

To effectively address excess production and excess capacity, the earlier-mentioned structural imbalances in the economy must be solved. In my opinion, to address the structural imbalance of the economy, it is necessary to start from the following aspects:

1. Adjust the development strategy to gradually replace the strategy of unbalanced development with the strategy of balanced development

Unbalanced development was one of the economic development strategies recommended for developing countries by development economists in the 1950s and

1970s, and the American scholar A.O. Hirschman is a major proponent of this theory. In his book *The Strategy of Economic Development* (1958), Hirschman argued that developing countries have limited capital, technology, and resources, so they should concentrate their limited capital and resources on developing certain industries with large "correlation effects" first, and then use them as an impetus to gradually expand investment in other industries and drive the development of other industries. Hirschman opposes the balanced development strategy, arguing that it is impractical and even a nightmare for developing countries to implement it, while unbalanced development is invaluable to the economic development process. He wrote,

> In a competitive economy, gains and losses are signs of imbalance, and our aim is to make the imbalance exist, not to make it disappear. To move the economy forward, the task of development policy is to keep tensions, disproportions, and imbalances.[5]

Some development economists believe that this unbalanced development strategy can be implemented not only in the process of industrial development of a country, but also in the process of regional economic development of a country, that is, to drive the economic development of other regions by giving priority to the development of one or some regions.

The economic development of the former Soviet Union followed a unbalanced development path. Since its founding over 70 years ago, China has basically pursued a strategy of unbalanced development. In the context of China's weak economic base, capital shortage, and technological backwardness, especially China's backward industrial development and great differences in regional economic conditions, the adoption of the strategy of unbalanced development is appropriate and has proved to be effective in practice. After more than 70 years of construction and development, China has been ranked among the world's economic powers, and this leapfrog development is not unrelated to the implementation of the strategy of unbalanced development.

However, when a country, especially a major country, has reached a certain stage of industrial and economic development, it needs to adjust its development strategy and switch from unbalanced development to a balanced development model, and it is not advisable to solidify the unbalanced development model for a long time. Focused investment in an industry may promote the development of this industry; however, if there is no corresponding investment in other industries, and other industries lag behind in development for a long time, the prioritized industries or fast-growing industries will inevitably have excess production and excess capacity due to the lack of sufficient demand support. This is also true for regional economic development. For example, due to the long-term implementation of the strategy of giving priority to the development of heavy industry, the structure of light industry and heavy industry in China's economy became seriously imbalanced at the beginning of the reform and opening up, and the proportion of light industry and heavy industry in the total industrial output value changed from 64.5% and 35.5% in 1952 to 43.1% and 56.9% in 1978 respectively, while light industry is the major demander of heavy industry products, and the lack of development of light industry will lead to insufficient demand for heavy industrial products, and heavy industry will fall into excess capacity, and people's life will be seriously affected. In order to correct the long-term one-sided strategy of developing heavy industry and solve the problem of structural imbalance between light industry and heavy industry, the Chinese government adopted the "six priorities" principle of supporting the development of light industry from 1979 to 1984 to accelerate and strengthen the development of light industry. Through several years of structural adjustment and development, the structure of light and heavy industries gradually became more reasonable. The current excess capacity in the steel, cement, and glass industries etc. in China's economy is largely due to three reasons: (1) some of the absolute excess capacity was not removed in time; (2) the international market reduced the demand for these products after the international financial crisis, resulting in a decline in exports of these products, and these products had to be returned to the domestic market for sale; (3) the decline in the investment and development of construction, automobile, real estate industries etc. as well as some light industries, which were originally the big demanders of steel, cement, and glass products. The third of these reasons led to a new structural imbalance of industries within the secondary industry.

One of the main reasons for the current overstocking of many industrial goods and urban commercial housing in the Chinese economy is the slow growth of farmers' income due to the lagging development of agriculture and rural areas, and the farmers' demand for industrial goods and urban commercial housing is insufficient, which means that the imbalance between the urban and rural economic structures has led to a part of excess production and excess vacant houses.

Although we can "strengthen areas of weakness" in our economic structure and development in the short term by implementing the strategy of unbalanced development and prioritizing development policies, in the long term, we should establish the concept of balanced or equilibrium development and use the concept of balanced or coordinated development to guide our long-term development plan (e.g. "Five-Year Plan"). In this way, our economy can truly achieve stable, coordinated, and sustainable development. With a long-term imbalance and imbalance in the economic structure, it is impossible to achieve stable and coordinated economic development.

After nearly 70 years of construction and development, China's national economic structure has become relatively complete and has a solid industrial and technological foundation, and its economic development and per capita income have reached the level of lower middle developed countries, which has raised the conditions for China's economic development to shift from unbalanced development to balanced development, while excess capacity and economic structural imbalance highlight the necessity and urgency of the shift in development strategy.

2. Pay attention to the balance between AD and AS

The balance between AD and AS includes both quantitative balance and structural matching and coordination.

For supply-side structural reform, it is necessary to shift the focus of reform and policy to the supply side, but it does not mean that in can abandon the demand management and demand restructuring, and it does not mean that when the supply-side problems are solved, the demand-side problems are naturally solved with it. Maintaining the balance between AD and AS in terms of quantity and structure is still the basic point of our economic work and macroeconomic policy. I have already discussed this point in Chapter 5.

The adjustment and upgrading of the supply structure is a medium- to long-term process that cannot be completed in the short term because it involves a series of deep-seated problems such as technology and equipment renewal, labor quality improvement, innovation, and institutional change. However, in the short term, we still need to maintain the medium- and high-speed growth of the economy, and to maintain the stable operation and normal development of the economy. To achieve these short-term goals, we still need to maintain the moderate growth of AD and do a good job in regulating AD to make it compatible, balanced, and coordinated with the AS and its growth.

For a long time in the past, China's economic growth was "investment-led", i.e. realizing the high input of factors or resources through high investment, thus supporting high economic growth. The long-term implementation of this extensive mode of development pattern has not only resulted in a lack of coordination between economic development, environmental protection, and social development, but also inevitably led to the imbalance of economic structure and excess capacity in some industries.

Therefore, in order to make the AD and AS structurally coordinated through supply-side structural reform, it is necessary to change this "investment-led" type of economic growth, transform economic development from relying mainly on factor inputs to technological progress, innovation, knowledge accumulation and application, and giving full play to institutional advantages, mobilizing the enthusiasm of individuals, enterprises, and the government, and improving the efficiency of resource allocation. In terms of the AD structure, we should make raising consumer demand, especially residential consumer demand, the focus of reform and adjustment.

3. Reduce resource misallocation through further market-oriented mechanisms for correcting resource misallocation

According to microeconomics principles, efficient resource allocation (Pareto optimal) must satisfy the marginal condition that the marginal conversion rate of any two goods produced by producers is equal to the marginal substitution rate of any two goods purchased by consumers. The marginal conversion rate (MRT_{XY}) of two kinds of goods (assumed to be X and Y) is equal to the ratio of the amount of change in the two goods, i.e., $MRT_{XY} = dY/dX$; under conditions of resource scarcity, increasing the production of one product (e.g., Y) requires decreasing the production of another product (e.g., X), therefore, increasing the opportunity cost $\left(C_X^o\right)$ of producing one unit of Y is to give up a certain amount of X, and the amount of X given up can be measured by the increased cost of producing one unit of X (i.e. the marginal cost of producing X Mc_X). And thus, from the supply side, the marginal conversion rate can be expressed as the inverse of the opportunity cost of producing the two goods and the inverse of the marginal cost, i.e.

$$MRT_{XY} = \frac{dY}{dX} = \frac{C_x^o}{C_y^0} = \frac{MC_x}{MC_y} \tag{7.1}$$

The marginal substitution rate (MRS_{XY}) of the two goods is equal to the ratio of the amount of change of the two goods, i.e. $MRS_{XY} = dY/dX$, and according to the law of diminishing marginal utility, the ratio of the amount of change of the two goods is in turn equal to the inverse of the ratio of the marginal utility of the two goods, i.e.

$$MRS_{XY} = \frac{dY}{dX} = \frac{MU_X}{MU_Y} \tag{7.2}$$

If from the perspective of the supply side, in a perfectly competitive market, the product is priced according to "marginal cost", i.e. $P_x=MC_x$, and from the demand side, the consumer will determine the price he is willing to pay according to the "marginal utility" provided by the good, i.e. $P_x=MU_x$, then:

$$MRT_{XY} = \frac{dY}{dX} = \frac{MC_X}{MC_Y} = \frac{P_x}{P_y} = \frac{MU_X}{MU_Y} = MRS_{XY} \tag{7.3}$$

Formula (7.3) shows that the Pareto optimal allocation of resources is achieved if the price of any product is equal to both the marginal cost on the supply side and the marginal utility on the demand side; i.e., it satisfies both the profit maximization condition of the producer and the utility maximization condition of the consumer.

Formula (7.3) also implies that resource allocation is efficient if the marginal returns obtained from the production of any product by a certain amount of resources are equal, i.e., $P_X \times d_X = P_Y \times d_Y$.

Thus, misallocation of resources is a situation in an economy where a certain amount of resources is used in the production in different industries or different enterprises, and the marginal returns of their products are not equal; or the price of such a product is not equal to its marginal cost, or its price is not equal to the marginal utility it provides to consumers.

Resource misallocation is also manifested that in some industries or in the production of some products, some resources or factors are over-allocated and others are under-allocated.

Based on the data from China for 1998–2005, India for 1987–1994, and the United States for 1977, 1987, and 1997, Hsieh and Klenow (2009) measured the impact of resource misallocation on the manufacturing TFP in these three countries. They found that if the resource allocation efficiency in China and India reached the level of the United States, the manufacturing TFP in China and India could increase by 30%–50% and 40%–60%, respectively. They projected that if resource misallocation in China, India, and the United States could be completely eliminated, the aggregate output in these three countries would increase by 115%, 127%, and 43%, respectively.[6] Stefano and Marconi (2016) used the methodology of Aoki (2012) to estimate the data of 26 sectors in China from 1980 to 2010 and found that China's TFP could increase by 25–35%. By incorporating the dynamic distortions in factor markets within the analytical framework and considering the entry and exit behavior of enterprises, Hsieh and Klenow (2009) found that TFP in manufacturing could be increased by 33.12% if distortions in the labor market are improved. Using Aoki's framework, Han Guozhen and Li Guozhang (2015) found that improvements in labor allocation distortions contributed 9.1% to the growth of total industrial TFP. It can be seen that resource misallocation in China's economy is serious and the efficiency loss caused by resource misallocation is significant. This also implies that there is a great potential to increase aggregate output by reducing or eliminating resource misallocation to improve TFP.

The main reasons for resource misallocation are as follows:

1. Labor market distortion

The labor market distortions are mainly manifested by the fact that the price (wages) of labor is chronically higher or lower than the marginal productivity of labor, and the actual amount of labor employed deviates from the amount employed when profit or utility is maximized. The main causes of labor market distortions are institutional factors that impede the free movement of labor, such as the household registration system that restricts the transfer of labor from the rural or agricultural sector to the urban or industrial sector (Hayashi & Prescott, 2008; Ge et al., 2013); gender discrimination (Gustafsson & Li, 2000); ownership differences and market segmentation (Mueller, 1998; Depalo et al., 2015); insufficient development of social networks and insurance markets (Munshi & Rosenzweig, 2016); etc.

2. Financial (or capital) market distortion

Financial or capital market distortions are mainly manifested in the incomplete development of financial markets, financial frictions, and financial repression leading to misallocation of capital and entrepreneurial talent across industries and enterprises (Jeong & Robert, 2007; Buera & Yongseok, 2013).

The "debt-to-equity swap" is a method invented by the Chinese government to reduce debt leverage in response to the negative impact of the 1998 Southeast Asian financial crisis on China's economy and in the process of resolving the chain debts of state-owned enterprises. This method has solved some major problems faced by state-owned enterprises in their survival and development, such as insolvency, high debt costs, and high leverage, so it has some positive significance. However, the debt-to-equity swap and government-led mergers and reorganizations have also enabled some of the "zombie enterprises" to survive, causing the problematic enterprises to transfer their debt burdens to the high-quality enterprises receiving mergers and reorganizations, and to state-owned commercial banks or financial institutions with government background. This actually "dilutes" or averages out the excessive debt burden of some state-owned enterprises in the whole society.

More importantly, the debt-to-equity swap has given some state-owned enterprises and institutions and even local governments a wrong signal, making them have a wrong expectation: they are not afraid of incurring more debts, not afraid of not being able to repay the debts; anyway, it will be solved eventually by the government through write-off, or debt-to-equity swap, or merger and reorganization. The massive debts generated by the expansion tide of Chinese colleges and universities through merger (construction of new campuses one after another) at the end of the 20th century and the beginning of the 21st century were finally paid by the government, which is an example of the success of universities' borrowing the strategy of debt-to-equity transfer from state-owned enterprises. In recent years, many local governments have raised a large amount of debt inspired by the debt-to-equity swap of state-owned enterprises. Now, some highly indebted local governments are looking forward to the State Council's policy to "blow away" their debts.

3. Inappropriate policies lead to market distortions

This distortion refers to the misallocation of factors of production or resources caused by the implementation of inappropriate policy measures by the government, such as the government's inappropriate pricing of certain products, the tax incentives, fiscal subsidies, entry restrictions, and differential tariffs adopted by the government to support and protect the prioritized development of certain industries or enterprises. Caballero et al. (2008) studied the phenomenon of resource misallocation in Japan due to the creation of "zombie enterprises" as a result of the "debt moratorium" policy. They pointed out that in the period of economic recession, the governments of some countries will require commercial banks to postpone the debts of enterprises that have lost money and should go bankrupt in order to reduce public censure, and commercial banks are willing to do so in order to meet capital adequacy requirements, which leads to the emergence of zombie enterprises. The emergence of zombie enterprises, on the one hand, allows labor and capital that should have been released through enterprise bankruptcy to continue to be allocated in inefficient or even ineffective enterprises, and on the other hand, prevents potential competitors with high efficiency from entering the industry or enterprise by raising wages and depressing product prices, thus perpetuating resource misallocation.

According to the report of *Shenzhen Special Zone Daily* on May 21, 2017, the Department of Intensive Care Unit (ICU) of the First Affiliated Hospital of

Shantou University Medical College received a patient who was poisoned by dichlorvos on the night of May 18, and the patient was in a coma, confused, and in a critical condition when admitted to the hospital. To treat this patient with organophosphorus pesticide poisoning, 40–70mg of atropine should be injected intramuscularly or intravenously every 10–20 minutes, but the hospital did not have any large-size atropine of 5mg (1ml) each, but only 0.5mg (1ml) of atropine each, and no large-size atropine was available in other hospitals. The First Affiliated Hospital of Shantou University Medical College urgently mobilized the medical staff to break open the glass ampoule of 0.5mg (1ml) of atropine by hand. It was necessary to break 800 ampoules per hour to save this patient, until the next morning when the patient was rescued, the medical staff broke 8,000 ampoules in total!

This case is a misallocation of resources caused by improper government pricing and defects in the allocation system.

The reason why large-size atropine is out of stock is that the drug manufacturers are not willing to produce it, and the reason why the enterprises are not willing to produce is that: (1) The pricing department of the National Development and Reform Commission sets too low a price for atropine, and the enterprises make little profit or even no money from producing atropine; (2) although the final demander of atropine is the patient, the direct demander is the hospital, and the patients may use it only if the hospitals have purchase the same from the manufacturers. Since hospitals have to cover hospital expenses with medicine revenue, and the price of atropine is low, doctors and hospitals cannot make much money by using atropine, so hospitals do not purchase or try to purchase as few low-cost medicines as possible.

It is not only atropine that is often out of stock in the market or in hospitals, but also some other low-cost medicines that are often commonly used and even life-saving medicines are often out of stock, for example, as reported in the media over the years, penicillin, amoxicillin, gentamicin, acetylspiramycin, erythromycin, compound Danshen dripping pills, Qingyan dripping pills, Quick Acting Heart Reliever, Wangshi Baochi Pill, Fuke Qianjin Tablet, etc. are also often not found in hospital pharmacies. This indicates that the resource allocation of low-cost medicines is seriously inadequate.

In fact, this resource misallocation is not difficult to be corrected by deepening the reform: (1) Cancel the government pricing of such medicines and let the market mechanism set the price independently. (2) If for the sake of medication safety and to reduce the burden of patients, the government pricing department can use the cost-plus-pricing method to price such drugs based on the investigation of the production cost of enterprises, so that enterprises can make reasonable profits. (3) Reform the medical and pharmaceutical system so that the costs and benefits generated by medical and pharmaceutical services are reasonably distributed among drug manufacturers, hospitals, and patients, and so that the needs of the final demanders of medicines (patients) are truly reflected in the prices of medicines. The practice of China's National Healthcare Security Administration in recent years of centralized procurement of some bulk, commonly used medicines based on negotiated pricing with drug manufacturers is worthy of promotion.

4. Information incompleteness leads to market distortion

Information asymmetry, information distortion, and information incompleteness may lead producers and investors to make wrong decisions or lead economic actors to make adverse choices, thus causing resource misallocation and consequently TFP loss and reduction in total output.

Resource misallocation is a common phenomenon in market economies, but the degree of resource misallocation varies in different market economies and at different stages of development. But in general, the degree of resource misallocation in China's economy is higher than that in developed market economies. The reasons for this mainly include: (1) As China has not been moving towards a market economy for a long time, the market price mechanism is still in the process of growth and development, and the price mechanism is not strong enough to regulate the allocation of resources to an efficient level. (2) The degree of market competition is insufficient. On the one hand, this is due to the existence of different forms of monopolies in China's economy, such as ownership monopoly, industry monopoly, and monopoly of key resources, which cause price distortion and prevent the market from pricing at marginal cost; on the other hand, there are institutional barriers to the flow of labor and resources, and there are strong rigidities and frictions in the labor market and other factor markets, making it difficult to form average profit margins among industries and factor prices and to equalize factor prices among industries, which leads to over-allocation of labor and capital in some industries and enterprises and under-allocation in some industries and enterprises. (3) Excessive government intervention and inappropriate intervention. In China, resource misallocation is not only caused by improper or even wrong policies such as macroeconomic policies, price policies, industrial policies (such as preferential development policies and various preferential and subsidy policies), and regional development policies, but also by the human reasons such as the arbitrary decisions of government officials. The misallocation of resources caused by the arbitrary decisions of officials may be more common. (4) The credit rationing and credit constraint in the financial market cause the misallocation between the supply of credit funds and the demand for credit funds in terms of quantity and structure, resulting in the misallocation of liquidity in the real economy and the virtual economy. (5) China's labor market is underdeveloped and highly distorted. At the present stage, the collective labor–capital bargaining system has not yet been formed in China's labor market, and there is no institutional arrangement of industrial unions in China, and laborers are engaged in decentralized negotiations with enterprises on labor conditions and wages and benefits as individual subjects or "atomic" subjects; the free mobility of the labor force is not yet high.

Therefore, to solve the problem of excess production and excess capacity caused by resource misallocation, we must continue to promote market-oriented reforms, further develop market mechanisms, increase the degree of competition and the level of marketization, and reduce the government's inappropriate intervention and excessive intervention. (1) Further reform the price determination mechanism by letting the market determine the prices of goods, service items, and factor prices that can be determined by the market, so as to further rationalize the price relations and eliminate price distortions. (2) Increase the free mobility of individuals and factors of production, especially the free mobility of individuals from the bottom to the top of the society, in different regions and industries (markets) through deepening reforms. Without the free mobility of labor and factors of production in the production of different products in different markets, full competition in the market economy cannot be formed, and full competition is an effective way to optimize resource allocation and improve labor productivity and factor productivity. (3) Continue to substantially reduce the government's power of approval, thereby reducing excessive and improper government intervention and arbitrary decisions by government officials. (4) Deepen the reform of the financial system and capital market to improve the level of financial prudential supervision, and thus reduce the misallocation of funds and capital. (5) Give full play to the decisive role of the market mechanism in resource allocation.

5. Adjustment, optimization, change, and upgrading of the economic structure

The supply-side structural reform should first address the serious imbalance in China's economic structure, and then on this basis, reform and upgrade the economic structure. Solving the imbalance of economic structure requires adjusting and optimizing the economic structure.

The main directions of the adjustment and optimization of China's economic structure are: (1) Adjust and optimize the industrial structure. On the basis of strengthening the secondary industry, especially the equipment manufacturing industry, vigorously develop the tertiary industry, continue to increase the proportion of the tertiary industry in the national economy, continue to reduce the proportion of the primary industry in the national economy, and at the same time, improve the structural reform of the agricultural supply side, and through deepening the reform of the agricultural production and operation system, through vigorously developing the agricultural infrastructure and through continuously improving the technical level and modernization of agricultural production, strengthen China's agriculture to lay a foundation for the sustainable development of the national economy. (2) Adjust and optimize the urban and rural economic structures. Vigorously promote the construction of new rural areas and beautiful villages, significantly increase the income level of farmers through agricultural development and agricultural modernization, and change the appearance of rural areas to achieve coordinated and balanced development between urban and rural areas. The dual pattern of modernized cities and backward villages should not exist for a long time. (3) Adjust and optimize the regional economic structure. In recent years, the development gap between the eastern, central, and western regions of China has narrowed in some aspects; the central region especially is developing faster, but the development gap between the western region and the eastern region is still large, and the three northeastern provinces have been lagging behind in recent years and there are many problems. How to accelerate the development of the western regions and northeastern provinces is the key direction of the regional economic structural adjustment. (4) Adjust and optimize the relationship between the real economy and the virtual economy (the structure of the two). It is the key to weaken the virtual economy, reduce the bubbles, and reverse the situation of "moving of capital away from the real economy to the virtual economy". Among them, reducing the debt ratio of local governments and enterprises, controlling housing prices and stabilizing the real estate market, and reducing production costs of enterprises are the three key points for adjusting and optimizing the relationship between the real economy and the virtual economy.

In the process of the adjustment and optimization of economic structure, it is necessary to further change and upgrade the economic structure. Change and upgrading should be one of the important goals of the supply-side structural reform. Without the change and upgrading of economic structure, the results of economic structural adjustment that have been achieved may be lost and cannot be consolidated.

Main focuses of economic structural change and upgrading:

1. Strengthen China's manufacturing industry, especially the high-end equipment manufacturing industry

The manufacturing industry is the mother of other industries, the skeleton of an economy, and the basis for the development of other industries. If a country's manufacturing industry is not developed and strong, it is difficult for this country's economic development to take an independent and autonomous path, and the economic strength of this country can hardly be said to be strong. The size of a country's GDP and per capita income are important, but this does not mean that this country has strong economic power and foundation, competitiveness, and sustainable development ability, such as some countries which become rich because they are rich in oil, natural gas, tourism resources, services, or other resource endowments. A "rich country" is not the same as a "strong country". China is known as the "world factory" in the manufacturing industry, and China's manufacturing industry is already at the top of the world in terms of scale, but its quality (technological content and competitiveness) is not yet in the top echelon of the world's manufacturing industry. According to the judgment of Miao Wei, the then–Minister of the Ministry of Industry and Information Technology of China, China is still in the third echelon of the four echelons of global manufacturing industry, and is not ranked among the world's manufacturing powers.[7]

In the supply-side structural reform, we should get rid of a wrong concept: China's manufacturing industry has been very developed and has excess capacity; the urgent task of China is to accelerate the development of the tertiary industry to increase improve the proportion of it in the national economy. In fact, the development of the tertiary industry and the strengthening of the manufacturing industry is not contradictory. The upgrading of the manufacturing quality will not only provide a better material and technological foundation, but also open up more and larger markets for the development of the tertiary industry. For example, the development of intelligent equipment manufacturing can not only better arm the tertiary industry, but also provide more entrepreneurial opportunities and employment opportunities for the tertiary industry.

The key to making China's manufacturing industry stronger is to improve the scientific and technological level and process level of China's manufacturing industry and improve the precision and quality of manufacturing products, and to achieve this goal, it is necessary to arm the manufacturing industry with new technologies and new processes, promote the combination of industry, academia, and research, promote the industrialization of scientific and technological achievements, promote the inflow of talents and skilled craftsmen into the manufacturing industry, and make them rooted in manufacturing industry and dedicate to the manufacturing industry, which in turn requires the coordination of system (especially the distribution system) reform and policy adjustment.

2. Improve the scientific and technological level of agriculture and industry to realize their modernization

China has started its industrialization process since the mid-1950s and has now achieved industrialization, but it cannot be said that China has completed industrialization. Industrialization is a dynamic concept and a dynamic process. With the development and progress of science and technology and with the advent of a new round of industrial revolution, the connotation of industrialization is constantly upgraded; industrialization needs to be constantly modernized and deepened. There is no end for industrialization.

China's further industrialization is not to pave the way or expand the scale of industrial production, but to improve the technological content and grade of industrialization, and the level of industrial modernization, to integrate information and communication technology and intelligent manufacturing technology into industrialization, and to vigorously implement innovation projects, talent projects, and craftsmanship projects. Industrialization also needs to "make up for weaknesses". For example, the high-end manufacturing and the precision level of industrial products are our "weakness".

Both the first and second generations of the CPC leadership put forward the goal of "four modernizations", namely, to modernize China's agriculture, industry, national defense, and science and technology by the end of the 20th century. Now, it is mainly agricultural modernization that is holding back the achievement of this goal. China's agricultural modernization level is not high, and agriculture is still "subsistence" agriculture in some places, where farmers' income is only enough for food and clothing.

China's agricultural modernization requires a three-step approach: (1) Implement and complete the decision of the CPC Central Committee and the State Council on winning the battle against poverty and achieve the target of lifting more than 70 million rural poor people out of poverty by 2020. On July 1, 2021, Chinese President Xi Jinping announced that this target had been achieved. (2)

Strengthen the construction of rural infrastructure, further promote the activities of bringing science and technology to the countryside, bringing knowledge and talents to the countryside, providing industrial support to agriculture, and supporting the development of rural areas by urban areas, promote the structural reform of the agricultural supply side, increase the policy support for the "agriculture, rural areas and farmers", so as to improve agricultural production, revitalize the rural economy, and improve the income and living standards of farmers. (3) Deepen the reform of the rural land system, agricultural production system, agricultural product price system, and rural grassroots organization system and governance structure, and implement the strategy of integrated and balanced development of urban and rural areas to make agriculture, rural areas, and farmers enter the track of sustainable development of the national economy as a whole.

3. Through reform and innovation, truly develop the real economy and reduce the false prosperity of the virtual economy

Changing the relationship between real economy and virtual economy requires numerous and complex changes and upgrades. The main focus is to increase the supply of high-quality financial assets, such as accelerating the securitization of high-quality credit assets, developing new investment channels, deepening reforms and developing capital markets, stimulating long-term investment, and curbing short-term speculation. Improve the profitability and competitiveness of enterprises in the real economy by liberalizing and revitalizing, reducing burdens and costs, and direct more talent, technology, and capital to the real economic sectors through reforms and policy adjustments. Adjust and further reform the tax sharing system, for example adjusting the tax sharing ratio between the central government and local governments; adjusting the tax structure, reforming the land transferring fees system; expanding the tax sources of local governments by adding new taxes (e.g. real estate tax); changing the situation that local governments have "more powers over affairs but less powers over finance, and serious overdraft of the powers over finance by the powers over affairs", and at the same time, delegating some local government affairs to the market or intermediaries and social organizations, so as to reduce the burden of local governments and make them gradually get rid of the land finance dependency of "raising money by selling land".

4. Seize the commanding height of the new round of scientific and technological revolution

A new round of scientific and technological revolution is coming. From historical experience, countries that have taken the lead and dominated in every major wave of technological revolution have become strong countries in science and technology, economy, and military. If China can seize the commanding height in the upcoming technological revolution, it will certainly give rise to a number of technological innovations, new industries, and new forms of business, which will drive the change, transformation, and upgrading of the economic structure. In the short run, we will be able to completely get rid of the negative impact and influence of the current round of international financial crisis and COVID-19 on China's economy, and move towards a steady rebound and prosperity; China's supply-side structural reform and the transformation of economic development mode will have a reliable material and technical foundation. In the long run, China will have a reliable material and technical guarantee to move from an economic giant to an economic power.

To take a place in the new round of scientific and technological revolution, we must first select the main direction and breakthrough, and then organize scientific research forces to focus on tackling key problems. When selecting the main direction and breakthrough, we should concentrate the wisdom of the Chinese scientific community, formulate necessary selection procedures, and consider the comparative advantages of China's scientific and technological forces and their feasibility. Second, implement the national scientific and technological research system of combining "industry, academia, research and government". For conventional scientific and technological innovation, the implementation of the system of combining "industry, academia and research" is appropriate and effective. But for major scientific and technological breakthroughs for seizing the commanding height of the new scientific and technological revolution, this system may not be strong and useful enough; it should be replaced by the system of combining industry, academia, research, and government, especially the central government. The system of combining industry, academia, research, and government is a scientific and technological research system led, organized, and implemented by the government, which is a system of concentrating human (especially scientific and technological experts), material, and financial resources on major and critical scientific and technological projects at the national level for a certain period of time, just like the research and development of "missiles, nuclear bombs, and the artificial satellite".

Notes

1 The quality of some Chinese products is not up to standard (for example, a few biochemical indicators of some Chinese-made milk powder exceed the standard); the low price of foreign products and the lack of information dissemination are also the reasons that lead some Chinese residents to buy abroad.

2 In 2010, China surpassed Japan in terms of GDP and became the world's second largest economy.

3 In these 14 years, the significant declines in investment growth in 1989–1990 and 1999–2000 were caused by social unrest and the Southeast Asian Financial Crisis, respectively, and the lower growth rate of investment than consumption since 2015 was caused by a relative excess of supply and a deteriorating international economic environment.

4 In 1958, the added value of China's secondary industry in GDP (36.%) exceeded that of the primary industry (34%) for the first time, but in 1961–1965 and 1967–1969 the proportion of the primary industry was again higher than that of the secondary industry.

5 [U.S.] Hirschman, A. O. (1991). *The Strategy of Economic Development*, translated by Pan Zhaodong and Cao Zhenghai. Beijing: Economic Science Press, 59.

6 Hsieh, C. T., & Klenow, P. J. (2009) "Misallocation and Manufacturing TFP in China and India", *Quarterly Journal of Economics*, 1403–1448.

7 Miao Wei believes that the global manufacturing industry has basically formed a four-tier echelon development pattern: the first echelon is the global science and technology innovation center led by the United States; the second echelon is the high-end manufacturing field, including the EU and Japan; the third echelon is the middle- and low-end manufacturing field, including mainly some emerging countries; the fourth echelon is mainly resource-exporting countries, including OPEC (Organization of Petroleum Exporting Countries), and other countries in Africa and Latin America. See "China's Manufacturing Is in the Third Echelon of Global Manufacturing" on www.chinanews.com, November 18, 2015.

8 Three-step strategy of supply-side reform (3)

Radical treatment

The reasons for the imbalance of economic structure are very complex, but they may be divided into four main categories: First, the adjustments in product structure, production structure, and industrial structure lag behind the changes in AD and its structure caused by changes in consumer preferences and income. Second, the changes in AD and its structure lag behind the changes in AD and its structure caused by changes in production technology. Third, the supply and its structure cannot be adjusted accordingly with the change of demand and its structure due to system defects or system rigidity. The so-called system rigidity means that the system cannot be adjusted accordingly with the changes in the quantity and structure of demand, such as the planned economic system. Fourth, structural imbalance in an economy caused by external demand shocks or supply shocks. The first three categories of reasons are within an economy and are the internal reasons of structural imbalances in the economy; the fourth category of reasons are external shocks from an economy and are external reasons. In the era of economic globalization, open economies are vulnerable to structural imbalance triggered by external shocks. In terms of internal reasons, the first two types of structural imbalances are regular phenomena in the process of economic development, because consumer preferences, income, and production technology are constantly changing. These two types of structural imbalances are also normal phenomena, because it is these two types of structural imbalances that cause structural adjustments to optimize and upgrade the economic structure and achieve a new equilibrium between supply and demand at a higher level. This new equilibrium will be broken in the process of changes in consumer preferences, income, and production technology, so as to enter the next round of structural imbalances and structural adjustment, and then optimization and upgrading. The economic structure is constantly optimized and upgraded in the process of "equilibrium—imbalance—adjustment—new equilibrium—imbalance again—adjustment— . . .", and economic development is also realized in this process of structural adjustment and upgrading. Unlike the process of economic growth, which is mainly the growth of aggregate output, the process of economic development is a process of continuous adjustment and upgrading of the economic structure and the change of economic system.

DOI: 10.4324/9781003367000-11

In a well-developed market economy, the first two types of structural imbalances can usually be adjusted through the automatic regulation of the market mechanism, but when there are major changes in production technology and consumer demand, the regulation of the market mechanism becomes incompetent; when the market mechanism cannot show its regulating effect and the structural imbalances accumulate to a certain extent, economic crises or major economic fluctuations will occur. Since the first economic crisis caused by excess production broke out in Britain in 1825, all previous economic crises have been generated in this way.

The reasons for the first two types of structural imbalances can be independent, but are often associated with the third type of reasons—system defects or system rigidity. Among the many reasons for the structural imbalances in the economy, system reasons are the fundamental and decisive factors. The imbalances in China's industrial structure, regional economic structure, and urban–rural structure at the present stage have system reasons, the reasons of development strategies determined by the current system, as well as historical reasons. For example, in recent years, China's financial and real estate industries have been highly profitable, speculative, over-leveraged, and over-bubbled, but the responsibility for this does not lie mainly with financial and real estate enterprises, because making more money and making more profits are their pursuit of goals and their natural instincts. The question is why they can make such high profits. Why is it so easy for them to make so much profits? We can see over the years, in China, a real estate developer, whether he is well educated and whether he has any expertise, as long as he can get land approvals, he will be able to make a lot of money. What's the secret of getting rich? A singer or film star may obtain an annual income of tens of millions or even hundreds of millions yuan by singing or acting in movies. Are their contributions dozens or even hundreds of times greater than those of the scientists who developed the quantum computer, Huawei's founder Ren Zhengfei, or Tu Youyou's team of scientists? This requires questioning the system. Does the system provide a fair and just competitive environment? Does the system selectively provide some resources, some opportunities to specific people or specific enterprises? Does the system create rents, create opportunities for arbitrage? Does the system leave gaps and loopholes in some areas?

The system determines how people behave, how resources are allocated, how production is organized, and how the production results are distributed, thus determining the efficiency of resource allocation, micro-efficiency and macroeconomic performance, the severity of economic structural imbalances, and the size of economic fluctuations.

The economic structural imbalances caused by system defects or system rigidities can be divided into two cases: first, the defects of the economic system itself become the reasons for economic structural imbalances; second, system defects and system rigidities hinder the automatic regulation of the market mechanism, resulting in the failure of the function of the market mechanism to regulate the structure, so that the first two types of structural imbalances will break out in the form of financial crisis or (and) economic crisis when they accumulate to a certain extent.

As early as the second half of the 19th century, Marx and Engels systematically analyzed the relationship between the capitalist system and the economic structural imbalance and even the economic crisis in a series of treatises. They argue that the inherent flaw of the capitalist system is the contradiction between capitalist private ownership and the socialization of production. One of the characteristics of the capitalist system is that "the production of surplus value is the immediate purpose and the decisive motivation of production".[1] This characteristic determines that capitalist production is featured with the fact that "production is carried out without regard to the existing boundaries of consumption, and production is limited only by capital itself".[2] "Capitalist production strives for nothing more than the extraction of as much surplus labor as possible. . . . Thus, in the very nature of capitalist production lies production regardless of the limitations of the market".[3] However, the socialization of production has resulted in the dramatic expansion of production and the accelerated growth of aggregate output, which led to the uncoordinated production and consumption, or AS and AD, in terms of quantity and structure, and eventually to an economic crisis of excess production. According to Marx,

> What constitutes the basis of modern excess production is just the unstoppable development of the productivity and the resulting mass production, which takes place under conditions in which, on the one hand, the consumption of the majority of producers is limited to the range of necessities, and, on the other hand, the profits of the capitalists become the boundary of production.[4]

Thus, in Marx's view:

> The most fundamental reason for all real crises is nothing more than the poverty of the masses and their limited consumption, and capitalist production, in spite of this situation, seeks to develop the productivity as if only the absolute consumption capacity of society is the boundary of the development of productivity.[5]

The structural imbalance of China's economy since 2012 is the result of the intertwined and mixed effects of the previously given four types of reasons, but the main reason is from systems. To dig out the root of the structural imbalance of China's economy and eradicate the foundation of excess capacity, we must start with the systems and comprehensively deepen the reform of current systems.

It should be noted that the system reasons for the structural imbalance of China's economy at this stage are fundamentally different from those for capitalist excess production. The structural imbalance of China's economy is mainly caused by system defects and system rigidities that hinder the development of the market system and the automatic regulation of the market mechanism, that is, the second case of the economic structural imbalance caused by the earlier-mentioned system reasons.

China's economic system is now in the process of transition from a highly centralized planned-economic system to a socialist market economic system. On the one hand, there are remnants of the planned-economic system and frictions between the old and new systems; on the other hand, the market economic system is still under construction and is still a "semi-market economy". Under this "semi-market economy" system, the regulation of the market mechanism is still insufficient, the regulation of the efficacy is not in place; at the same time, the market mechanism is also bound or even suppressed by the traditional systems, and cannot properly play its decisive role and regulation function in the allocation of resources. Therefore, China's current system defects and system rigidities have their own particularity or "Chinese characteristics".

Being fully aware of the defects and rigidities of the existing systems, the Communist Party of China and the Chinese government made the decision on "deepening the reform comprehensively" at the Third Plenary Session of the 18th CPC Central Committee in November 2013, to "resolutely eliminate the shortcomings of various systems and mechanisms" through comprehensively deepening reform. The goal of the reform is to "form a complete, scientific, standardized and effective system, so as to make all aspects of the system more mature and stereotyped".[6] This decision proposes that "the overall goal of comprehensively deepening reform is to improve and develop the socialist system with Chinese characteristics". Among them, in terms of the economic system reform,

> We shall deepen the reform of economic system by closely sticking to the decisive role of the market in resource allocation, to uphold and improve the fundamental economic system, accelerate the improvement of the modern market system, the macroeconomic regulation and control system and the open economic system, accelerate the transformation of the pattern of economic development, and speed up the construction of an innovation-oriented country, so as to promote the economy to develop in a more efficient, fairer and more sustainable way.[7]

Compared with the reform started in 1979, the new round of reform "focuses more on whether the reforms are systematic, holistic and collaborative" and has "reached the crucial stage and waded into the deep water zone", so it is a major reform, and a revolution in terms of economic system and supply-side structural reform.

Comprehensively deepening system reform and improving and developing China's socialist economic system are the highlight and finale of supply-side structural reform, and the fundamental way to solve China's economic structural imbalance and eliminate excess capacity.

To solve the supply-side structural problems through system reform, we need to promote system reform, system construction, and system innovation in various aspects.

I. Overall positioning of system reform

In a market economy, people's economic activities are motivated by self-interest and are spontaneous and autonomous, and the process of interpersonal transactions is complex and the results of transactions are full of uncertainties. System is a set of rules formulated or spontaneously formed by people about mutual transactions between individuals. These rules restrain and inhibit opportunistic behaviors, arbitrary behaviors, and self-serving behaviors at the expense of others in the process of individual transactions, and punish those who violate the rules, so as to make people's behaviors conform to a certain order, make the cooperation between people easy, and make the results of transactions predictable, thus promoting division of labor, transactions, innovation, and wealth growth. While systems are not a sufficient precondition for economic growth, reasonable or appropriate systems are a necessary precondition for economic growth. "The need for appropriate institutional arrangements is to provide a framework for interpersonal cooperation in markets and in organizations, and to make such cooperation more predictable and trustworthy".[8] Harold Demsetz said of the function of property rights systems, "Property rights are a social instrument whose importance lies in the fact that they help a person form reasonable expectations when dealing with others". One of the main functions of property rights is to "guide people to achieve incentives that internalize externalities to a greater extent".[9]

In the construction of China's socialist market economic system, we should first comprehensively deepen the reform of the existing "semi-market economy" system and carry out system innovation at the same time. The objectives of such system construction and system innovation are as follows:

1. Transform individual profit motives into economically and socially beneficial behaviors. The driving mechanism of economic growth is the individual's desire for self-improvement, that is, people's self-interest motives; the braking or restraining mechanism of economic growth is human reason and competition. Whether a system is efficient and can promote the increase of national wealth depends on whether the system can generate a mechanism that transforms the strong desire of individuals for self-improvement into behaviors that are beneficial to society.
2. Minimize the risks of investment and innovation activities and maximize the compensation for the risks of these activities, closely link the contributions of economic entities with their rewards, and the institutional systems shall contain arrangements for institutional mechanisms to reduce or diversify (or dissolve) individual investment and innovation risks.
3. The market (mechanism) plays a decisive role in resource allocation, and plays a leading role in regulating the relationship between AD and AS and in adjusting the economic structure. The market is a good mechanism for allocating resources, and the market mechanism also has the function of adjusting the structure.

4. Maximize the enthusiasm and creativity of individuals, enterprises, and governments. This requires a system of effective property rights arrangements, a system of contribution-based distribution, effective legal protection of contracts, full individual freedom, and a disciplined and motivated government in which individuals and governments keep their promises.
5. Form a fair and just competitive environment. A fair and just competitive environment is required for the production and operation of enterprises and for personal life and talent growth. A system that cannot create a free, fair, and just competitive environment is not a good or efficient system.

To achieve the previously given objectives, it is required to carry out a series of system reforms and constructions are needed, especially the reform and construction of a property rights (including intellectual property rights) system, legal system, price system, and distribution system, and to strengthen the construction of beliefs and morality. A society without common beliefs and moral codes is bound to be incohesive, and will be full of inevitable conflicts and frictions, and the transaction costs of economic activities are bound to be high. Under China's socialist system, a major system innovation that is faced by the construction of China's socialist market economic system and that must be solved in practice is how to effectively protect private property rights and private legal property or wealth, and how to scientifically construct the property rights system of state-owned enterprises and the public property rights system to make the state-owned or public property rights system compatible with the market economy. In the context of China's history and culture, it is a major difficulty of reform to switch the predictability and harmonizability of economic activities and interpersonal interactions from the current reliance more on trust in personal relationships and loyalty to personal authority to more loyalty to formal rules and the rule of law.

Since the reform and opening up, the profit motive of individuals has been fully released, and "putting money above everything else" is the classic expression of this profit motive in modern Chinese language. "Hustling and bustling, all for benefits" (*Records of the Grand Historian—Biographies of Extremely Wealthy Businessmen*), "Heaven destroys those who do not look out for themselves", and "Human beings die in pursuit of wealth, and birds die in pursuit of food" are the ultimate Chinese expressions of this profit motive. "Putting money above everything else" is now not only the belief of many people, but also the action guide for many people to engage in activities. Getting money and getting rich through one's own labor, struggle, and contribution is unquestionable, legitimate, and should be encouraged. The problem with China's current system is that people's self-interest motivation has been stimulated, but the braking mechanism or restraint mechanism for self-interest motivation has not been established accordingly, and the braking mechanism or restraining mechanism is still weak or even ineffective in some cases. We have not yet developed a mechanism that may transform the strong desire of individuals for self-improvement into behaviors that are beneficial to society or internalize the externalities in the profit-seeking process. As a result, we see many uncivilized, immoral, and even illegal and criminal phenomena:

benefiting oneself at the expense of others, cheating, making and selling fake products, secretly discharging pollution, corruption, bribery, using power for personal gain, turning public property into private property, embezzling state-owned assets, and so on.

The formation of mechanisms to restrain individual self-interest motives relies mainly on market competition, the construction of the legal system, belief and morality, and the improvement of people's literacy and civilization. At present, the reform and construction of these systems in China are still in progress. Compared with the rate of economic growth, the reform and construction of these systems are lagging behind.

Through such system reform, construction, and innovation, establish an effective set of incentive-restraint mechanisms for economic activities, resource allocation mechanisms, mechanisms of selecting the superior and eliminating the inferior and mechanisms for economic structural adjustment, so that wealth growth and economic development may be realized on the basis of the role of these mechanisms. By comprehensively deepening reform,

> speed up the development of the socialist market economy, democratic politics, advanced culture, harmonious society and ecological civilization, release all the gushing vitality of the labor, knowledge, technology, management and capital, give full play to all sources of social wealth, and make more development benefit shared by all the people in a fairer way.[10]

II. Advancing system reform around four aspects

The supply-side structural reform should be a comprehensive and deepening reform of the existing system, of which the key is to solidly promote system reform and innovation around the following four aspects.

1. Reforming and reconstructing the relationship between government and market

For quite a long time after the founding of the People's Republic of China, China has been implementing a highly centralized planned economic system, under which resource allocation, economic operation, and economic development are dominated or even controlled by the government, and the market mechanism is basically ineffective in the process of resource allocation and economic operation. The long-term implementation of the highly centralized planned economic system resulted in the chronic shortage of supply, inefficient resource allocation, and frequent structural imbalances in the economy. The reason for the failure of this highly centralized planned economic system was that under such a system, the resource allocation could be performed "as planned"—because there was a large national top-down government planning department responsible for formulating detailed development plans, production plans, employment plans, material allocation plans, and product distribution plans, but it was difficult to do so "proportionally" because the quantity and proportion of AS (what and how much to produce) were determined by the quantity and structure of demand from consumers and producers, and ultimately by the quantity and structure of consumer demand, and it was impossible for the government planning department to get such demand information. The supply proportion and production scale determined by the planning department were usually based on past experience, limited information, and the will of the plan makers, thus often resulting in a quantitative and structural imbalance between supply and demand. Thus, we can see that under the planned economic system, supply shortage was the normal state of economic life when the level of productivity development was low; while when the productivity development reached a certain level, the coexistence of supply shortage and supply surplus has become the normal state of economic life.

Since 1953, China has experienced seven rounds of serious economic structural imbalances and has correspondingly carried out seven nationwide large-scale economic structural adjustments: 1956, 1961–1965, 1979–1984, 1988–1991, 1998–2001, 2008–2010, and 2015 to the present.[11] The nature of these seven rounds of economic structural imbalance was different: the first round was mainly manifested in the proportion of agriculture to light industry and heavy industry, the proportion of defense industry to civilian industry, the proportion of coastal development to interior development, and the imbalance of the urban–rural proportion. The second round was the structural imbalance under the acute shortage of supply, which was mainly manifested in that AS was less than AD, and the supply of consumer goods (especially food) was in serious shortage. The third and fourth rounds were structural imbalances with the coexistence of shortage and surplus. On the one hand, some commodities and factors of production were undersupplied, leading to price increase, and on the other hand, some other commodities and factors of production were oversupplied, coupled with overheated investment and the price signal confusion caused by the coexistence of planned prices and market prices, leading to resource misallocation. The fifth and sixth rounds of structural imbalances were manifested in the relative excess of AS and disproportionate relationship between some key industries caused by external shocks and insufficient domestic demand. The seventh round was mainly manifested in excess production and excess capacity, and the main reason for excess was supply-side structural imbalance. These seven nationwide economic structural adjustments were initiated and led by the government and were carried out from top to bottom.

Since 1979, China has carried out eight rounds of macroeconomic control: 1979–1981, 1985–1987, 1989–1992, 1993–1997, 1998–2002, 2004–2007, 2008–2012, and 2015 to the present.[12]

These seven economic structural adjustments and eight rounds of macroeconomic control have achieved varying degrees of results, but each structural adjustment and each round of macroeconomic control were obliged to be carried out when the economic structural imbalance reached to a very serious extent that the economy could not operate normally, and enterprises and consumers complained a lot. Structural adjustment and macroeconomic control were seriously lagging behind, and the policy lag was too long.[13] Due to the lag of adjustment, each round of adjustment is costly both in time and money, and has many after-effects. From historical experience, China's previous structural adjustments have either gone too far or not in place. The main reason is that the government fails to obtain the complete information about the nature, causes, and extent of economic structural imbalances, and fails to grasp the dynamic changes in the economic structure. The "visible hand" of the government can not do a good job in resource allocation and economic structural adjustment. The fact is that after many rounds of structural adjustment and macroeconomic control, structural imbalances in China's economy still appear periodically and habitually, and the time spent on structural imbalance and adjustment has a tendency to gradually lengthen.[14]

The development practice of China's economy for more than 70 years and the practice of macroeconomic control have proved that there is no way to eliminate the cyclical imbalance of the economic structure from the root without reforming the planned economic system, removing the beliefs of the planned economy, and handling the relationship between the government and the market in a scientific and reasonable manner.

As we said in Chapter 4, the market mechanism has the function of automatic removal and self-rehabilitation. The so-called automatic removal is to remove excess capacity and remove backward products, technologies and enterprises. The so-called self-rehabilitation refers to the imbalanced proportional relationships in the economy being able to gradually become reasonable after a period of automatic adjustment of the market mechanism; and the declined or recessed economic growth may automatically rebound and recover after a period of self-rehabilitation. This function of automatic removal and self-rehabilitation is mainly realized through the competitive mechanism of selecting the superior and eliminating the inferior and the incentive mechanism of the economic parties to pursue the maximization of their own interests. This function of market mechanism is not only the function of spontaneous adjustment and automatic optimization of economic structure, but also the function of self-stabilization of economic fluctuations. We should look at this function from both sides. On the one hand, every economic crisis or recession will bring about the destruction of productivity, that is, the destruction of production capacity and part of the wealth, but at the same time it also has a good side: it may clear the excess production capacity and eliminate low-quality products and backward enterprises, and thus provide an opportunity for the optimization and upgrading of economic structure. Therefore, if we say that the economic crisis destroys productivity, it mainly destroys backward productivity; if we say that it destroys production capacity, it mainly destroys backward production capacity. Of course, the automatic removal and self-rehabilitation function of the market mechanism has its own limitations, which is that it cannot guarantee regular full employment, fair and just distribution of income and wealth, automatically correct major disproportionate relationships and large economic structural imbalances, and automatically maintain coordinated and sustainable economic, environmental, and social development. We don't want to have a big world-wide crisis like the one in the 1930s, a typical outcome of major disproportionate relationships and big economic structural imbalance, which, once they happen, often destroy the backward production capacity together with the advanced production capacity at that time. We should try to avoid any major economic crisis. However, it is difficult for us to avoid general economic fluctuations. In fact, there is no need to avoid them, because economic fluctuations themselves have the function of automatic removal and spontaneous adjustment. At the same time, the process of economic fluctuations is also a process of squeezing out the economic bubble, a process of metabolism of micro cells in the economic system, a process of reshuffling of all kinds of markets and a process of adjustment of economic relations and economic structure. Through this automatic removal of the market mechanism, spontaneous adjustment and squeezing of bubbles, the economic structure can be continuously adjusted, optimized, and upgraded.

This automatic removal and spontaneous adjustment function of the market is the self-protection and self-healing function of the economy, which is the same as a person coughing and sneezing with a cold and fever; coughing and sneezing are the self-protection reactions of the human body, while fever is the process of the human body clearing the viruses and infections. The government's improper intervention in economic fluctuations can cause sequelae and even poisoning to the economy, just as a person takes good medicine as soon as he gets a cold. Keynesian economics is essentially a kind of economics and policy system to deal with economic depressions and economic fluctuations. For most of the second half of the 20th century, western market economy countries used Keynesian prescriptions to manage economic fluctuations. As a result, although the great depression, as in the 1930s, did not reappear again, the economic cycle was deformed: economic fluctuations no longer occurred regularly and periodically, but irregularly; the four stages of boom, recession, depression, and recovery that the economic cycle originally presented have become blurred, and the recession and depression stages were greatly shortened; the intervals between economic fluctuations were lengthened.[15]

In China's economic discourse system, we use neutral or pleasant words such as "economic structural imbalance", "chaos of economic order", "economic overheating", "market weakness", "excess capacity", "economic downturn", etc. to refer to economic fluctuations and recessions in China, and generally do not use the term "economic crisis". Whenever there is an economic overheating or economic downturn in the China, the government will use policy and administrative measures to intervene. Most of the time, these interventions have suppressed inflation or prevented further recessions, but they have also inhibited the economy's automatic removal and self-adjustment functions, making the market mechanism unable to give full play to its role of selecting the superior and eliminating the inferior, thus leading to long-term distortions in some economic relationships and long-term imbalances of the economic structure.

In order to re-understand and correctly position the relationship between the government and the market under the new normal of economy, we must re-understand the nature and role of economic fluctuations (or economic cycle) and the function of market mechanism.

From the founding of the People's Republic of China to the mid-1990s, the prevailing view in China's economic circles was that market mechanisms and market regulation were spontaneous, blind, and anarchic, and that the market lagged in adjusting structural imbalances in the economy. Obviously, we need to re-examine and re-understand this view today.

The function of the market mechanism is based on the individuals' pursuit of the maximization of their own interests and on the basis of their spontaneous and free activities, and thus in this sense, the regulating role of the market mechanism is spontaneous and anarchic. However, this spontaneous mechanism is an automatic mechanism of resource allocation, which is a good mechanism and an advanced mechanism compared with the manual mechanism or human intervention (e.g. government control). The regulation of this automatic mechanism is not blind; it has a purpose, which is to direct the resource allocation to the Pareto optimum; the market regulation seems to be disorderly or anarchic, but in fact it is orderly. Through competition, and through institutional and ethical constraints, the spontaneous activities of disorderly individuals are transformed into an orderly economic order, which is illustrated by Adam Smith's principle of the "invisible hand". Compared with the government's adjustment of economic structural imbalance, the structural adjustment of market mechanism is also automatic, and the selecting of superior and eliminating of inferior in market competition are carried out at anytime and anywhere, which is much faster and more timely than the government's structural adjustment.

Of course, we cannot say that the market mechanism functions perfectly. Microeconomics has analyzed the various causes of market failure, Keynes and his followers have revealed the causes of non-full employment and economic fluctuations, and some economists have argued that the market mechanism fails in coordinating the decentralized individual actions to achieve a more desirable macroeconomic equilibrium (e.g., full employment), i.e., there are coordination failures[16] in the market mechanism. Perhaps the greatest shortcoming of the market mechanism is its inability to address the issue of fair and equitable distribution of income and wealth and to ensure the realization of normalized full employment.

Understanding is the forerunner of action. Without right understanding, it is difficult to have the right action. If our understanding of the function and role of the market mechanism still stays on the traditional concept that the market is "spontaneous, blind, and anarchic", it is impossible for us to really let the market play a decisive role in the allocation of resources in practice. If we believe that the government is smarter and better than the market, we cannot sincerely rely on the market mechanism to allocate resources. On the other hand, if we cannot see the defects and failures of the market mechanism, we will slip into the illusory world of liberalism and neoliberalism, because the economic world in the liberal and neoliberal systems is still stuck in the perfectly competitive world of the 18th–19th centuries, which is far away from us. Of course, if we don't realize that government can also fail, we cannot correctly delineate the boundary between market and government, and cannot correctly deal with the relationship between market and government.

Since the second half of the 20th century, the real-world market economy has not operated purely on the principle of the "invisible hand", and governments have assumed certain responsibilities in the operation and development of the economy. The real version of the market economic system is actually a mixed economic system combining market regulation and government intervention. Today, the ability of a market economy country to solve the major relationship between efficiency and fairness and how effective it is depend to a large extent on how it handles the relationship between market and government.

On the issue of the relationship between market and government, the key is not whether the government should intervene, but how the government intervenes, how the government makes scientific decisions in economic activities, and how to act effectively and fairly.

As we said earlier, China's market economy is fundamentally different from that of western countries; that is, what China is building is a socialist market economy with Chinese characteristics, and it is an innovation of the market economic system by the Chinese Communists. Since such market economy is "socialist", it cannot be separated from public ownership, state-owned enterprises, fair distribution, common wealth, and government plan (or planning) regulation; since it is a market economy, it must play the decisive role of market mechanism in resource allocation, and the market mechanism must play its function of automatic regulation, automatic removal, and spontaneous adjustment. Therefore, the nature of the socialist market economic system determines that the relationship between the market and the government in China's market economy is different from the "big market, small government" relationship described in western economics, and that the relationship between market and government is not antagonistic. Both the market and the government should have their own position, role, and space to play their role. In China's socialist market economy, the status and role of the government are mainly derived from: (1) The nature of the socialist market economy. (2) The market mechanism is not fully developed and perfect at this stage; the market mechanism is still relatively weak and the regulation is still difficult to be in place. (3) Market mechanism failure. In other words, the necessity and inevitability of government intervention in China's market economy are not entirely due to market failure, which is not exactly the same as the reasons why government intervention is needed in western market economies.

The Decision of the Central Committee of the Communist Party of China on Several Major Issues concerning Comprehensively Deepening Reforms provides a good explanation of the principles on how to reform and adjust the relationship between market and government in China's economy:

> The reform of the economic system is the focus of comprehensively deepening reforms. The core is to correctly handle the relationship between government and market so as to help the market play a decisive role in the allocation of resources and help the government better play its role. The market determining the allocation of resources is the general law of market economy. Therefore, to perfect the system of socialist market economy, we must follow

> this law and put forth efforts to solve the imperfection of the market system and the excessive intervention and the lack of regulation by the government.[17]

The Decision also makes a good positioning for the functions of the market and the government in the socialist market economy:

> We must actively and prudently advance market-oriented reform in breadth and depth, greatly reduce the government's direct allocation of resources, and promote the allocation of resources on the basis of market rules, market prices, market competition to achieve maximum benefit and efficiency optimization. The government's role and responsibilities mainly include maintaining the stability of macro-economy, strengthening and optimizing the public services, safeguarding fair competition, reinforcing market regulation, maintaining the market order, promoting sustainable development, advancing the common prosperity and making up for market failure.[18]

The key is how to turn the content of the Decision into reality and implement it in the supply-side structural reform.

Based on the development economists' summaries of the experiences of dozens of countries that have developed over the past few decades, P.A. Samuelson summarized the role of government in the development of a market economy as follows:

> The role of government is critical to establishing and maintaining a healthy economic environment. Governments must respect the rule of law, emphasize the validity of contracts, combat corruption, and make their policies conducive to competition and innovation. Government investment in conventional social capital, such as education, health care, communications, energy, and transportation, can play an important role, but it must rely on the private sector in those industries in which the government has no comparative advantage. The government should resist the temptation to keep all production at home, and firmly promote the opening of foreign trade and foreign investment, all of which will help all sectors of the national economy quickly keep pace with the international advanced level.[19]

Milton Friedman argues that

> the government should maintain law and order, define property rights, act as an instrument by which we change property rights and other rules of the game, adjudicate when disputes arise over the interpretation of rules, enforce contracts, promote competition, provide a monetary framework, engage in activities to eliminate technological monopolies, overcome various neighborhood effects (a type of external effect—quoter) that are recognized as important enough to warrant government intervention, and assist private charities and ordinary families in the protection of the incapacitated (mental patient or children).[20]

Samuelson and Friedman, the leader of neoconservatism and the leader of neoliberalism respectively in western economics since the second half of the 20th century, respectively, have sharply opposed each other on the question of whether to intervene in the economy, but their positions on the role of government in the market economy are virtually the same.

The market economic system can better solve the problem of resource allocation efficiency, but it cannot automatically solve the problems of full employment and fair and just distribution. The spontaneous operation of market economy and free competition may lead to underemployment, resulting in an increasing concentration of income and wealth in the hands of a few people, and thus leading to a polarization between rich and poor. Both Marx and Keynes recognized this consequence. The goal of China's socialist market economy is to achieve common prosperity and to realize the "Chinese Dream". China's market economy should be more fair and just than the capitalist market economy, so the government also undertakes the responsibility of creating a fair and just institutional environment, a fair and just market order, and a fair and just distribution system in the process of reform and development, as well as safeguarding fairness and justice.

To properly handle the relationship between market and government, it is certainly necessary to redefine the boundary between the market and the government in the process of comprehensively deepening reform, to reposition the functions, status, and roles of the market and the government, to adapt the roles of the market and the government to the requirements of the new normal of China's economic development, and more importantly, to reduce the government's control over the allocation of resources, to institutionalize or regularize government decision-making and policy-making, to reduce the randomness in the process of government decision-making and in the process of policy implementation, to reduce the personal discretion of officials in decision making and policy formulation, to reduce the capricious behavior of officials in accordance with their own preferences or pursuit of interests, and to reduce the occurrence of major officials replacing policies or even laws and regulations with their speeches, instructions, and proposals. From the historical experience since the founding of the People's Republic of China, the words and actions of government officials, especially those with decision-making power, overriding the democratic centralized decision-making system and above the law, are often one of the main reasons for resource misallocation and economic disasters.

An important element in handling the relationship between government and market under the new normal is that the local government gradually fades out of the leading role in economic development.

Since the Third Plenary Session of the 11th CPC Central Committee shifted the focus of Party-wide work to socialist modernization, China's economic development has been jointly led by two main bodies or dual leading roles—local governments (mainly the city-level and county-level governments) and enterprises. This is part of the characteristics of China's economic system and economic development model. Professor Shi Z. F. summarized this characteristic as a "three-dimensional market system", meaning that China's market economic system consists of three bodies: the central government, local governments, and enterprises. He called the market system of developed countries, which consists of government and enterprises, as the conventional market system. According to Professor Shi, in the process of China's economic development, "The local government, as a competitive economic entity system, is almost as important as the system of competitive enterprises". This market economic system with Chinese characteristics has generated extraordinary investment power, which has enabled the China's economy to achieve an extraordinary growth rate and will continue to maintain this extraordinary growth until 2049.[21]

It is undeniable that local governments have contributed to the high growth of China's economy at an average annual rate of nearly 10% over the 30 years from the reform and opening up to 2010. Local governments have boosted to or even directly promoted economic growth and development in terms of infrastructure construction, project investment, enterprise establishment, investment attraction, internal guidance and external connections, credit support and guarantee, and creation of market environment and market conditions (e.g., providing preferential policies).

However, we should recognize that the local governments' leading role in economic development is an inevitable requirement and result of China's transition from a highly centralized planned economic system to a socialist market economic system, and is a historical transition phenomenon. Before the reform and opening up, there were no enterprises in the sense of economics in China, and the government was the only economic entity, and enterprises were only the subsidiary production units of the government; for quite a long time after the reform and opening up, enterprises, as the main entities of market competition and the main players in economic development, were still in the process of cultivation and development, and needed the supports and conditions provided by governments, and the governments were also habitually acting as an economic entities. However, after the initial establishment of the socialist market economic system, local governments should, in the process of improving the socialist market economic system, gradually fade out of the leading role of economic development and reduce the direct allocation of resources. Economic development should be the one-man show of enterprises, not the two-man show of enterprises and governments.

From the theory and practice of market economy, there is a clear division of labor between governments and enterprises in a market economy, and there is a boundary between the scope of their activities, although this boundary is dynamically changing and constantly adjusted. Simply put, in a mature market economy, enterprises mainly produce private goods, and the government is responsible for providing system environment or system supply, legal protection, public goods, and social services; the government does not need to and should not produce private goods. However, at present, local governments in China still take up a considerable number of tasks of producing private goods. For example, local governments are responsible for determining what kind of projects are to be launched, what kind of enterprises are to be set up, the locations of plants, the output of a certain product, the growth rate of regional GDP . . . and so on. This means that the local government has squeezed out the market activity space of some enterprises and robbed them of their "rice bowls". This is what scholars often call government "overstepping". It is not hard to understand that the more resources local governments allocate directly mean the less resources enterprises and the market can allocate. The local governments' greater role in economic development and more powerful position in the operation of the market mean the more limited and squeezed role of enterprises and market mechanisms.[22] However, if the local government occupies the leading position and plays a strong role in the economic operation, it is unlikely to cultivate a developed market economic system and to form an internationally competitive group of entrepreneurs and enterprises.

Some of the contradictions, drawbacks, malpractices, and even crimes that have emerged in China's economic and social development are directly or indirectly related to the "overstepping" and powerful position of local governments, such as the repeated construction and blind investment caused by the competition between local governments, "matchmaking", or even taking the place of others in the introduction of foreign investment, illegal land acquisition, disorderly demolition, quick work regardless of the cost, promotion of projects and production regardless of the environmental and ecological cost, uncontrolled financing scale and debt scale of local governments, data fraud, bribery . . . and so on. The main reasons for the generation of corrupt and greedy government officials and for the occurrence of series of corruption cases are that our current system provides them with too many resources and give them too much power, so they can rely on these resources and power to set up, create and seek rent, and to conduct power-for-money deals; the local government, as the leading role of economic development, provides space and stage for the corruption of such officials. The expansion of local governments and civil service is closely linked to the excessive resources and power controlled by local governments, and to the fact that local governments themselves are the leading roles of economic development.

All major economic overheating and inflation in China after the reform and opening up have been inextricably linked to the extraordinary investment power of local governments. An important reason for these non-efficient, unconventional market behaviors of local governments is that local governments do not need to be cost-constrained or budget-constrained in any economic activity as enterprises are, and local governments (leaders) do not need to bear the risk of investment failures and operating losses. Although local governments in China are subject to budget constraints, they can solve the debts by generating extra-budgetary income, selling land to increase revenue, raising funds through urban investment and construction companies or even capital raising, and applying for "bailouts" from the central government, increasing transfer payments or even "write-off". More importantly, local governments have the motivation to maximize GDP (and tax revenue) and its growth rate, but not the motivation to maximize profits or minimize costs, so they do not need to conduct cost–benefit comparisons or pursue cost minimization or benefit maximization when engaging in economic activities. To eliminate these disorders, it is necessary to deepen reforms to gradually withdraw local governments from the leading role in economic development, and make local governments play a role compatible with China's socialist market economic system. As clearly pointed out in the Decision of the Central Committee of the Communist Party of China on Several Major Issues concerning Comprehensively Deepening Reforms:

> The government's role and responsibilities mainly include maintaining the stability of macro-economy, strengthening and optimizing the public services, safeguarding fair competition, reinforcing market regulation, maintaining the market order, promoting sustainable development, advancing the common prosperity and making up for market failure.[23]

This definition applies to both the central government and local governments. If economic development is a kind of ball game, then its athletes can only be enterprises, the government can neither be an athlete, nor a referee, but only a servant—picking up the balls, pouring tea, handing towels and cleaning the ground for athletes, that is, to providing services and security for enterprises and residents. This is just the concept of "streamlining administration, delegating powers, strengthening regulation and improving services" proposed by the State Council.

From the development experience and practice since the reform and opening up, the places where economy has developed faster and better in China are the places where the government plays a better role in supporting and serving enterprises, rather than the places where the local government plays the leading role. For example, Wenzhou and Taizhou in Zhejiang Province, Suzhou, Wuxi, and Changzhou in Jiangsu Province, and Shenzhen, Foshan, and Dongguan in Guangdong Province have realized rapid development with individuals and enterprises taking the lead with government support and services. On the contrary, many places where local governments play a leading role in economic development or where local governments are strong have not only failed to achieve rapid economic development, but have faced numerous economic and social problems, and many such cases can be found in central and western China.

Of course, it will take a longer process for local governments to fade away from the leading role in the economic development, and it cannot be completed in a short period of time. This involves not only the issue of path dependence, but also the issue of the changing role of local governments and enterprises in the process of establishing and improving the socialist market economic system. However, it is the direction of the reform and improvement of China's socialist market economic system for local governments to change from being the leading role in economic development to being the servant and guarantor of economic development. In my opinion, the day when local governments really fade out from the leading role in economic development is the day when China's socialist market economic system is completed. The conversion of local governments from athletes to servants in the economic development should be one of the important symbols of the completion of China's socialist market economic system.

As mentioned earlier, in China's socialist market economic system, the government is not just a "night watchman", but also plays its own role and influence in the resource allocation and economic operation, which is one of the characteristics of China's socialist market economy that differ from the western capitalist market economy. However, the key question here is how to "better play the role of the government" in the process of playing the decisive role of the market in resource allocation. This is a major issue that must be answered in theory and solved in practice.

In my opinion, in order to play the role of the government, the following reforms may be needed: (1) Establish relevant systems for economic decision-making and government resource allocation, rely on the system for project approval, land development, credit extension, economic policy formulation and adjustment, setting or adjustment of non-market-determined product and service prices, and eliminate the approval by one person. (2) For the approval of major projects, prior feasibility assessment and demonstration shall be conducted by a third party or an independent organization (such as an expert committee, an investment advisory and evaluation agency, or a national think tank) which shall have no interest in the project applicant (bidder) and employer, and which shall be determined not by the project approving party, but through competitive bidding. (3) The project leader responsibility system shall be implemented for major projects. After the implementation of the project, mid-term inspection and evaluation and later inspection and acceptance shall be carried out, and the financial and administrative responsibilities of the project leader should be pursued if the project is unqualified. The approver shall be responsible for the major projects approved by him. (4) Accountability system shall be implemented for the approval of major projects: the approver who violates the project approval system or rules or procedures shall be held accountable, and the approvers and implementers shall be held accountable for the failure of major investment or significant project losses caused by non-irresistible reasons. (5) For the setting or adjustment of the non-market-determined product and service prices, it is required to hold hearings based on extensive consultation and full search for demand information; representatives attending the hearings must be randomly selected from the supply and demand sides of these products and services, and cannot be designated or assigned by the department holding the hearings.

In short, what China wants to establish is a socialist market economic system, and in this market economic system, the functions and roles of the government will be different from those of the governments in western market economies. How to fix the boundary between market and government in China's socialist market economy, how to define the functions and roles of market and government, and how to better play the role of government in the process of playing the decisive role of market allocation of resources will be an important system innovation facing the supply-side structural reform.

2. Reforming and improving the distribution system

The reform of the distribution system mentioned here includes the reform of the income distribution system and the reform of the wealth (property) possession system. At present, China has both the problem of excessive gap in income distribution and the problem of unfair possession of wealth. Since the reform and opening up, especially the implementation of "maintaining close oversight on the large state-owned enterprises and subjecting smaller ones to market competition" in the state-owned economy and the restructuring and reorganization of state-owned enterprises, as well as since the implementation of the marketization of real estate market and the development of real estate at the end of the 20th century, social wealth has been rapidly concentrated to some people, and some people have accumulated quite astonishing wealth. According to the *2014 China Wealth Report: Outlook and Strategies*, released on February 22, 2014 by the China Household Finance Survey Center of Southwestern University of Finance and Economics, the assets owned by the top 10% of Chinese households accounted for 63.9% of the total assets of Chinese households in 2013. According to the data provided in this Report, the Gini coefficient of national household assets in 2013 was 0.717, and although this figure is lower than in 2011, it is still higher than the Gini coefficient of Chinese household income distribution,[24] which indicates that the inequality of wealth possession in China is much higher than that of income distribution. Notably, this Report found that in terms of reasons for getting rich, only 56.1% of the wealthy households in the top 1% of assets became wealthy through entrepreneurship; only 37% of the top 5% of wealthy households became wealthy through entrepreneurship, while nationally only 14.1% of households became wealthy through entrepreneurship.

The unreasonable distribution of income and wealth is not only an important reason for the lack of domestic demand in China, especially the lack of consumer demand, but also an important factor for the intensification of social conflicts, so it is one of the important elements of comprehensively deepening reform.

What is the relationship between income and wealth distribution and supply-side structural reform? The answer is: they are related to whether AD and AS can match and balance each other quantitatively and structurally.

From the microeconomics perspective, the production of one product will bring certain income to its producer and thus create demand for another product. For example, a person is a producer in the clothing market and a demander in the food market, and when he uses the income obtained from the production of clothes to buy food, the production of clothes creates demand for the production of food; in turn, the production of food also creates demand for the production of clothes. However, from the perspective of macroeconomics, the extent to which AS or production can create its own AD depends on the capacity to pay; the capacity to pay of an economic society depends on the distribution system of that society and, ultimately, on the ownership of the means of production or property rights system of that society. By introducing the system factors, we find that both AS and AD are influenced or conditioned by such factors. The system acts on both supply and demand; this action may be unbalanced and asymmetric for both supply side and demand side. The strength of the action of systems on both supply side and demand side depends on the nature and structure of the systems. Some systems promote supply but constrain demand; for example, the capitalist system in its ascendancy created more productivity in the 100 years since its establishment than the sum of the productivity previously created by mankind, but the AD did not grow in tandem. Marx pointed out that the basic contradiction of the capitalist system will inevitably lead to the contradiction between the tendency of production to expand indefinitely and the relative shrinkage of demand for which working people have the ability to pay. Some systems are conducive to releasing demand but constrain the growth of supply capacity; for example, there is a general underproduction or shortage of supply under a planned economic system. From the perspective of system or production relations, the reason why the growth of effective demand lags behind the growth of supply capacity is that the distribution system under a certain economic system is flawed. For example, income and wealth are unfairly distributed, the rich have money but are unwilling to consume more—because their consumption is near or at the physical and psychological needs, while the poor desire to consume more but cannot afford to consume—because they have limited income and wealth, which results in a disconnection between the consumption needs (from the poor) and the ability to pay (possessed by the rich), preventing a portion of consumption needs from being converted into effective demand. Thus, if the aggregate output produced by an economy with the available technology and resources cannot be fully converted into effective demand through an appropriate distribution system, it will lead to inconsistent and out-of-sync growth in supply capacity and demand capacity, and thus to widespread excess production. The error of Say's Law is not in the assertion that "supply will create its own demand", but in the fact that it abstracts away the influence of the system on supply and demand, and discusses the relationship between AS and AD in a general sense.

Since the late 1990s, China's economic development has been plagued by the lack of domestic demand. If we reduce the degree of inequality in income distribution and wealth possession through the reform of the distribution system to make the distribution fairer and more reasonable, it will significantly increase the average propensity to consume of residents and thus expand their consumption demand. Take the data of 2015 as an example: the urban residents' per capita disposable income was RMB 31,194.84, the per capita consumption expenditure was RMB 21,392.36, and the average propensity to consume was 0.69; the rural residents' per capita disposable income was RMB 11,421.71, the per capita consumption expenditure was RMB 9,222.59, and the average propensity to consume was 0.81. The propensity to consume of rural residents was 0.12 higher than that of urban residents; if the per capita disposable income of rural residents is raised to 80% of that of urban residents, i.e., to RMB 24,955.87, the per capita consumption expenditure of rural residents will increase to RMB 18,716.90 (= 24,955.87 × 0.75, assuming that the average propensity to consume decreases to 0.75 after the increase in rural residents' income), the per capita consumption of rural residents will increase by a net RMB 9,494.31 (=18,716.90–9,222.59); based on China's rural population of 603.46 million in 2015, the consumption demand of rural residents will increase by a net RMB 5,729.436 billion, which will bring the expenditure-based GDP to RMB 7,564.376 billion in 2015, an increase of 8.20% over the actual expenditure-based GDP achieved in 2015 (RMB 69,910.94 billion)!

The reform of China's distribution system includes the reform of the current income distribution system and the wealth possession system. At present, the reform of wealth possession system seems not to be paid enough attention in theory, and little has been done in practice. For example, the issue of whether to levy an inheritance tax has been discussed and debated in Chinese academic circles for years, and there is still a wide divergence of views. The legal document for levying a property tax (which is actually a tax on high wealth holders) is still in the process of drafting, and there are still many controversies about whether and how to levy a property tax.

In the opinions of most Chinese residents, the biggest unfair distribution in China is the unfair possession of wealth. The so-called unfair possession of wealth refers to the use of power, status, relations and even illegal means, such as embezzlement of state-owned assets, bribery, power-for-money deals, etc., and the use of seemingly legal but illegal capital operations to possess part of the social wealth. Some people have an amazing scale of wealth, and their wealth growth is often beyond the reach of even very successful entrepreneurs.

This unfair possession of wealth is linked to the inadequacy of the legal system, lax implementation of the rule of law, unregulated competition, and corruption of a few government officials in China's current economy, and is the result of system defects. These system defects are also the root causes of excess production and excess capacity. As Samuelson pointed out:

> If an economy is full of vicious competition, serious pollution, or government corruption, it will of course only produce less than what that economy could have produced if "there were no such problems" or it will produce a whole lot more of the wrong goods. All of these will leave consumers worse off than they would have been. These problems are a consequence of the failure to allocate resources efficiently.[25]

The basic elements of reforming and improving China's distribution system are to effectively implement the principles of distribution based on labor and contribution in the field of primary income distribution, while taking care of the weak and some special groups in need of help in the process of redistribution, so as to improve the social security system. Improve the taxation system, the property rights system, and the system to punish corruption, so as to eliminate the systemic root causes of illegal acquisition of income and possession of wealth through power and power-for-money deals. Make people get fair development opportunities through reforms, reduce the unfairness in people's starting point through measures such as developing education, health care, and urbanization, and thus narrow the gap in income distribution and wealth possession to a socially tolerable and acceptable range.

3. Building and improving incentive mechanism and innovation mechanism

It is a consensus among modern economists that technological progress is the main contributor to modern economic growth. Technological progress comes from innovation. If the growth of labor and capital inputs is the traditional power source of economic growth or supply growth, then innovation is the new power and new source of economic growth or supply growth. Technological inventions and innovations are by nature random and difficult to control, but they are closely linked to individual initiative, adventurous spirit, and knowledge accumulation that are shaped by incentive–constraint mechanisms. Although enthusiasm and some kind of call can also stimulate individual initiative and adventurous spirit, effective incentive–constraint mechanisms are needed to maintain individual initiative, adventurous spirit, and knowledge accumulation in a stable and continuous way.

A certain incentive–constraint mechanism is embedded in a certain system or rules. Proper system arrangements can make individual efforts and contributions commensurate with their rewards, reduce the transaction costs of productive and innovative activities, improve the predictability of activity results, and impose penalties on the violations of rules. Therefore, a good system is one that can promote invention and innovation.

Fairness in access to education, employment opportunities, and development, and fairness in distribution are related to the effective mobilization of individual initiative and creativity, and the degree of fairness in these areas is determined by the nature of the system or the soundness of the system.

Entrepreneurs are also individuals in the market economy, but they are individuals with special abilities, that is, they have entrepreneurial talent or entrepreneurship. To provide new impetus for supply growth and to promote effective supply increase and optimize economic structure, we must vigorously cultivate entrepreneurship.

One of the main elements and goals of China's supply-side structural reform is to mobilize individual initiative, foster entrepreneurship, and promote technological innovation and enhance economic vitality through the construction of systems to provide new impetus for supply growth.

The property rights protection system based on clear property rights, the patent system, the legal arbitration system, the reasonable tax system and tax rate, the fair and just distribution system, the scientific education and training system, the scientific talent selection system, the independent spirit and personality, and the free and open social atmosphere are all effective ways and necessary environments for fostering invention, innovation, mobilizing individual initiative, and cultivating entrepreneurship.

4. Reforming and improving the land system

Land is one of the four factors of production and is the carrier of all human economic activities. According to the current law, land in China is "state-owned" and "collectively owned" (rural land), and it is the local government that exercises "state-owned" and "collectively owned" land rights, and therefore land in China is actually owned by the government. An important basis or means for the local government to achieve its political and economic goals is its control over land, an important resource. Local governments can increase their fiscal revenues by selling land directly (the so-called "land finance"), or attract investment by providing cheap or even free land to enterprises, thereby increasing regional GDP and local tax revenues.

The reform of the land system during the period of Liberation War made hundreds of millions of toiling masses follow the Communist Party with determination, mobilized millions of farmers to support the front, go to the front and fight alongside the PLA, and inspired them to send their children to join the army and the war. The first land reform before and after the founding of the People's Republic of China greatly stimulated the enthusiasm of the farmers to engage in agricultural production and to build the country; the farmers' feelings toward the Communist Party at that time were really like the song "follow the Communist Party with all my heart", and the farmers who were given land felt deeply that they had become masters of the country. The household contract responsibility system implemented at the beginning of reform and opening up was actually a land system reform movement, which could be regarded as the second land reform after the founding of New China. Farmers who have the land contract right have the right to use and profit from the land. The household contract responsibility system not only quickly solved the problem of food and clothing for the vast majority of farmers, but also enabled China's agriculture and rural areas to achieve stable and greater development by mobilizing the initiatives of farmers, laying a system foundation for the subsequent "demographic dividend".

The development of China's agriculture, rural areas, and farmers seems to have hit a bottleneck and is stagnant in recent years. The main reason for this may be that after more than 30 years of implementation of the household contract responsibility system, the marginal benefits (or marginal utility) of this system are diminishing, and the economic growth potential of the household contract responsibility system has almost been fully realized, while our land system has not been further reformed and improved. The widespread abandonment of land in many rural areas is a manifestation of farmers' dissatisfaction with the land system and their alienation from the land.

To fundamentally solve the problems of "agriculture, rural areas, and farmers", we need to implement the third land system reform to further bring farmers and land ownership, and the right to use and benefit from land together and bring farmers and land closer together. At present, some rural areas are implementing the reform of land rights confirmation system, which is a positive exploration to deepen the land system reform. According to the productivity standard proposed by Comrade Deng Xiaoping, all reform initiatives that are conducive to agricultural growth, rural development, and farmers' prosperity can be boldly tried.

The development and modernization of "agriculture, rural areas, and farmers" may provide China's economy with greater development space, greater rural market demand, and greater and more lasting driving force, which may be much greater than the driving force generated through the construction of several special zones or new areas.

We still have much to do and many hurdles to overcome in system reform, construction and innovation, such as the reform of state-owned enterprises, reform of the financial system and capital market, reform of the social security system, reform of the education and scientific research system, and so on. The system reform and innovation in China's supply-side structural reform will be a challenging but significant process. The success of China's supply-side structural reform will promote the improvement of the socialist market economic system. The establishment and improvement of China's socialist market economic system will be a major achievement of human market economic system innovation.

III. "Three Engines" of new driving force for economic growth

Since the founding of New China, China's economic growth has been driven by high accumulation, high investment, and high consumption, which is unsustainable with high accounting costs and opportunity costs. In the process of supply-side structural reform, we need to find new driving forces for China's economic growth.

From the supply side, promoting economic growth and increasing effective supply can be achieved by moving the AS curve to the right; in the short run, changes in the prices of factors of production and changes in production technology may affect production costs in opposite ways (directions), thus moving the short-run AS curve in the opposite direction. Specifically, if production technology remains unchanged and the prices of factors of production (e.g., wage rates) increase, the short-run AS curve will move to the upper left. This is because higher prices of factors of production will cause higher production costs, making the same output to be sold at a higher price. If the prices of factors of production remain unchanged and the production technological progress moves the production function curve to the right, it indicates that the same amount of employment can produce more output and that the marginal productivity of labor increases. The increase in labor productivity will make the average cost of production lower, which causes a rightward movement of the short-run AS curve; at this time, the same output can be sold at a lower price, or enterprises are willing to produce more output at the same price level.

The short-run right movement of the AS curve includes a rightward movement of the steep part of the AS curve and a downward movement of the smooth part of the AS curve, and the reasons for the movement of these two parts of the AS curve are different.

In terms of the movement of the short-run AS curve, the reasons for the movement of its steep part and smooth part are different. If the quantity of resources and machinery and equipment increases or the level of production technology increases, the productive capacity of the economy will increase,

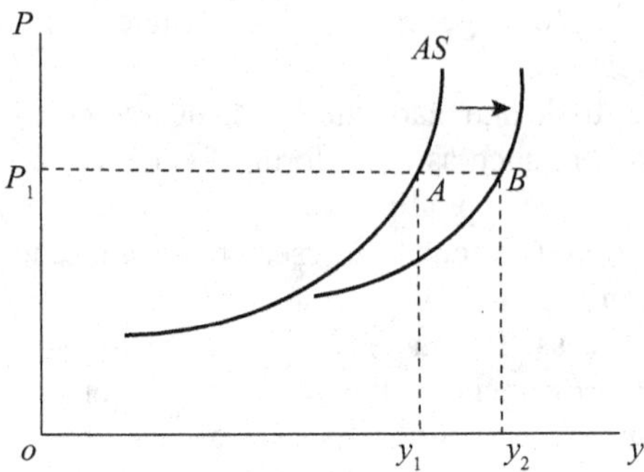

Figure 8.1 Movement in the steep part of the short-term AS curve

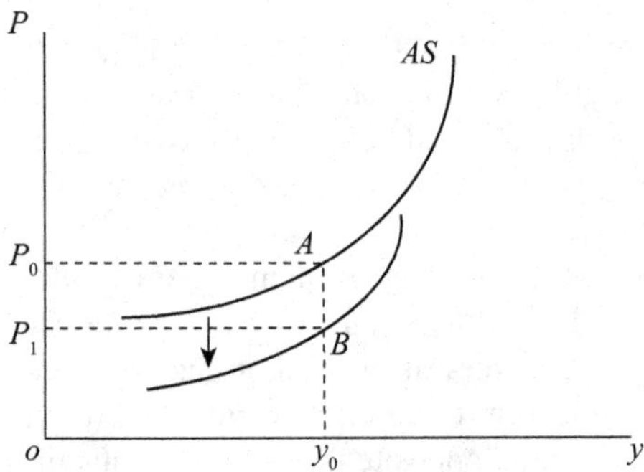

Figure 8.2 Movement of the smooth part of the short-term AS curve

which causes the steep part of the short-run AS curve to move to the right and the smooth part changes very little (see Figure 8.1). This means that producers are willing to produce more output at the same price level. If the quantity of resources, machinery and equipment, and production technology remain unchanged, and the efficiency of labor increases (e.g., workers are more motivated and their quality and skills improve), the gentle part of the short-run AS curve will move down and the steep part will change very little (see Figure 8.2). In this case, producers will be willing to supply products to the market at a lower price. The former is a horizontal effect of the AS change—mainly affecting output—while the latter is a vertical effect of the AS change—mainly affecting price. A rightward movement of the overall AS curve then has both horizontal and vertical effects.

This gives us an insight into the search for new driving forces for economic growth, i.e., the quality and efficiency improvement of factors, structural optimization and upgrading, and TFP improvement constitute the "Three Engines" of new driving forces for economic growth.

1. Quality and efficiency improvement of factors

The quality improvement of factors is mainly to improve the quality and skills of workers, to improve the physical capital and land quality, and to nurture and develop entrepreneurial talent or entrepreneurship, thereby improving production efficiency.

In the process of "cutting overcapacity, reducing excess inventory, deleveraging, lowering costs, and strengthening areas of weakness", capital will be upgraded; through the supply-side structural reform of agriculture, the quality of land will be improved and enhanced. The key to improving the quality of factors in China's economy is how to improve the quality and skills of workers, i.e. how to improve the quality and grade of human capital, and how to cultivate and give play to entrepreneurship. In the factors of production, workers and entrepreneurs are the human factors (human capital) which are the living and dynamic factors.

There is still much room and great potential for quantitative accumulation and qualitative improvement of human capital in China, especially for the vast number of front-line workers and hundreds of millions of migrant workers, most of whom are not yet highly educated and skilled, and have not received vocational training, and many of whom are still educated at junior high school or below, and a certain proportion of whom are illiterate. If all of them can become skilled workers, their labor productivity and efficiency will be greatly improved, and China's TFP will have a reliable human capital base for stable growth.

In the current process of "cutting overcapacity, reducing excess inventory, deleveraging, lowering costs, and strengthening areas of weakness" and in the process of mergers and reorganization of enterprises, there will be part of the workers unemployed or transferred, the state can take advantage of this opportunity to implement the "full staff training program", the government, educational institutions, social organizations, and enterprises work together to organize these unemployed or transferred workers for vocational skills training, so as to make them acquire new or better skills, and transform them into skilled workers.

2. Structural optimization and upgrading

The structural optimization mentioned here includes the optimization of economic structure and the resource allocation. Through comprehensively deepening reform, we can optimize the AD and AS structure, industrial structure, supply chain structure, urban and rural structure, virtual economy and real economy structure, ownership structure, market structure, and so on; meanwhile, we can reduce the degree of resource misallocation and improve the efficiency of resource allocation.

As mentioned earlier, there are many structural imbalances and resource misallocations in China's economy, but looking at it from another perspective, it shows that there is a lot of room for China's economy to improve its supply capacity and economic growth potential by optimizing its economic structure and correcting resource misallocation.

The focus of China's economic structural optimization and upgrading is mainly on optimizing and upgrading the industrial structure, promoting the modernization of agriculture and rural areas, and reducing resource misallocation.

The upgrading of industrial structure is realized mainly by implementing Made in China 2025 to achieve deep industrialization, industrial modernization, and intellectualization of production and service industry, and by strengthening the equipment manufacturing industry to improve the technical level and competitiveness of China's industry, so as to use the upgraded version of industry as the material and technical basis to upgrade the technical level of the three industries and improve the technical connotation and efficiency level of the economic structure.

By deepening the reform of the rural land system, developing and improving the agricultural and rural infrastructure, and guiding capital, entrepreneurs, and technological personnel to enter the rural areas to start businesses, China's agricultural and rural development can keep pace with modernization to fundamentally change the imbalance of China's urban and rural structures and enable the coordinated and balanced development of agriculture and industry, and rural and urban areas. The modernization of agriculture and rural areas will increase the average productivity of China's economy and provide a reliable and powerful source of power for China's stable and sustainable economic growth. At present, the per capita disposable income of rural residents in China is about 40% of that of urban residents, and the average propensity to consume of the former is about 0.12 higher than that of the latter. If the per capita disposable income of rural residents is raised to about 70% of that of urban residents, the demand side of China's economy will be significantly improved, the contradiction of supply surplus will be significantly alleviated, and the medium- and high-speed growth of China's economy will be supported by strong and effective demand.

As discussed earlier in this monograph, reducing resource misallocation can increase China's TFP by 25%–35% (Marconi, 2016); while reducing monopoly, increasing the degree of competition, and giving play to the decisive role of market mechanism in resource allocation are the fundamental ways to reduce resource misallocation and improve resource allocation efficiency.

3. Improvement of TFP

The main ways to improve TFP are to promote technological progress, especially independent innovation; to promote the popularization and accumulation of scientific and cultural knowledge; and to increase the accumulation of human capital.

To promote innovation and technological progress, the education of the whole society must reach a certain level and the accumulation of knowledge must reach a certain height; there must be a democratic, fair, and harmonious social environment; independent and free academic discussion is the scientific research environment necessary for invention and innovation, and critical thinking and skepticism are the scientific research modes necessary for invention and innovation; there shall be a perfect distribution system to motivate individuals and enterprises to engage in invention and innovation; and there shall be an appropriate arrangement of institutional mechanism to disperse or compensate the risks of invention and innovation.

The improvement of TFP through autonomous technological innovation cannot be achieved through short-term efforts; it requires long-term system reform and innovation to nurture these factors that affect autonomous innovation. Since autonomous innovation is a random event, it is highly risky and uncertain. Therefore, China's autonomous innovation should take advantage of the system advantage of being able to centralize scientific research forces and resources, and for major projects, adopt a national system for the R&D and technological innovation, and at the same time, implement an organizational model that combines national innovation with individual and corporate innovation by encouraging and supporting individual and corporate R&D and innovation through incentive mechanisms and policy guidance. To improve TFP in the short run, we also need to make efforts in eliminating market distortions, reducing resource misallocation, optimizing the economic structure, reducing government intervention and policy mistakes, mobilizing individuals and enterprises, and improving incomplete information, etc.

Notes

1 Marx & Engels. (2012). *Selected Works*. Vol. 2. Beijing: People's Publishing House, 2012, 650.
2 Marx & Engels. (1973). *Collected Works*. Vol. 26 (II). Beijing: People's Publishing House, 1973, 594.
3 Marx & Engels. (1973). *Collected Works*. Vol. 26 (II). Beijing: People's Publishing House, 1973, 596.
4 Marx & Engels. (1973). *Collected Works*. Vol. 26 (II). Beijing: People's Publishing House, 1973, 603–604.
5 Marx. (2004). *Capital*. Vol. 3. Beijing: People's Publishing House, 548.
6 *Decision of the Central Committee of the Communist Party of China on Several Major Issues Concerning Comprehensively Deepening Reforms*. Beijing: People's Publishing House, 2013, 7.
7 *Decision of the Central Committee of the Communist Party of China on Several Major Issues Concerning Comprehensively Deepening Reforms*. Beijing: People's Publishing House, 2013, 3–4.
8 [Germany] Kasper, W., & Streit, M. E. (2002). *Institutional Economics: Social Order and Public Policy*. Beijing: The Commercial Press, 24.
9 [USA] Demsetz, H. (1991). *Toward a Theory of Property Rights. Property Rights and Institutional Changes*. Shanghai: SDX Joint Publishing Company, 97–98.
10 *Decision of the Central Committee of the Communist Party of China on Several Major Issues Concerning Comprehensively Deepening Reforms*. Beijing: People's Publishing House, 2013, 3.
11 See Chapter 10 of this monograph for details. The economic structural adjustment that began in 1956 was aborted by the "anti-rightist" movement in 1957.
12 The supply-side structural reform started at the end of 2015 also includes macroeconomic control.
13 Fang, F. Q. (2009). "Shorten the Policy Time Lag and Improve the Level of Macroeconomic Control", *Teaching and Research*, (7), 5–10.
14 Fang, F. Q. (2014) "Reconstruction of China's Macro-economic Control System from the Perspective of Great Reform", *Economic Theory and Business Management*, (5), 5–27.
15 Fang, F. Q. (2019) *Main Schools of Modern Western Economics*. 3rd Ed. Beijing: China Renmin University Press, 77–78.

16 Diamond, Peter A. (1981) "Mobility Costs, Frictional Unemployment, and Efficiency", *Journal of Political Economy*, 798.

Diamond, Peter A. (1982). "Aggregate-Demand Management in Search Equilibrium", *Journal of Political Economy*, 882.

Cooper, Russell, and John, Andrew (1988). "Coordinating Coordination Failures in Keynesian Models", *Quarterly Journal of Economics*, 441–463.

17 *Decision of the Central Committee of the Communist Party of China on Several Major Issues Concerning Comprehensively Deepening Reforms*. Beijing: People's Publishing House, 2013, 5–6.

18 *Decision of the Central Committee of the Communist Party of China on Several Major Issues Concerning Comprehensively Deepening Reforms*. Beijing: People's Publishing House, 2013, 6.

19 [USA] Samuelson, P. A., & Nordhaus, W. D. (2014). *Economics* (II). 19th Ed., translated by Xiao Chen et al. Beijing: The Commercial Press, 916.

20 Friedman, M. (1962). *Capitalism and Freedom*. Chicago: University of Chicago Press, 34.

21 Shi, Z. F. (2013). *Extraordinary Growth: China's Economy from 1979 to 2049*. Shanghai: Shanghai People's Publishing House, 35–36.

22 After the Third Plenary Session of the 18th CPC Central Committee, Jiangsu Province proposed the "strong government + strong market" development model, which is considered to be the development practice in Southern Jiangsu after the reform and opening up, and this model has a universal practical effect. They stressed that "strong government + strong market" is integrated and unified, and is constantly interactive and evolving in the development practice. However, they also explained that "strong government" means that the government plays an important role in creating an environment, providing services, guiding the direction, and regulating supply and demand through macroeconomic control; "strong government" is the guardian of "strong market" and should provide opportunities for the market to give play to its advantages. According to this explanation, such "strong government" is actually "effective government", "service-oriented government", and "guardian government", which is not much different from the definition of the status and role of government in the market economy in economics textbooks.

23 *Decision of the Central Committee of the Communist Party of China on Several Major Issues Concerning Comprehensively Deepening Reforms*. Beijing: People's Publishing House, 2013, 6.

24 According to the data released on the website of the National Bureau of Statistics of China on January 20, 2014, the Gini coefficient of China's resident income was 0.473 in 2013.

25 [USA] Samuelson, P. A., & Nordhaus, W. D. (2014). *Economics* (I). 19th Ed., translated by Xiao Chen et al. Beijing: The Commercial Press, 6–7.

9 Initial results achieved by supply-side structural reform

China's supply-side structural reform was officially launched nationwide in 2016, and by the time the global pandemic of COVID-19 hit in the spring of 2020, the reform had been in progress for four years. Since the COVID-19 pandemic, coping with the shock of the epidemic has become a top priority for most countries, as it has been for China. However, China's supply-side structural reforms are still in progress and deepening.

I. Progress over the past six years

Over the past six years, especially from 2016 to 2019, China's supply-side structural reform has been continuously promoted and deepened, and a series of results have been achieved.

1. Initial results of "cutting overcapacity, reducing excess inventory, deleveraging, lowering costs, and strengthening areas of weakness"

The Central Economic Work Conference held in December 2015 listed the optimization of domestic production capacity, the innovation of growth drivers, the implementation of enterprise burden reduction, the promotion of real estate destocking, and the prevention of financial risks as the five key tasks in 2016, and proposed to "deeply promote 'cutting overcapacity, reducing excess inventory, deleveraging, lowering costs, and strengthening areas of weakness' to advance the substantial progress of the five tasks".

In 2016, the year when China's 13th Five-Year Plan was launched, the CPC Central Committee and the State Council listed "vigorously promoting structural reform" as one of the three key tasks that must be vigorously promoted during the 13th Five-Year Plan period, and included it in the Outline of the 13th Five-Year Plan for National Economic and Social Development. In the Report on the Work of the Government 2016, it was proposed that 2016 was "the year of tackling structural reform", and one of the key tasks in 2016 was to

> strengthen supply-side structural reform; accelerate the fostering of new driving forces for development; strengthen traditional comparative advantages;

DOI: 10.4324/9781003367000-12

> cut overcapacity, reduce excess inventory, deleverage, lower costs, and strengthen areas of weakness; . . . we should get off to a good start in economic and social development during the period covered by the 13th Five-Year Plan.

Through the efforts of many parties, the "cutting overcapacity, reducing excess inventory, deleveraging, lowering costs, and strengthening areas of weakness" in 2016 has achieved initial results: First, the steel and coal industries are the two key industries for cutting overcapacity. The annual plan for 2016 was to cut steel capacity by 45 million tons and coal capacity by 250 million tons. In 2016, more than 65 million tons of steel capacity and 290 million tons of coal capacity were actually withdrawn, and the coal stocks of coal enterprises decreased by 40.77 million tons year-on-year, down 32%. These two key industries have exceeded their annual targets for cutting overcapacity and started to turn losses into profits. The member enterprises of China Iron and Steel Association posted a loss of RMB 52.9 billion in the first 11 months of 2015 and a profit of RMB 33.1 billion in the first 11 months of 2016, and coal enterprises' profits also increased by 1.1 times. In the process of cutting overcapacity in the steel and coal industries, 180,000 workers in the steel industry and 620,000 workers in the coal industry need to be resettled. By the end of 2016, nearly 700,000 workers had been reemployed, and the diverted workers generated during cutting overcapacity had been properly resettled. Second, the government supported migrant workers to buy houses in urban areas, and increased the proportion of monetized resettlement of shantytowns transformation, and achieved positive results in real estate destocking. The unsold area of commercial housing has been declining month by month since January 2016. Third, it promoted enterprise mergers and reorganizations, developed direct financing, and implemented market-based and law-based debt-to-equity swaps; as a result, the debt-to-asset ratio of industrial enterprises has decreased. Fourth, the government has introduced measures such as cutting taxes and fees, lowering contributions to endowment insurance, medical insurance, unemployment insurance, work-related injury insurance, childbirth insurance and housing accumulation funds, and lowering electricity prices to help reduce costs in the real economy. Fifth, it achieved positive results of the work of strengthening areas of weakness by stepping up the efforts to strengthen areas of weakness to handle a number of urgent and long-term major matters.

In the process of "cutting overcapacity, reducing excess inventory, deleveraging, lowering costs, and strengthening areas of weakness", constantly adjust the relationship between the government and the market, and actively explore the path of market-oriented reform of institutional mechanisms. For example, explore the establishment of a medium- and long-term contract system, reserve capacity system, increase/decrease-linked and reduced displacement index trading system, minimum and maximum inventory system, and the system for preventing abnormal price fluctuations through the joint efforts of the government, industry, and enterprises, etc.

As a key task of the supply-side structural reform, "cutting overcapacity, reducing excess inventory, deleveraging, lowering costs, and strengthening areas of weakness" has been generally accepted by local governments and enterprises. In addition to the remarkable overcapacity cutting results achieved in the steel and coal industries, the overcapacity cutting in cement, flat glass, and shipbuilding industries is also being actively promoted, with many local governments and enterprises taking the initiative to reduce, optimize the stock, and guide the increment. The supply-side structural reform of agriculture, the revitalization of the real economy, the cultivation of new kinetic energy, the transformation and upgrading of traditional industries are being actively promoted.

By the end of 2019, China's supply-side structural reform has achieved a series of phased results. (1) In 2015, China's steel industry suffered losses across the board. Through reforms such as resolving the overcapacity, it exceeded the upper target of cutting overcapacity of 150 million tons specified in the 13th Five-Year Plan two years ahead of schedule, and also outlawed more than 100 million tons of "substandard steel", turning losses into profits. By 2019, the industry's efficiency reached the highest level in history. (2) From 2015 to 2019, through cutting overcapacity and reducing excess inventory, China's industrial capacity utilization rate rose to 76.6% by the end of 2019, an increase of 0.1 percentage points over the previous year. The capacity utilization rate of the mining industry and raw material industry in 2019 were 74.4% and 76.9%, respectively, both rising to the highest point in the past seven years. Among them, the capacity utilization rate of the steel industry was 80.0%, higher than the average value since the survey was available in 2006. (3) The micro leverage ratio declined, and enterprise inventory turnover accelerated. At the end of November 2019, the asset–liability ratio of industrial enterprises above designated size stood at 56.9%, a year-on-year decrease of 0.3 percentage points, and that of state-owned holding enterprises was 58.4%, a year-on-year decrease of 0.5 percentage points; the inventory turnover days of finished goods were 17.3 days, a year-on-year decrease of 0.2 days. The growth rate of macro leverage ratio remained low, dropping from 6.7% in June 2016 to 2.4% at the end of 2019, and even negative from the third quarter of 2018 to the first quarter of 2019. (4) By reducing costs, the business tax, which had been levied for 66 years, has been withdrawn from the historical stage, and the burden of corporate taxes and fees has been further reduced, with a cumulative total of about RMB 7.6 trillion of new tax cuts and fee reductions from 2016 to 2020.

2. *Significant tax cuts and fee reductions*

Premier Li Keqiang proposed in his government work report in March 2016 that the government deficit for 2016 was projected to be RMB 2.18 trillion, an increase of RMB 560 billion over last year, meaning the deficit-to-GDP ratio will rise to 3%. The increase in government deficit was projected primarily to cover tax and fee reductions for enterprises, a step that would further reduce their burdens. Since then, the State Council, as well as the Ministry of Finance and other relevant departments, have repeatedly introduced policies and measures to reduce taxes and fees, starting a large-scale tax and fee reductions. To summarize, the list of tax cuts and fee reductions in 2016 is as follows.

Tax cuts: comprehensively replace business tax with value-added tax, which may reduce taxes for enterprises by more than RMB 500 billion throughout the year.

The executive meeting of the State Council on March 18, 2016 decided that, in order to further reduce the burden of enterprises and promote the transformation and upgrading of economic structure, from May 1, 2016, the pilot program of collecting value-added tax in lieu of business tax would be extended to the construction industry, real estate industry, financial industry, and living service industry, and the value-added tax contained in new real estate of all enterprises would be included in the scope of deduction. On April 30, 2016, the State Council issued the Circular on Effectively Extending the Pilot Program of Collecting Value-added Tax in Lieu of Business Tax across the Country and the Circular on the Transitional Proposals for Adjusting the Division of Value-added Tax Revenue of the Central Government and Local Governments after Comprehensively Promoting the Pilot Collection of Value-added Tax in Lieu of Business Tax, requiring governments at all levels to carry out the work in a smooth and orderly manner to ensure that the tax burden of all industries would only be reduced but not increased.

Fees reductions. The fee reductions include a number of policy initiatives.

1. Reduce periodically the social insurance payment rates and the housing provident fund deposit ratio, reducing the burden of enterprises by RMB 100 billion per year.

On April 20, 2016, the Ministry of Human Resources and Social Security and the Ministry of Finance jointly issued the Circular on Periodically Reducing Social Insurance Payment Rates, deciding to periodically reduce social insurance payment rates. The main measures are as follows: within two years from May 1, 2016, in provinces (regions or cities) where the required contribution rate for employers to the basic endowment insurance of enterprise employees is more than 20%, such required employer contribution rate shall be reduced to 20%; in provinces (regions or cities) where such required employer contribution rate is 20% and the cumulative balance of the basic endowment insurance fund for enterprise employees by the end of 2015 is sufficient to pay for more than nine months of such contributions, the required employer contribution rate may be periodically reduced to 19%; and the overall unemployment insurance payment rate may be reduced periodically by 1–1.5% on the basis of the one-percentage-point reduction in 2015 wherein the individual contribution rate shall not exceed 0.5%.

The Ministry of Housing and Urban-Rural Development and the National Development and Reform Commission and other departments jointly issued a document requiring that within two years from May 1, 2016, any housing provident fund deposit ratio higher than 12% shall be regulated and adjusted, which shall not exceed 12%. Enterprises with production and operation difficulties can not only reduce the deposit proportion, but also apply for a suspension of deposit of housing provident fund.

2. Clean up and standardize government fund charges to reduce the burden of enterprises by RMB 26 billion per year.

The main measures are as follows: since February 1, 2016, reduce the collection standard of new vegetable field development and construction funds and the forestation funds to zero, cease the collection of price regulation funds, integrate and consolidate seven governmental funds such as the reservoir migrant support funds, and cancel the local government funds established in violation of regulations. Extend the exemption scope of educational surcharges, local educational surcharges, and water conservancy construction funds from the current payment obligors whose monthly taxable sale or turnover is not more than RMB 30,000 to those whose monthly taxable sale or turnover is not more than RMB 100,000. The exemption policy is valid for a long time.

3. Extend the exemption scope of 18 administrative and institutional fees.

On April 28, 2016, the Ministry of Finance and the National Development and Reform Commission jointly issued the Circular on Extending the Scope of Exemption of 18 Types of Administrative and Institutional Fees, which stipulates that since May 1, the scope of exemption of 18 types of administrative and institutional fees from which small and micro businesses are currently exempted shall be extended to cover all enterprises and individuals. The types of fee exempted include 11 types of agricultural fees, such as the quarantine fees for domestic plants and the examination and approval fees for new veterinary drugs; six types of fees charged by quality supervision departments, such as the fees for certificates of public measurement standards and the fees for authorized assessment of measurement, and the forest right survey fees charged by forestry departments.

4. Reduce electricity prices twice, reducing the burden of enterprises by RMB 47 billion.

Since January 2016, the average on grid price of coal-fired thermal power in China has been reduced by about RMB 0.03 per kWh, and the average sales price for general industry and commerce in China has been reduced by about RMB 0.03 per kWh. Since September 2016, the average electricity price for general industry and commerce has been reduced by RMB 0.0105 per kWh, and the average electricity price for large-scale industry has been reduced by RMB 0.011 per kWh.

5. Significant reduction of the bank card swiping charges.

In order to further reduce the operating costs of merchants, the National Development and Reform Commission and the People's Bank of China decided to reduce the bank card swiping charges from September 6, 2016. The main contents include: reduce the rate of service fee charged by the issuing banks; reduce the rate of network service fee; adjust the capping control measures for the service fee and network service fee charged by the issuing banks; implement preferential measures for the service fee and network service fee rate charged by issuing banks to some merchants; the acquiring service fee shall be subject to market adjusted price, and the acquirer shall negotiate with the merchant to determine the specific rate.

These tax and fee reduction policies and measures achieved remarkable results that year. In 2016, the tax burden of enterprises was reduced by more than RMB 570 billion. In 2016, the Ministry of Finance, together with relevant departments, issued a series of policies and measures to reduce fees and burdens. A total of 496 chargeable funds were cancelled, suspended, exempted, and reduced, reducing the burden on enterprises and individuals by more than RMB 150 billion per year. In 2016, further strengthened the clearing and reform of chargeable funds, and cancelled, suspended, and integrated seven government funds such as the new vegetable field development and construction fund; extended the exemption scope of educational surcharges, local educational surcharges, and water conservancy construction funds from the current payment obligors whose monthly taxable sale or turnover is not more than RMB 30,000 to those whose monthly taxable sale or turnover is not more than RMB 100,000; and extended the scope of exemption of 18 types of administrative and institutional fees from which small and micro businesses are currently exempted to cover all enterprises and individuals. Through these measures, the burden on enterprises and individuals was reduced by about RMB 27 billion a year.

From 2016 to 2019, one of the key contents of fiscal policy was to reduce taxes and fees. After the outbreak of COVID-19 in 2020, fiscal expenditure has increased, and stabilizing growth has become the primary objective of the macro economy. However, tax and fee reductions have not stopped, and have been continuously promoted. According to the data from China's Ministry of Finance, in the six years since 2016, the cumulative scale of tax and fee reductions in China has exceeded RMB 8.6 trillion, of which the new tax and fee reduction in 2021 exceeded RMB 1 trillion.[1]

3. Continuous advancement of "delegation, regulation, and services"

"Delegation, regulation, and services" is the abbreviation of streamlining administration, delegating more powers, improving regulation, and providing better services. "Delegation" means that the government streamlines administration and delegate power to lower the access threshold. "Regulation" means to promote fair competition by reforming and innovating government regulatory systems and measures. "Services" mean to improve the quality and efficiency of government services and create a convenient business and social environment.

On May 12, 2015, China's State Council held a National Teleconference on Promoting the Streamlining Administration, Delegating More Powers and Improving Regulation and Function Transformation, and first introduced the concept of "delegation, regulation and services" reform. In March 2016, Premier Li Keqiang proposed in the Report on the Work of Government that we should continue to streamline administration, delegate more powers, improve regulation, and provide better services, so as to continuously improve the efficiency of the government. Thus, the process of "delegation, regulation, and services" reform was started.

In May 2016, the State Council issued the Key Focus of the Work of Promoting the Reform of Streamlining Administration, Delegating More Powers, Improving Regulation and Providing Better Services in 2016, which made arrangements for the "delegation, regulation, and services" reform in 2016. This document puts forward three key tasks. First, continue to streamline administration and delegate power, continue to deepen the reform of the administrative review and approval regime, thoroughly advance the reform of the investment approval regime, effectively carrying out the reform of professional qualifications, continue to advance the reform of the commercial system, actively carry out the clean-up reform and supervision and inspection in respect of fees and charges, expand the autonomy of universities and research institutes, further streamline administration and delegate powers to lower levels by making government affairs more open, and further bring forth market vitality and social creativity. Second, strengthen regulatory innovation, implement fair regulation, promote comprehensive regulation, explore prudential regulation, promote fair competition among all kinds of market players, and promote social fairness and justice. Third, optimize government services, improve the efficiency of "mass entrepreneurship and innovation" services, improve the supply efficiency of public services, improve the efficiency of government services, so as to accelerate the formation of a more attractive international, legalized, and convenient business environment.

Since 2016, the State Council, the National Development and Reform Commission, the Ministry of Finance, the Ministry of Public Security, the Ministry of Industry and Information Technology, the Ministry of Commerce, and other ministries and commissions have continuously issued policies and measures on "delegation, regulation, and services" reform, and irregularly organized the supervision on the implementation of such policies. Almost every year, the State Council formulates plans and specific measures for the division of key tasks in deepening the reform of "delegation, regulation, and services", and guides and urges all ministries and commissions of the State Council and local governments at all levels to solidly promote the reform and make it come into effect. For example, in March 2021, the State Council made it clear that the specific measures for deepening the reform of "delegation, regulation, and services" in 2021 mainly include: First, improve the employment environment. Reduce the number of vocational qualifications for admission and promote the socialization of vocational skills level recognition. Support the healthy development of new forms of employment. Promote flexible employment and occupational injury protection pilot, expand the coverage of work-related injury insurance, and protect the legitimate rights and interests of flexibly employed personnel. Second, promote the reduction of links, materials, time limit, and expenses involved in enterprise approval. Accelerate the whole electronic process of trademark and patent registration and application. Reduce the customs clearance and inspection rate of law-abiding and compliant enterprises and low-risk commodities. Reduce and consolidate port charges. Third, support the expansion of domestic demand. Clean up the illegal restrictions on the relocation of second-hand cars, and reasonably relax the market access of tourism, homestay, and so on. Fourth, optimize the supply of services for people's livelihood. Promote the "cross-provincial handling" of more service matters related to people's livelihood. Promote the development of elderly care institutions, and introduce social forces to expand their capacity and improve their operation and service quality. Fifth, further promote fair regulation. Adhere to the combination of delegation and regulation, take fair regulation as the necessary guarantee for streamlining administration and delegating power, implement departmental regulation responsibilities, improve regulation rules and standards, establish a benchmark system of administrative discretion, innovate and strengthen in-process and ex-post regulation, and strictly regulate those involving people's life and health and public safety. Through deepening reform, release vitality, perform fair regulation and provide efficient service.

4. Overall results of supply-side structural reform

In the Report on the Work of Government in May 2020, Premier Li Keqiang summarized the results of supply-side structural reform since 2016 as follows.[2]

- The economic structure continued to improve, and the development priorities of regions are better aligned. Total retail sales of consumer goods exceeded RMB 40 trillion, and consumption continued to serve as the main engine driving growth. Advanced manufacturing and modern services registered rapid growth. Grain output reached 665 million metric tons. For the first time, permanent urban residents exceeded 60% of the population; progress was made in implementing major development strategies for regions.
- New growth drivers became stronger. A number of major innovative achievements were made in science and technology. Emerging industries continued to grow; upgrading in traditional industries accelerated. Business startups and innovation continued to surge nationwide, with an average net increase of over 10,000 businesses per day in 2019.
- Major headway was made in reform and opening up. Supply-side structural reform was further advanced, and breakthroughs in reform were made in key areas. We cut taxes and fees by RMB 2.36 trillion in 2019, going well beyond our target of RMB 2 trillion, with manufacturing and micro and small businesses benefiting most. The reform of government bodies was completed. The "delegation, regulation, and services" reform steadily advanced. The Science and Technology Innovation Board, or STAR Market, was established. The joint efforts to pursue the Belt and Road Initiative (BRI) yielded

fresh results. Regulations for the implementation of the Foreign Investment Law were adopted, and the China (Shanghai) Pilot Free Trade Zone Lin'gang New Area was established. Foreign trade and investment remained stable.

- Pivotal progress was achieved in the three critical battles. Decisive achievements were made in poverty alleviation—the rural poor population was reduced by 11.09 million in 2019, and the poverty headcount ratio fell to 0.6%. Pollution prevention and control efforts continued, with further reductions in the discharge of major pollutants and overall improvements in the environment. The financial sector remained stable.
- Living standards continued to improve. Per capita disposable personal income topped RMB 30,000. Basic old-age insurance, health insurance, and subsistence allowance standards were raised. Further progress was made in the construction of urban government-subsidized housing and the rebuilding of dilapidated houses in rural areas. The number of students in compulsory education receiving living allowances increased by almost 40%, and enrollments at vocational colleges grew by one million in 2019.

At the Ceremony Marking the Centenary of the Communist Party of China, General Secretary Xi Jinping solemnly declared to the world that

> through the continued efforts of the whole Party and the entire nation, we have realized the first centenary goal of building a moderately prosperous society in all respects. This means that we have brought about a historic resolution to the problem of absolute poverty in China, and we are now marching in confident strides toward the second centenary goal of building China into a great modern socialist country in all respects.[3]

In a large developing country with a population of more than 1.4 billion, eliminating absolute poverty and building a moderately prosperous society in all respects should be the greatest achievement of supply-side structural reform.

II. New challenges

The six-year supply-side structural reform has achieved a series of initial results, and some of the results are quite significant, but there are also some challenges.

1. Changes in the international situation have increased the uncertainty

Since the implementation of supply-side structural reforms in China, the international situation has undergone many significant changes. First, populism, isolationism and trade protectionism have prevailed, international relations have become increasingly fragmented, disagreements and confrontations among some countries have intensified, the operation of WTO rules has been hindered, trade activities and investment activities have been unduly restricted, and economic globalization has reversed. Second, COVID-19 since 2020 has severely impacted most economies in the world, leading to an overall recession in the world economy and a trend of localization, regionalization, and decentralization of global supply chains. The epidemic, which has lasted for three years, has caused not only millions of deaths, but also a large number of business deaths, and the economies of some countries have reached the brink of collapse. Third, the intensification of the conflict between Russia and Ukraine since February 2022 has led to the outbreak of the Russo-Ukrainian War. This war has further escalated originally tense international relations, and the mutual sanctions between some countries have forced the disruption of many international economic and trade relations, exacerbating the energy supply shortages and inflation. The deterioration of the international environment has made the external environment of China's supply-side structural reform, opening up to the outside world, and economic development more severe and complex, with increased pressure and costs for reform and opening up, economic development, and increased external risks and uncertainties. It will be a major challenge for China to respond to these major changes in external factors, adjust the deployment of supply-side structural reform, continue to deepen reform and expand opening up, and ensure the stability and moderate growth of China's economy.

2. *There is a long way to go to strengthen areas of weakness*

Among the five reform tasks of "cutting overcapacity, reducing excess inventory, deleveraging, lowering costs, and strengthening areas of weakness", the difficulty of "cutting overcapacity, reducing excess inventory, deleveraging and lowering costs" is relatively small, and results can be achieved in the short run. However, "strengthening areas of weakness" is not only difficult and heavy, but also difficult to be completed in place in the short run.

More than six years after the implementation of the supply-side structural reform, a lot of positive progress has been made in "strengthening areas of weakness", but many aspects of the areas of weakness still exist and need to be strengthened. At present, China's economy still has obvious weaknesses in key core technology research and development, cultivation of new driving forces for economic development, construction of modern service industries and livelihood projects, prevention of returning to poverty after eliminating absolute poverty, coordinated urban-rural and regional development, optimization of business environment and mobilization of market players' enthusiasm, etc., especially in system innovation and technological innovation.

China is still a developing country with weak scientific and technological strength, enterprise competitiveness, and national competitiveness, and China's economy in general is still in the middle and low end of the international division of the labor industrial chain and value chain, the quality of the supply system is not high, and its weakness in high-end technology and high-end equipment research and development and manufacturing is prominent. To achieve high-quality development of China's economy, we must gather and integrate the factor resources conducive to high-quality development, and gradually make up for these weaknesses through reform, research, and development.

We have weaknesses in system innovation and technological innovation, and the continuous promotion of system innovation and technological innovation is the key to solve weaknesses in all aspects. This suggests to us that, to fundamentally solve a series of weaknesses in China's economic development, we must solidly and continuously promote reform and opening up, and continuously deepen reform in a comprehensive manner; and in the process of reform and opening up, give full play to the enthusiasm of both the market and the government, vigorously develop science and technology and advanced manufacturing industries, focus on tackling key core technologies and high-end equipment, and form a number of independent and autonomous innovations to forge new momentum for China's economic development.

3. How to grasp the dynamic changes of economic structure

As mentioned earlier in this monograph, the economic structure changes dynamically, while the basic content of supply-side structural reform is to adjust, optimize, and upgrade the economic structure, therefore, it is a major challenge that how to continuously adjust the policy measures of supply-side structural reform with the changes in the economic structure itself, especially the timely adjustment of the content, strength, and scope of "cutting overcapacity, reducing excess inventory, deleveraging, lowering costs, and strengthening areas of weakness", and how to realize this appropriately.

China's supply-side structural reform is government-led, and the "cutting overcapacity, reducing excess inventory, deleveraging, lowering costs, and strengthening areas of weakness" is mainly implemented by administrative means, while the reform decisions made by the government and the "cutting overcapacity, reducing excess inventory, deleveraging, lowering costs, and strengthening areas of weakness" policies and measures introduced are based on the past economic structure. It is difficult for the government to predict the future changes in the economic structure caused by such reform, and to identify the changes in the economic structure itself, which may cause a mismatch between the reform initiatives and the changes in the economic structure, and even generate new structural imbalances and imbalances between supply and demand.

At the beginning of the supply-side structural reform, China's coal industry is one of the two key industries with excess capacity and inventory. The State Council and relevant ministries and local governments focused on the implementation of "cutting overcapacity and reducing excess inventory" in the coal industry, issued targets of cutting overcapacity and reducing excess inventory of key coal mines each year, and forcibly closed some small-scale coal mines. And the local governments and coal mining companies that failed to complete the task of cutting overcapacity will be "held accountable" or punished. The implementation of these policies and measures did have a quick effect, and the coal industry achieved outstanding results in cutting overcapacity in 2016–2018. However, later, due to the rise of trade protectionism and international trade friction, China's coal imports decreased, and coupled with the expansion of production scale and increased demand for coal in some coal-using industries, the coal industry reversed from relative oversupply to undersupply, leading to several increases in coal prices. Since the outbreak of the epidemic in 2020, the undersupply of coal has intensified and coal prices have further increased. In 2021, the average price of steam coal in China was RMB 1,044 per ton, up 81.3% from the previous year. The significant increase in coal prices led to a significant increase in the production costs of coal-fired power generation enterprises and cement enterprises nationwide, resulting in reduced profits and even losses for many of such enterprises.

The practice of cutting overcapacity in the coal industry tells us that, the supply-side structural reform, including "cutting overcapacity, reducing excess inventory, deleveraging, lowering costs, and strengthening areas of weakness", cannot be completely led by the government and cannot simply rely on administrative means; instead, we shall play the role of both the market and the government at the same time. For China at this stage, how to deal with the relationship between the market and the government, and how to play the role of the market and the government in resource allocation and economic structural adjustment, is an important issue that must be paid attention to. This point will be further analyzed in Chapter 11.

The epidemic has caused a major impact on China's economy and supply-side structural reform, while the epidemic has also changed the structure of the world economy and China's economy. How to deal with the changes in the economic structure and supply chain in the post-epidemic era is a problem that China's economic development and supply-side structural reform cannot avoid. The Outline of the 14th Five-Year Plan (2021–2025) for National Economic and Social Development and Vision 2035 of the People's Republic of China proposes that China's future reform and development should "pursue development with a focus on quality improvement, promote supply-side structural reforms as the main task and make reforms and innovation the primary driving force", and the key is how to turn these plans and goals into practical results.

Notes

1 See *China Financial and Economic News*, March 7, 2017.

2 See the Report on the Work of Government of Premier Li Keqiang at the Third Session of the 13th National People's Congress on May 22, 2020, *People's Daily* on May 29, 2020.

3 Xi Jinping's Speech at a Ceremony Marking the Centenary of the Communist Party of China on July 1, 2021, *People's Daily*, July 2, 2021.

Part III

Theories

This part focuses on answering the following questions: What is the theoretical source of China's supply-side structural reform? Is it Say's Law? Is China's supply-side structural reform theoretically based on supply-side economics and Reaganomics? What is the guiding significance and inspiration of Marx's theory of supply for China's supply-side structural reform? Why should China's supply-side structural reform choose the dual path of market-oriented reform and government reform (government transformation)?

DOI: 10.4324/9781003367000-13

10 Theoretical origin and development of supply-side structural reform

"Supply-side structural reform" has been a hot topic of research and discussion in Chinese academia in recent years. These discussions mainly involve two major categories of issues. One is why and how to improve the supply-side structural reform of China's economy; the other is what is the theoretical source and basis of supply-side reform. The first category of issues mainly involves the design or practical operation of the reform policy program, while the latter category involves the basic theoretical issues. The first three parts of this monograph mainly resolve the former type of issues, and this chapter focuses on the latter type of issues.

In the discussion of the latter category of issues, some Chinese scholars trace the theoretical source of supply-side structural reform to Say, a French economist in the early 19th century, while others argue that the theoretical basis for China's supply-side structural reform comes from the American supply-side economics or Reaganomics in the 1970s. In the author's view, these understandings are not in line with historical facts.

First of all, we need to clarify the relationship between the theory of supply-side structural reform and the theory of supply: The two are related and intersect, but they are not exactly the same. The core of theory of supply is what factors determine the AS capacity, while the core of supply-side structural reform is reform—how to improve the AS structure and increase the AS capacity and quality through reform. Secondly, we need to distinguish between the theory itself and the source of the theory. The formation of any economic theory has a process and a source, so the study of a certain theory cannot be separated from the source of this theory. However, the source of a theory is not the same as the theory itself, and it takes a long process and the study of several generations of scholars from the emergence to the formation of a theoretical system.

I. The source of supply theory is classical economics

Throughout the history of economics, it is easy to see that the emphasis on the importance of supply over demand and on the study of supply has been the tradition of economics before Keynes, especially the classical economics of England and France.[1] The idea of "labor creates wealth" was generally accepted by

DOI: 10.4324/9781003367000-14

classical economists. From the perspective of analysis, classical economics is the economics of supply or a system of economics that focuses on the analysis of supply.

Classical economics arose during the period of the rise of the capitalist market economy and the establishment of the capitalist system, a period of transition from workshop handicraft industry to machine industry. In this period of great transition and change, it was already evident that a great deal of goods and wealth came from the factory production process rather than from the circulation process (commerce or trade), and it needed to find a theoretical foundation for the capitalist system. As the spokesmen of the nascent industrial bourgeoisie, the classical economists sought to find the source of social wealth and commodity value, the economic basis of the capitalist system, in the production process, that is, the supply side. Therefore, they focused the perspective of economic research to the supply side, and penetrated the "scalpel" of political economy into the capitalist commodity production process, thus overturning the mercantilist doctrine that "wealth comes from circulation (trade)".

W. Petty (1623–1687), the founder of English classical political economy, recognized that the value of commodities was created by labor and believed that the value of money was also determined by labor. It was Petty who came up with the famous maxim "labor is the father of wealth, and land is the mother of wealth". The original words of Petty are: "Land is the mother of wealth, while labor is the father and the active element of wealth".[2] Labor and land are what we today call the two factors of production that determine supply, and Petty correctly recognized that labor is the dynamic, living factor that governs the other factors of production on the supply side. One of the basic views of modern supply economics, that "the division of labor increases labor productivity, which in turn lowers the cost of production", was also originally proposed by Petty.

> For example, to weave cloth, one combs it, one spins it, another weaves it, another draws it, another arranges it, and finally another flattens it and packs it. The cost of this division of production must be lower than that of just one individual clumsily doing all the work.[3]

The idea expressed previously is the same as the famous "pin making" example given by Adam Smith in *The Wealth of Nations* to illustrate the economic effects of division of labor and specialization. Scientific and technological progress, innovation, and improvement in the quality and skills of workers are important factors in increasing supply or output and driving economic growth, which is almost a consensus among economists today and has become the policy orientation of most countries. This idea was clearly discussed in the book *Political Arithmetick* written around 1672 (and published in 1690) by Petty. He said:

> Some people who, because of their skills, are able to do many jobs that many people who do not have the skill can do. For example, if a man uses a grinder to grind grain into flour, the amount he can grind will be equal to the amount

> that twenty people can pound with a stone mortar. The number of copies a printer can print will be equal to the number of copies a hundred people can copy out by hand.[4]

Petty correctly recognized that improved resource allocation would improve efficiency and increase supply and income. He said:

> Barren land full of shrubs can be finished to grow flax or clover, so that its value will increase a hundredfold. For the same piece of land, if it is used for building a house, it a provide a hundred times more rent than if it is used as pasture.[5]

This idea of Petty's is still true today. Accelerating technological progress, promoting technological innovation, facilitating industrial transformation and upgrading, and formulating and implementing appropriate policies are still important elements of China's current supply-side reform.

In France at the end 17th century and the beginning of the 18th century, agriculture was the main industrial sector of the national economy and the sector with the most prominent economic problems. The mercantilist policy pursued by the French government at that time led to the serious depletion of the agricultural economy. Therefore, French classical economics broke with mercantilism at the beginning and went to the path of physiocracy. Pierre Boisguillebert (1646–1714), an early representative of French classical economics, not only emphasized that "all wealth comes from the cultivation of the land", but also realized that the correct proportion between industrial sectors should be maintained and that free competition could make the total social amount of labor (i.e., the total amount of resources available—quoter) to be allocated to each industrial sector in the correct proportion.[6] The French physiocratic school saw social wealth as the agricultural products produced through the cultivation of the land and believed that the real source of social wealth was agriculture. From today's perspective, this view is obviously one-sided, because agriculture is only one of the sectors that produce wealth, but it studies the source and growth of social wealth from the supply side rather than the demand side. The famous Quesnay's Economic Table discussed for the first time in the history of the development of economics the process of reproduction and circulation of total social capital, which is in fact the relationship between what we today call AS and AD, and the Economic Table confirmed that the total products (AS) produced by agriculture in a year is the starting point of the economic cycle.

A. Smith (1723–1790) is recognized as the founder of the classical system of political economy and the originator of modern economics. The entire theoretical system of *The Wealth of Nations* begins with the analysis of the division of labor. Smith regarded the division of labor as the greatest contributor to the increase in the labor productivity. The first chapter of *The Wealth of Nations* begins by stating, "The greatest improvement in the productive powers of labor, and the greater part of the skill, dexterity, and judgment with which it is anywhere directed, or applied, seem to have been the effects of the division of labor".[7] He used the example of the trade of the pin-maker to illustrate that the division of labor greatly increased the labor productivity. Moreover, Smith further recognized that the division of labor not only improves the labor productivity of individual workers and increases the output of individual firms, but also promotes industrial development and efficiency in a country at the macroeconomic level. He said, "This separation, too, is generally called furthest in those countries which enjoy the highest degree of industry and improvement".[8] A well-developed division of labor combined with a well-governed country will lead a country to general prosperity. "It is the great multiplication of the productions of all the different arts, in consequence of the division of labor, which occasions, in a well-governed society, that universal opulence which extends itself to the lowest ranks of the people".[9]

According to Smith, labor is the source of national wealth, and there are only two ways to increase national wealth: one is to improve the labor productivity, and the other is to increase the number of useful workers; and the development of division of labor, the use of machinery, and the improvement of labor allocation will promote the improvement of labor productivity, and the increase of capital accumulation will increase the number of useful workers employed; so the growth of wealth of a country depends on the speed of development of division of labor and the amount of capital accumulation. Smith wrote that:

> The annual produce of the land and labor of any nation can be increased in its value by no other means but by increasing either the number of its productive laborers, or the productive powers of those laborers who had before been employed. The number of its productive laborers, it is evident, can never be much increased, but in consequence of an increase of capital, or of the funds destined for maintaining them. The productive powers of the same number of laborers cannot be increased, but in consequence either of some addition and improvement to those machines and instruments which facilitate and abridge labor; or of a more proper division and distribution of employment.[10]

In Smith's analysis of supply and the reasons for the growth of national wealth (i.e., economic growth), the most enlightening points are the following: (1) The division of labor will greatly increase the labor productivity, and the development of the division of labor depends on the expansion of the scope of market transactions; therefore, so to promote the division of labor, is necessary to develop markets and market systems, because

> as it is the power of exchanging that gives occasion to the division of labour, so the extent of this division must always be limited by the extent of that power, or, in other words, by the extent of the market.[11]

(2) The more developed a country's manufacturing industry is, the more prosperous its agriculture will be,[12] the more developed its domestic and foreign trade will be, and the higher the level of urbanization will be. (3) The driving mechanism of

a country's economic growth is the individual's desire for self-improvement, that is, people's self-interest motives; the braking mechanism (or constraint mechanism or protection mechanism) of a country's economic growth is human reasoning and competition. Whether a country's system is efficient and can promote the increase of national wealth depends on whether the system can generate a mechanism that transforms the strong desire of individuals for self-improvement into behaviors that are beneficial to society. The following words in *The Wealth of Nations* are often quoted:

> But man has almost constant occasion for the help of his brethren, and it is in vain for him to expect it from their benevolence only. He will be more likely to prevail if he can interest their self-love in his favor, and show them that it is for their own advantage to do for him what he requires of them. Whoever offers to another a bargain of any kind, proposes to do this. Give me that which I want, and you shall have this which you want, is the meaning of every such offer; and it is in this manner that we obtain from one another the far greater part of those good offices which we stand in need of. It is not from the benevolence of the butcher, the brewer, or the baker that we expect our dinner, but from their regard to their own interest. We do not beg for mercy from them, but resort to their self-interested intentions.[13]

Smith's following words seem to be under-quoted, but it's equally important: "The greater part of his occasional wants is supplied in the same manner as those of other people, by treaty, by barter, and by purchase".[14] The "treaty" and "barter" used here can be understood as a mechanism arrangement that transforms the strong desire of individuals for self-improvement into a system that is beneficial to society, i.e., the arrangement of the market economy system. (4) A system of free competition will promote the growth of national wealth and social progress, and the economy and society should remove the system barriers in this regard and limit the functions and role of government to the necessary extent. Smith believed that a system that restricts manufacturing and trade "retards, instead of accelerating, the progress of the society towards real wealth and greatness; and diminishes, instead of increasing, the real value of the annual produce of its land and labor".

> All systems either of preference or of restraint, therefore, being thus completely taken away, the obvious and simple system of natural liberty establishes itself of its own accord. Every man, as long as he does not violate the laws of justice, is left perfectly free to pursue his own interest his own way, and to bring both his industry and capital into competition with those of any other man, or order of men.[15]

As can be seen, *The Wealth of Nations* explores the sources of economic growth from the supply side, providing a more systematic analysis of supply economics. Today, our discussion of supply-side structural reform is still inseparable from the analysis of the factors such as division of labor, capital accumulation, labor, labor productivity, manufacturing development, market development, urbanization, and system change, and the relationship between them. These ideas elaborated by Smith in *The Wealth of Nations* are especially theoretically relevant to our supply-side structural reform today.

David Ricardo (1772–1823) highly summarized the reasons for the growth of a country's national wealth as the invention of machines, technological progress, the development of the division of labor, and the development of markets. Ricardo wrote that

> by the invention of machinery, by improvements in skill, by a better division of labor, or by the discovery of new markets, where more advantageous exchanges may be made, a million men may double or treble the amount of riches, of "necessaries, conveniences, and amusements," in one state of society, that they could produce in another,[16]

and that, "By continuously increasing the facility of production, we . . . not only add to the national riches, but also to the power of future production".[17] It is easy to see from these two passages that Ricardo, who lived in the early 19th century, had little difference from modern economists in his understanding of the factors affecting the growth of an economy's supply capacity.

In summary, we have reason to believe that the whole classical economics is the initial supply economics, which has conducted a more systematic and in-depth study of supply and its determinants. Marx once clearly pointed out that classical economists attached importance to the analysis of supply without paying much attention to demand,

> some economists like Ricardo regarded production and the self-accretion of capital as one and the same thing directly, and thus they were neither concerned with the limits of consumption nor with the limits of circulation itself due to the necessity of expressing equivalent values at all points, but paid attention only to the productivity of development and the growth of the industrial population, and only to supply and not to demand.[18]

Although the mainstream economics after Ricardo was called vulgar economics by Marx, it still inherited the tradition of classical economics of attaching importance to supply and emphasizing supply analysis on the question of whether supply or demand takes the first place. Therefore, it can be said that the emphasis on supply and supply analysis has been the tradition of western mainstream economics before the Keynesian Revolution.[19] It is for this reason that Keynes, who later emphasized AD analysis and created the theory of effective demand, complained that classical economics had done an exhaustive AS (function) analysis without any AD analysis. "The great puzzle of effective demand with which Malthus had wrestled vanished from the economics literature",[20] and "from the time of Say and Ricardo the classical economists have taught that supply creates its own demand".[21] The supply-side economics that emerged in the United States in the late 1970s also openly admitted that the source of their theory was classical economics.[22]

II. How to view Say's Law

In his book *A Treatise on Political Economy* published in 1803, Say systematically discussed the relationship between production (supply)[23] and demand, arguing that supply determines demand, supply creates demand, supply takes precedence over demand, and demand increases with the increase of supply. Say's argument is that people produce for consumption, and that the producer offers one product to the market in exchange for another product he needs; therefore, "a product is no sooner created, than it, from that instant, affords a market for other products to the full extent of its own value".[24] "Money performs a momentary function in this double exchange; and when the transaction is finally closed, it will always be found, that one kind of commodity has been exchanged for another".[25] "In every community the more numerous are the producers, and the more various their productions, the more prompt, numerous, and extensive are the markets for those productions; for price rises with the demand".[26] This argument of Say was summarized by later economists as "Say's Law". Keynes expressed Say's Law in *The General Theory* as "supply creates its own demand".[27] It can be seen that Say's Law inherits the tradition of classical economics of England and France, which attaches importance to supply, and develops "supply determines demand" into "(aggregate) supply and (aggregate) demand must be equal" or "buying and selling must be balanced".[28]

The further question is, what is the original intention of Say's Law, what are its implied assumptions, and what is its relationship with the supply-side structural reforms we are discussing today?

The main purpose of Say's Law is to prove that as long as there is no interference with production, there will be no general excess production, because "production creates demand for products",[29] more supply will create more demand, and AS and AD will always be balanced (or equal). Say wrote that: "there must needs be some violent means, or some extraordinary cause, a political or natural convulsion, or the avarice or ignorance of authority, to perpetuate this scarcity".[30] Say's Law implies that the market mechanism is sensitive and effective, and that it can automatically achieve equilibrium between AD and AS at the full employment level, without a shortage of effective demand and thus without a economic crisis of general excess production.

There are four assumptions implied by Say's Law. (1) The market price mechanisms are fully elastic, and their automatic regulation can ensure that various markets are cleared in a timely manner. (2) The automatic regulation of interest rate can ensure that all the part of current income (savings) that is not used for consumption can be converted into investment, which is based on the assumption that the interest is the return on savings and the cost of investment, and that interest rates have complete elasticity. (3) Money is neutral, and is only a medium of transaction. The changes in quantity of money only affects nominal variables in the economy, but not real variables. (4) The distribution system in the economic society can ensure that the aggregate output and the corresponding total income are converted into an equal amount of effective demand.

Having determined that there would be no general excess production, Say opposed government intervention in economic activity and government stimulation of consumption through policy instruments to expand AD. He believed that "one kind of production would seldom outstrip the other, and its products be disproportionally cheapened, were production left entirely free".[31] "The encouragement of mere consumption is no benefit to commerce; for the difficulty lies in supplying the means, not in stimulating the desire of consumption".[32] Therefore, according to Say's Law, an economy's main concern and effort to increase should be supply or production; demand is not a problem, and it naturally follows the growth of supply.

Marx categorized Say as a bourgeois vulgar economist, and he criticized Say's Law in the first volume of *Capital*. Marx argued that Say's Law made two mistakes. First, capitalist commodity production is secretly replaced by simple commodity production, while the two kinds of production have fundamentally different purposes. The purpose of the former production is for surplus value or profit, while the latter production is for its own consumption, and capitalist commodity production has the potential to expand blindly without regard to the limits of consumption demand. Second, Say further changed the commodity–money exchange relationship into a barter relationship. In the process of barter, the "selling" of one commodity is also the "buying" of another commodity, that is, "one thing for another", and the selling and buying are necessarily equal or balanced. In the process of commodity–money exchange, the selling and buying are separated in time and space under such case, if a producer sells a product here and now to get money, he does not necessarily buy another product immediately with the money he earned. This can lead to money deposits, disconnections between buying and selling, and imbalances between supply and demand. When money has the function of a means of payment, the buyer and seller are no longer "making a payment at the time of delivery"; the buyer of a commodity does not have to pay money immediately, but can defer the payment (e.g., "on credit"). The formation of this debt chain further strengthens the possibility of the occurrence of economic (financial) crisis. The basic contradiction of the capitalist mode of production turns this possibility into a reality. In his critique of Say's Law, Marx wrote:

> The method of the apologists for economics has two characteristics. First, simply remove the distinction between the circulation of commodities and the direct exchange of products, equating the two. Second, try to reduce the relations between the parties to capitalist production to the simple relations arising from the circulation of commodities, thus denying the contradictions of the capitalist production process.[33]

Later, in his *General Theory* (1936), Keynes made Say's Law the main object of criticism. According to Keynes, Say's Law implies that AD is equal to AS at all levels of output, and that the AD function (curve) and the AS function (curve) overlap, and that "this is equivalent to the proposition that there is no obstacle to full employment".[34] In his *General Theory*, Keynes denied Say's Law from the different perspectives of money wages, commodity prices and stickiness or rigidity of interest rates, as well as the non-neutrality of money; he used the theory of MPC diminishing, the theory of diminishing marginal efficiency of capital, and the theory of liquidity preference trap leading to sticky interest rates to prove that savings are not automatically and equivalently converted into investment, and concluded that Say's Law could not established. Keynes argued that the underemployment and excess production caused by the highly developed production capacity and insufficient effective demand are the normal state of capitalist economies, and that the equilibrium of AS and AD at the level of full employment is only an exceptional or contingent situation.

So, what do we make of Say's Law today? Say's Law's claim that there is no possibility of universal excess production is not theoretically and logically valid, as both Marx and Keynes pointed out, although they argued from different perspectives. If the capitalist market economy was still in its booming period in Say's time and the economic crisis of excess production had not yet shown its face, economic crises have periodically assailed human economic life since the first economic crisis of general excess production in human history broke out in England in 1825. The economic practice of the past 200 years has also failed to confirm the intent of Say's Law. But Say's Law holds that supply is decisive and first in the relationship between supply and demand, and that supply creates demand, and it is an idea that holds in the long run if we put aside system factors based on production relations and look mainly from the development of productivity—because, in the long run, AS is the main decisive factor for the growth of aggregate output (economic growth). However, this idea was not put forward initially by Say, but had already appeared in classical economics, and it seems to have become an axiom in economics.[35] Generally speaking, in the long run, from the perspective of macroeconomics, the available resources and technologies are certain, and thus the potential aggregate output is certain (the long-run AS curve is vertical); and assuming that the prices and wages of the factors of production can be freely and fully adjusted, the effective demand can adapt to the AS capacity, and the potential aggregate output can be produced under the condition of full employment. In the long run, supply not only creates the object of demand (consumption), but also creates income, i.e., the ability to pay, and the income that people do not spend in the current period will always be used for future consumption. From the microeconomic point of view, people's needs or desires are infinitely diverse in the long run, and the production or supply of new products will always transform people's potential needs into realizable demands or satisfy them in a more comfortable, convenient, and inexpensive way, while products that are not suitable for people's needs will sooner or later gradually exit the market and stop being supplied. In fact, it is not that the supply may instantly create the demand for itself, but that the supply may transform the potential needs of people into realizable needs or satisfy people's needs in a better way, thus transforming needs into demands. Before the emergence of cell phones, people mainly relied on fixed telephones, faxes, and telegrams for communication. After the emergence of cell phones, a huge market demand for cell phones soon developed because they were more convenient and comfortable than traditional communication tools.

However, this transformation of potential needs into effective demand is supported by a corresponding release of ability to pay. Thus, while supply can transform people's potential needs into realizable demand in the long run, the extent to which supply can create its own demand depends on the ability to pay. The ability to pay of an economic society depends on the distribution system of that society and, ultimately, on the ownership of the instruments of production or property rights system of that society. By introducing the system factors, we find that both AS and AD are influenced or conditioned by such factors. The system acts on both supply and demand; this action may be unbalanced and asymmetric for both the supply side and demand side. The strength of the action of systems on both the supply side and demand side depends on the nature and structure of the systems. Some systems promote supply but constrain demand; for example, the capitalist system in its ascendancy created more productivity in the 100 years since its establishment than the sum of the productivity previously created by mankind, but the AD did not grow in tandem. Some systems are conducive to releasing demand but constrain the growth of supply capacity, for example, there is a general underproduction or shortage of supply under a planned economic system. From the perspective of system or production relations, the reason why the growth of effective demand lags behind the growth of supply capacity is that the distribution system (distribution relations) under a certain economic system (production relations) is flawed. For example, income and wealth are polarized, the rich have money but are unwilling to consume more—because their consumption is near or at the physical and psychological needs, while the poor desire to consume more but cannot afford to consume—because they have limited income and wealth, which results in a disconnection between the consumption needs (from the poor) and the ability to pay (possessed by the rich), preventing a portion of consumption needs from being converted into effective demand. Thus, if the results (actual aggregate output) produced by an economy with the available technology and resources cannot be fully converted into effective demand (production demand and living demand) through an appropriate distribution system, it will lead to the asymmetric growth of supply capacity and demand capacity, and its continuous development will lead to general excess production. The error of Say's Law is not in the assertion that "supply creates its own demand", but in the fact that it abandons the influence of social system on supply and demand, and discusses the relationship between AS and AD in a general sense; and that it denies the possibility of a general economic crisis of excess production under the capitalist system, regardless of the short and long term, based on the assertion that "supply creates its own demand".

As we can see previously, Say's Law is not a theory for discussing supply-side structural reform, nor is Say the originator of supply theory. China's supply-side structural reform is to "improve the quality and efficiency of the supply system, enhance the driving force of sustained economic growth, and promote the overall leap of China's social productivity" through reform and reshaping of the supply power,[36] which is not directly related to Say's Law, which advocates that "supply creates its own demand".

III. Marx's theory of supply

The main purpose of Marxian economics was to dissect the structure of the capitalist economy to demonstrate the historical temporary nature of the capitalist system, but in his economic works, Marx also addressed a range of supply analysis issues such as the status and role of supply, the determinants of supply, and the relationship between supply and demand.

Unlike Adam Smith, who lived in the age of workshop and handicraft industry, Marx lived in an era when the industrial revolution in England had been completed, France and Germany had also set off waves of industrial revolution, and heavy industry in particular had gained rapid development in Europe. The industrial revolution greatly increased the social productivity and greatly promoted the development of the capitalist commodity economy. This enabled Marx to observe more clearly the position and role of production or supply in the overall socio-economic life, and to discover the importance of industrialization, science and technology, education, division of labor, and collaboration in promoting supply in the process of the development of capitalist market economy. And, with the eventual establishment of the capitalist mode of production and the economic crisis of excess production that followed, there was a realistic basis for rethinking the effectiveness of Say's Law. Importantly, Marx stood in the position of the vast number of wage workers and was adept at dissecting the social system and economic activities of the era in which he lived with materialistic dialectics and the historical materialism. These subjective and objective conditions made Marx's analysis of production or supply surpass in many respects the English and French classical economics.

As early as when writing the economic manuscript 1861–1863, Marx outlined the main causes of the growth of AS or economic growth. "The expansion of production year by year is achieved for two causes: first, the increasing growth of capital invested in production; second, the increasing improvement of the efficiency of the use of capital".[37] Obviously, the "expansion of production year by year" that Marx refers to here is economic growth, of which the first cause is the determinant of economic growth as stated in the Harrod-Domar model of the 1930s–1940s,[38] and the second cause is the neoclassical economic growth model that Robert Solow and Trevor Swan described independently as the determinant of economic growth in 1956.

Division of labor, collaboration (cooperation), specialization, capital accumulation, science and technology, economies of scale (mass production), industrialization, and labor productivity are not only essential concepts for the analysis of supply theory, but also important factors that determine and affect AS. In his treatise, Marx made a more systematic analysis and discussion of these supply factors.

In the first volume of *Capital* and his economic manuscripts 1875–1985, Marx fully affirmed the role of scientific and technological progress in increasing labor productivity. "It is clear at a glance that large industry, by incorporating huge natural forces and natural science into the process of production, is bound to raise the labor productivity considerably".[39] The economic effects of scientific and technological progress and its innovations are highlighted by the savings in the consumption of labor and other resources in promoting economic growth or development, with economic growth (the creation of wealth) depending more and more on technological progress and its applications (innovations) and less and less on the consumption of labor and resources. Marx wrote:

> With the development of large industry, the creation of real wealth depends less on the time of labor and the amount of labor consumed, and more on the power of the agents employed in the time of labor, and the agents themselves—their great efficiency—are not in proportion to the direct labor time spent in producing them, but depend on the general level of science and technological progress, or rather on the application of this science to production.[40]

Moreover, scientific and technological progress increases and strengthens the capacity of capital to expand, allowing a certain amount of capital to acquire greater production capacity and promote social progress.

> Just as the utilization of natural wealth can be enhanced by simply raising the tension of labor, science and technology give capital, which performs its functions, an expansion capacity that does not depend on a certain amount of it. At the same time, this expansion capacity acts counteractively on that part of the original capital which has entered the stage of renewal. Capital combines without cost in its new form the social progress achieved behind its old form.[41]

Marx's Introduction to *A Contribution to the Critique of Political Economy* analyzes the dialectical relationship between the four links of the process of social reproduction: production, distribution, exchange, and consumption. Among them, production plays a decisive role; without production, there would be no objects of distribution, exchange, and consumption. Production, distribution, exchange, and consumption

> constitute members of a single whole, differences within a single unity. Production predominates both over itself in the antithetical determination of production and over the other moments. With it the process always starts afresh. It is self-evident that exchange and consumption cannot be predominant. Similarly for distribution as the distribution of the products. But as distribution of the factors of production, on the other hand, it is itself a moment of production. A specific production thus determines a specific consumption, distribution and exchange as well as the specific relations of these different

> moments to one another. Production in its one-sided form, of course, is in its turn determined by the other moments.[42]

For example, when the size of the market increases, the scale of production also increases, and the division of labor in society becomes finer and more developed. In terms of the relationship between production and consumption, "Production mediates consumption, for which it makes the material and which would be without an object in its absence". Thus, in this respect, production creates and produces consumption. "But consumption also mediates production by creating for the products the subject for whom they are products. The product only obtains its last finish in consumption". "Products only become realistic products in consumption", and "consumption creates new production demand, that is, it creates the conceptual intrinsic motivation of production, which is the premise of production".[43] It can be seen from Marx's point of view that, although supply or production takes precedence and plays a decisive role in the relationship between production (supply) and consumption (demand),[44] supply and demand are interdependent and mutually influential, with demand constraining supply and reacting to supply.

More importantly, Marx also promoted the decisive role of supply and supply structure to the level of production relations or systems for analysis, which is more profound than the relevant analysis of classical economists. When talking about the relationship between the four links of production, distribution, exchange, and consumption, Marx pointed out that:

> before distribution becomes the distribution of products, it is 1) the distribution of the instruments of production, and 2) which is another determination of the same relation, the distribution of the members of society among the various types of production (the subsumption of individuals under definite relations of production). It is evident that the distribution of the products is merely a result of this distribution, which is comprised within the very process of production and determines the structure of production. To examine production apart from this distribution which is included in it is obviously an empty abstraction.[45]

In other words, the nature of the system or relations of production determines the structure of the allocation of resources (the distribution of the instruments of production and the distribution of the members of society among the various types of production),[46] and thus the structure of supply (production), and the structure of the distribution of income (the distribution of products), is nothing but a necessary consequence of the structure of relations of production and the structure of supply. Marx always linked wealth and its production to the concrete socio-historical form of the mode of production, and by wealth and wealth production he always meant wealth and wealth production under a certain mode of production and exchange, and not wealth and its production in the abstract. Marx wrote: "When the question is to understand the particular nature of a certain mode of social production, it is precisely these forms alone that are important. . . . These forms are decisive for material wealth itself".[47]

Marx also elaborated in detail the total supply–demand relationship in the economic system in the third volume of *Capital*. Marx defines (aggregate) supply as "the products that are on the market, or that can be supplied to the market",[48] and (aggregate) demand as "the demand for goods that appears on the market" and "the actual social demand". The distinction is made between "the demand for goods that appears in the market" and "the actual social needs", which is today called "AD" and "effective demand" in macroeconomics. Marx pointed out that the size of AD in an economy is determined by the distribution relations of a society and the economic status of different classes. He wrote: " 'Social needs', that is to say, what regulates the principle of demand, are essentially determined by the mutual relations of the different classes and their respective economic positions".[49] As can be seen, Marx combined the analysis of AD and the analysis of system supply in terms of the nature of the structure, where the scale of AD and its structure are ultimately determined by the characteristics of the systems and their structure, and the systems determine the distribution relations and the proportion of distribution.

In the third volume of *Capital*, Marx further discussed the need for the structure of AS to fit and match the structure of AD. He wrote:

> The total products can be sold only if they are produced in the necessary proportions. This quantitative limit of the share of social labor time that can be used separately in each particular sphere of production is but a further development of the whole law of value, and it is obvious that necessary labor time here contains another meaning. Only such a large amount of labor time is necessary in order to satisfy social needs.[50]

According to this, the production of the aggregate social product (AS) must not only correspond to the AD in quantity, but also in structure, otherwise a part of the products produced will be in surplus and their value will not be realized because they are not suitable for the needs of society, and society does not recognize the production time spent on these products as necessary labor time. This discussion of Marx may be expressed in today's economic language as follows: only when the allocation of resources (i.e. "social labor time") is carried out according to the structure of social demand (i.e. the "necessary proportion" of social demand) can the products produced form an effective supply and then will the product be able to realize its value.

In the conditions of a commodity economy (market economy), by what mechanism is this proportional allocation of resources achieved? Marx's answer is competition, i.e. the market competition mechanism. Marx said: "By what amount is necessary labor time actually distributed among the different spheres of production? Competition constantly regulates this allocation, just as it constantly disrupts it".[51] Marx further pointed out that since capitalist commodity production is regulated by the law of surplus value and not by social needs, and since the limits of capitalist production are the profits of the capitalist and never the needs of the producer, this necessary proportion will often be disrupted and excess production is inevitable. "In every industry, each capitalist produces according to his capital, regardless of social needs, and especially regardless of the competitive supply of other capital in the same industry".[52] "Capitalist production is bounded by the profits of the capitalist, never by the needs of the producer".[53] "The bourgeois mode of production contains the limits of the free development of the productive forces—the limits exposed in the crisis, especially in the excess production which is the basic phenomenon of the crisis".[54] According to Marx, unlike capitalist production, social production based on the association of free men is regulated by social needs, so that only under a socialist system is it possible to allocate production (resources) in proportion.[55]

Marx's theory of supply and analysis of supply structure and its determinants have important theoretical guidance for our supply-side structural reform.

IV. Supply-side economics is mainly about policy programs

The basic idea of the supply-side economics, which was formed in the United States in the mid-to-late 1970s, is that it is production, not consumption, that generates income, and that without production there can be no consumption; in the relationship between supply and demand, supply is the "cause" and demand is the "effect". Therefore, the focus of economics and government policy should be on the supply side rather than the demand side. G. Gilder emphasized that "the source of wealth in capitalism is the supply of the economy. In western capitalist economies, this simple understanding is the core of all successful economic policies".[56] The representatives of the supply-side economics agree that the cause of economic stagnation and inflation in the United States in the 1970s was inadequate supply; and that the main cause of inadequate supply was too much government intervention in economic activity—ever-increasing government spending and taxes, more and more regulations; all of which prevented the free market system from stimulating the enthusiasm of work, savings, investment, and production. It is easy to see that the basic ideas of the supply-side economics come from classical economics.

The supply-side economics opposes the Keynesian demand determinism and demand management policies, arguing that the stagflation of the US economy is the result of the long-term implementation of Keynesianism. Gilder said, "In economics, when demand displaces supply in the order of priority, it inevitably results in economic stagnation and lack of creativity, inflation, and declining productivity".[57] The supply-side economics argues that Keynesian policies to stimulate AD are ineffective and harmful because demand itself does not produce anything. In the Keynesian view, if people don't buy, no one will produce for the market; the more people buy, the more products will be produced, so increasing AD through fiscal policy will increase GDP. However, Paul Craig Roberts argued that Keynesians have reversed the causal relationship between supply and demand, because "no matter how much aggregate demand increases, as long as work effort and investment fall, production will fall".[58]

The supply-side economics recognizes the truth of Say's Law. Gilder emphasized that "the central idea of Say's Law remains true: supply creates demand. There can be no such thing as an oversupply of total goods".[59] According to Arthur Betz Laffer, Say's Law is important not only because it summarizes the theories of the classical school, but also because it is convinced that supply is the only source that enables real demand to be supported, i.e., "people produce in order to consume" as Say put it. In Gilder's view:

> Say's law is important because it focuses attention on supply, on the capacity to stimulate or the investment of capital. It makes economists concerned first and foremost with the motives and stimuli of individual producers, turning them away from concentrating on distribution and demand and concentrating again on the instruments of production.[60]

Gilder reiterated the intent of Say's Law, that is, the spontaneous operation of a market economy will not result in a general excess production. He argued that, in the case of an economy as a whole,

> purchasing power and productivity can always be in equilibrium. There is always enough wealth in an economy to buy its products. There can be no surplus of goods caused by a shortage of aggregate demand. In summary, producers create the demand for their goods in the production process.[61]

Gilder emphasized, "This idea is obviously simple in many ways, but it contains many crucial economic truths and implications that Keynes and others have never refuted. These truths are the theoretical foundation of the supply-side economics".[62] He further emphasized that "Say's Law and its variants are the basic rules of the supply-side economics".[63]

It can be seen that the supply-side economics revived Say's Law and re-emphasized that Say's Law had the so-called truth, not because Say and Say's Law made any valuable analysis of the economy's AS capacity and the determinants of its growth, but in order to subvert Keynes' Law, which dominated economic theory and economic policy at that time, and to pull the attention of economists, government, and the public from the demand side back to the supply side. It was because the supply-side economics did not innovate much in economic theory, but merely reiterated the views of classical economics on supply and Say's Law; therefore, some scholars at that time regarded the emergence of the supply-side economics as the reincarnation of classical economics and the resurrection of Say's Law. A review by the Editorial Board of the Monthly Review in 1981 entitled "Comments on Supply Economics" pointed out that "Supply economics is a reincarnation of Say's Law" and "a genuine Atavism".[64]

The main influence of supply-side economics in the history of economics is policy research, on the basis of which a series of reform ideas and policy proposals to deal with economic stagflation have been put forward. So strictly speaking, supply-side economics is a kind of economic policy science. T. J. Hailstones in his book "A Guide to Supply-side Economics" suggests that "supply-side economics can be defined as a policy study that aims to stimulate economic growth and promote price stability through a variety of policy measures that affect the supply of goods and services".[65]

The core of the supply-side economics is to emphasize the mobilization of the enthusiasm of individuals and enterprises to promote the increase of supply. They argued that there are two main ways to mobilize the enthusiasm of individuals and enterprises. One way is the incentives for people's labor and investment enthusiasm that come from after-tax rewards for work, savings (investment), inventions, innovations, and entrepreneurial talent. People value net after-tax compensation rather than pre-tax compensation. In general, after-tax compensation rates vary in the same direction as people's enthusiasm. Thus, high tax rates discourage people from working, saving, and investing. Another way is a loose market environment. Some members of the supply-side economics argued that the economic system is like a spring, which is inherently tense, and that it curls and shrinks now that the government has put too much pressure or burden on it (e.g., high taxes and too many regulations), and that once these external pressures or burdens are removed, the economic system will regain its inherent tension like spring. In other words, the economy will now come alive if individuals and enterprises are unbundled and relieved of their burdens and free competition is restored. Based on these understandings, the supply-side economics has put forward two major policy propositions. (1) Reduce taxes, especially by cutting marginal tax rates. (2) Reduce government intervention, restore free competition, and drastically reduce the outdated, unnecessary regulations that hinder free competition. In short, the policy proposition of the supply-side economics is to reduce taxes and government regulations.

The supply-side economics further advocated privatization and market-based reforms to re-establish free markets, restore the resilience of market mechanisms and entrepreneurship, and promote economic growth. Gilder said,

> Throughout history, from Venice to Hong Kong, the fastest-growing countries or regions have emerged not from areas blessed with resources, but from countries (or regions) with full freedom of thought and private ownership of property. Two of the world's most economically prosperous countries (Germany and Japan—quoter) lost almost all their physical capital in World War II, but relied on the emancipation of entrepreneurs to re-emerge.[66]

As can be seen, the supply-side economics, represented by Arthur Betz Laffer et al., mainly put forward a set of policy ideas on how to solve the US economic stagflation, revive the economy, and increase supply, but there is little originality in their economic theory, and the theories of the supply-side economics are mainly borrowed from their predecessors or others.

V. Theoretical basis for China's supply-side structural reform

We can trace the theoretical source of supply analysis and supply-side structural reform back to classical economics in England and France; Say and Say's Law after classical economics may not be regarded as a source. Say's Law is to demonstrate that the spontaneous operation of a free market economy without government intervention will not result in an economic crisis of general overproduction. Say's Law is not a theory that argues why and how to carry out supply-side structural reforms. Marx's theory of supply is an important guide to how to carry out supply-side structural reform in China at this stage. The policy suggestions put forward by the supply-side economics, such as tax cuts, reducing government intervention, and rebuilding the market mechanism, are of reference value to China's supply-side structural reform.

However, we should see that China's economic situation in recent years is a very different from the economic situation when the supply-side economics was emerging. When supply-school economics was popular, the main maladies of American economy were stagflation, whereas China's economy is currently facing downward pressure on its economic growth rate. The main economic problems in the US at that time were stalled economic growth power (mainly in the form of negative growth of TFP), insufficient manufacturing capacity, and relative supply shortages, while the main difficulties of China's economy in recent years have been large excess capacity and the delay in effectively resolving excessive inventories. In recent years, China's economy has both supply-side and demand-side problems: on the one hand, there is excess capacity and excessive inventories, and on the other hand, there is a population of 600 million people with a monthly income of about RMB 1,000 whose basic living needs have not yet been met. The structural imbalance of China's economy and the weakening of its supply power are due to both institutional reasons and the transitional nature of China's economy in the process of "five transformations".[67] The supply-side structural reform of China's economy is not only a matter of economic structural adjustment, optimization and upgrading, but more importantly, a matter of reform and adjustment of the system or production relations.

The supply-side structural reform proposed by the Chinese government is mainly aimed at the problems that exist at the current stage of China's economic development and is based on the need for deeper reform and further development of China's economy, rather than from a ready-made economic theory. In fact, since the reform and opening up, the major reform measures and important policy adjustments introduced by the Chinese government have all started from China's national conditions and actual needs at that time, and from problems, rather than from a certain ready-made theory. This is because China's reform and opening up is a completely unprecedented initiative to establish a socialist market economy based on the breaking of the planned-economy system. It can be said that China's reform and its theoretical development are "problem-oriented". Therefore,

China's supply-side structural reform today needs to draw on the resources of ideas including classical economics, but also needs the support of the supply theory of Marxian economics, so as to innovate the socialist economic theory with Chinese characteristics in the light of China's actual situation, and on this basis to design a set of structural reform solutions and policy combinations that address the crux of China's economic problems.

Notes

1 The terms "classical economics" and "vulgar economics" mentioned in this chapter are based on Marx's definition.
2 Petty, W. (1981). *The Economic Writings of Sir William Petty*, translated by Chen Dongye, Ma Qinghuai and Zhou Jinru. Beijing: The Commercial Press, 12.
3 Petty, W. (1981). *The Economic Writings of Sir William Petty*, translated by Chen Dongye, Ma Qinghuai and Zhou Jinru. Beijing: The Commercial Press, 66.
4 Petty, W. (1981). *The Economic Writings of Sir William Petty*, translated by Chen Dongye, Ma Qinghuai and Zhou Jinru. Beijing: The Commercial Press, 12.
5 Petty, W. (1981). *The Economic Writings of Sir William Petty*, translated by Chen Dongye, Ma Qinghuai and Zhou Jinru. Beijing: The Commercial Press, 11–12.
6 *Pierre Boisguillebert: A Treatise on Grain. A Treatise on the Nature of Wealth, Money, and Taxation*, translated by Wu Chunwu, Beijing: The Commercial Press, 1979, 102–103.
7 Smith, A. (2001). *The Wealth of Nations* (I), translated by Yang Jingnian. Xi'an: Shaanxi People's Publishing House, 7–8.
8 Smith, A. (2001). *The Wealth of Nations* (I), translated by Yang Jingnian. Xi'an: Shaanxi People's Publishing House, 9.
9 Smith, A. (2001). *The Wealth of Nations* (I), translated by Yang Jingnian. Xi'an: Shaanxi People's Publishing House, 14.
10 Smith, A. (2001). *The Wealth of Nations* (I), translated by Yang Jingnian. Xi'an: Shaanxi People's Publishing House, 384.
11 Smith, A. (2001). *The Wealth of Nations* (I), translated by Yang Jingnian. Xi'an: Shaanxi People's Publishing House, 22.
12 Smith, A. (2001). *The Wealth of Nations* (I), translated by Yang Jingnian. Xi'an: Shaanxi People's Publishing House, 10.
13 Smith, A. (2001). *The Wealth of Nations* (I), translated by Yang Jingnian. Xi'an: Shaanxi People's Publishing House, 18.
14 Smith, A. (2001). *The Wealth of Nations* (I), translated by Yang Jingnian. Xi'an: Shaanxi People's Publishing House, 18.
15 Smith, A. (2001). *The Wealth of Nations* (II), translated by Yang Jingnian. Xi'an: Shaanxi People's Publishing House, 753.
16 *David Ricardo: On the Principles of Political Economy and Taxation*, translated by Guo Dali and Wang Yanan. Beijing: The Commercial Press, 1983, 232.
17 *David Ricardo: On the Principles of Political Economy and Taxation*, translated by Guo Dali and Wang Yanan. Beijing: The Commercial Press, 1983, 233.
18 Marx & Engels. (2012). *Selected Works*. Vol. 2. Beijing: People's Publishing House, 716.
19 Obviously, the "supply" mentioned here refers to the AS of one of the two groups of forces (supply and demand) that determine the aggregate output (national income, which Adam Smith called wealth), not the supply of one of the two groups of forces (supply and demand) that determine the price of goods; the former is a macroeconomic concept, while the latter is a microeconomic concept.
20 Keynes, J. M. (1999). *The General Theory of Employment Interest and Money*, retranslated by Gao Hongye, Beijing: The Commercial Press, 37.

21 Keynes, J. M. (1999). *The General Theory of Employment Interest and Money*, retranslated by Gao Hongye. Beijing: The Commercial Press, 23. It should be pointed out that Keynes' "classical economics" refers to the mainstream western economics in the period from Ricardo to Marshall and Pigou, which is different from the classical economics defined by Marx.
22 See Section IV of this chapter.
23 Economists tend to use the concept of "production" in three meanings: first, the production process, i.e., the process of input of factors or resources to the output of a product; second, the production capacity; and third, the result of production. The latter two meanings of production are what macroeconomics calls "potential aggregate output" and "actual aggregate output", which can be understood as "supply".
24 Say. (1963). *A Treatise on Political Economy*, translated by Chen Fusheng and Chen Zhenhua. Beijing: The Commercial Press, 144.
25 Say. (1963). *A Treatise on Political Economy,* translated by Chen Fusheng and Chen Zhenhua. Beijing: The Commercial Press, 144.
26 Say. (1963). *A Treatise on Political Economy,* translated by Chen Fusheng and Chen Zhenhua. Beijing: The Commercial Press, 147.
27 Keynes, J. M. (1999). *The General Theory of Employment Interest and Money*, retranslated by Gao Hongye. Beijing: The Commercial Press, 31.
28 Marx believed that Say's idea of "buying and selling must be balanced" was copied from another British classical economist, James Mull. See the *History of Economic Doctrine* (Revised Edition), by Lu Youzhang and Li Zongzheng. Beijing: China Renmin University Press, 2013, 200.
29 Say. (1963). *A Treatise on Political Economy*, translated by Chen Fusheng and Chen Zhenhua. Beijing: The Commercial Press, 142.
30 Say. (1963). *A Treatise on Political Economy*, translated by Chen Fusheng and Chen Zhenhua. Beijing: The Commercial Press, 145.
31 Say. (1963). *A Treatise on Political Economy*, translated by Chen Fusheng and Chen Zhenhua. Beijing: The Commercial Press, 145.
32 Say. (1963). *A Treatise on Political Economy*, translated by Chen Fusheng and Chen Zhenhua. Beijing: The Commercial Press, 149.
33 Marx & Engels. (2001). *Collected Works*. Vol. 44. Beijing: People's Publishing House, 136.
34 Keynes, J. M. (1999). *The General Theory of Employment Interest and Money*, retranslated by Gao Hongye. Beijing: The Commercial Press, 32.
35 Marx believed that in social reproduction, production determines distribution, exchange, and consumption, and production creates and produces consumption. The "production" here can be understood as "supply", the "consumption" can be understood as "demand", and the "reproduction" obviously refers to the long-term production process based on the expansion of reproduction. Keynesianism and New Keynesianism claim that "demand creates its own supply", but they admit that this is the conclusion of short-term analysis, and that in the long run it is supply that plays the decisive role. It is only that Keynes himself was not concerned with the long-term problem. Keynes famously said: "In the long run, we are all dead".
36 Xi Jinping's Speech at the 11th Meeting of the Central Leading Group on Financial and Economic Affairs on November 10, 2015, *People's Daily*, November 11, 2015 (1).
37 Marx & Engels. (1974). *Collected Works*. Vol. 26 (II). Beijing: People's Publishing House, 598.
38 This model was proposed by Roy F. Harrod and Evsey Domar independently proposed in 1939 and 1946 respectively.
39 Marx & Engels. (2001). *Selected Works*. Vol. 2. Beijing: People's Publishing House, 218.
40 Marx & Engels. (2001). *Selected Works*. Vol. 2. Beijing: People's Publishing House, 782–783.
41 Marx & Engels. (2001). *Selected Works*. Vol. 2. Beijing: People's Publishing House, 272.

42 Marx & Engels. (2001). *Selected Works*. Vol. 2. Beijing: People's Publishing House, 699.
43 Marx & Engels. (2001). *Selected Works*. Vol. 2. Beijing: People's Publishing House, 691.
44 The author believes that Marx's "production" here refers to the result of production, because it is only the result of production that "provides objects for consumption", so the "production" here can also be understood as "supply". Marx's "consumption" includes both production consumption and living consumption, and these two types of consumption together are what macroeconomics calls AD.
45 Marx & Engels. (1995). *Collected Works*. Vol. 30. Beijing: People's Publishing House, 37.
46 According to Marx, "the distribution of the instruments of production and the distribution of the members of society among the various types of production" is itself a social and economic system. But "the distribution of the instruments of production and the distribution of the members of society among the various types of production" obviously also has the meaning of "the allocation of resources (factors of production)".
47 Marx & Engels. (1974). *Collected Works*. Vol. 26 (I). Beijing: People's Publishing House, 308–309.
48 Marx & Engels. (2001). *Selected Works*. Vol. 2. Beijing: People's Publishing House, 485.
49 Marx & Engels. (2001). *Selected Works*. Vol. 2. Beijing: People's Publishing House, 480–481.
50 Marx & Engels. (2003). *Collected Works*. Vol 46. Beijing: People's Publishing House, 717.
51 Marx & Engels. (1974). *Collected Works*. Vol. 26 (I). Beijing: People's Publishing House, 234–235.
52 Marx & Engels. (1974). *Collected Works*. Vol. 26 (II). Beijing: People's Publishing House, 129.
53 Marx & Engels. (1974). *Collected Works*. Vol. 26 (II). Beijing: People's Publishing House, 602.
54 Marx & Engels. (1974). *Collected Works*. Vol. 26 (II). Beijing: People's Publishing House, 603.
55 Marx & Engels. (1974). *Collected Works*. Vol 26 (III). Beijing: People's Publishing House, 126.
56 *Selected Papers on Modern Foreign Economics* (17), compiled by The Commercial Press. Beijing: The Commercial Press, 1997, 16.
57 Gilder, G. (1985). *Wealth and Poverty*, translated by Chu Yukun et al. Shanghai: Shanghai Translation Publishing House, 45.
58 Roberts, P. C. (1997). *The Bankruptcy of Keynesian Model*, in the Selected Papers on Modern Foreign Economics (17) compiled by The Commercial Press. Beijing: The Commercial Press, 2.
59 Gilder, G. (1997). *Supply-side Economics*, in the Selected Papers on Modern Foreign Economics (17), complied by The Commercial Press. Beijing: The Commercial Press, 29.
60 Ture, N. (1997). *The Economic Effects of Tax Changes: A Neoclassical Analysis*, in the Selected Papers on Modern Foreign Economics (17) compiled by The Commercial Press. Beijing: The Commercial Press, 61.
61 *Selected Papers on Modern Foreign Economics* (17), compiled by The Commercial Press. Beijing: The Commercial Press, 1997, 21.
62 Gilder, G. (1997). *Supply-side Economics*, in the Selected Papers on Modern Foreign Economics (17), complied by The Commercial Press. Beijing: The Commercial Press, 21.
63 Gilder, G. (1997). *Supply-side Economics*, in the Selected Papers on Modern Foreign Economics (17), complied by The Commercial Press. Beijing: The Commercial Press, 30.
64 Monthly Review Editorial Office. (1984). *Comments on Supply Economics*, in the Selected Papers on Modern Foreign Economics (5) compiled by The Commercial Press. Beijing: The Commercial Press, 135.
65 Hailstones, T. J. (1982). *A Guide to Supply-side Economics*. Richmond, VA: Robert F. Dame, 3.

66 Quote from Hazlitt, T. W. (1997). *The Weakness of the Supply-side School: Criticism from the Austrian School*, in the Selected Papers on Modern Foreign Economics (17), compiled by The Commercial Press. Beijing: The Commercial Press, 113–114.

67 The "five transformations" include the transformation of economic pattern from "supply shortage" to "insufficient demand", the transformation of production mode from labor-intensive to capital-technology-knowledge intensive, the transformation of industrial structure from "secondary, tertiary and primary industries" to "tertiary, secondary and primary industries", the transformation of development driving force from investment to technology and innovation, and the transformation of economic system from "semi market economy" to "full market economy". Fang Fuqian. "China's Economy is Undergoing Five Transformations". *People's Tribune*, 2015.

11 Dual path of supply-side structural reform

Market-oriented reform and government reform

Since the Central Economic Work Conference in December 2009, which emphasized the need to "strengthen the economic structural adjustment and improve the quality and efficiency of economic development", "economic structural adjustment" has become a widely discussed topic and a hot topic in academic circles. Since Comrade Xi Jinping proposed the "supply-side structural reform" in November 2015, "supply-side structural reform" has become a hot topic instead of "economic structural adjustment". The basic problem to be solved by "supply-side structural reform" and "economic structural adjustment" is the same, that is, the imbalance of economic structure or unreasonable economic structure. However, "supply-side structural reform" is not only economic structural adjustment, but also a new round of reform and a revolution in the systems and mechanisms. If "adjustment" is to give China's economy "plastic surgery", then "reform" is to make a thoroughgoing change of China's economy; "adjustment" is mainly to repair and straighten out the imbalanced relationship in the economy, while "reform" is to further operate on the causes of the imbalanced economic relationship (system) on the basis of repair and straightening, and to transform and upgrade the economic structure. Therefore, compared with "economic structural adjustment", "supply-side structural reform" is a broader, deeper and stronger reform project.

In the discussion of supply-side structural reform in recent years, there seems to be a bias in Chinese academia: there are more discussions on the supply-side structural reform at the policy and operational levels, and less on it at the theoretical and institutional levels. Most of the articles that talk about "how" to carry out supply-side structural reform from the policy and operational levels advocate that the government should implement a policy of maintaining pressure and a differentiated industrial policy to adjust the focus and direction of government investment, and implement the "cutting overcapacity, reducing excess inventory, deleveraging, lowering costs, and strengthening areas of weakness" through administrative means or even by the operation of law. In short, they ask the government to do this and that, as if the structural adjustment and the implementation of supply-side structural reform are the government's business. The author believes that structural adjustment and supply-side structural reform cannot rely solely on the government; relying only on the government to implement measures

DOI: 10.4324/9781003367000-15

such as maintaining pressure and "cutting overcapacity, reducing excess inventory, deleveraging, lowering costs, and strengthening areas of weakness" cannot solve the root cause of the economic structural imbalance; the government's "visible hand" can solve some economic structural imbalance problems in the short run, for example, eliminate the excess inventory and excess capacity of some products through the government's top-down decomposition of indicators, so as to restore the balance between supply and demand of these product. However, supply-side structural reform and economic structural transformation and upgrading is a long-term and dynamic process, not just a problem of "cutting overcapacity, reducing excess inventory, deleveraging, lowering costs, and strengthening areas of weakness". How to solve the cyclical imbalance of China's economic structure, how to establish a long-term mechanism for economic structural adjustment, optimization, and upgrading, and how to make China's economy enter the track of a stable, medium or high-speed, and sustainable development are the key and main purpose of the supply-side structural reform. The author's basic view is that the core or key of the supply-side structural reform is to deal with the relationship between the government and the market, and truly implement the "decisive role of the market in the allocation of resources and better play the role of the government". To deal with the relationship between the government and the market, the supply-side structural reform should choose a dual path: on the one hand, further promote market-oriented reform and continuously improve the market-oriented degree of China's economy; on the other hand, accelerate government reform and promote government transformation.

I. Why should supply-side structural reform choose a dual path

Why should the supply-side structural reform of China's economy choose such a dual path of market-oriented reform and government reform? There are at least three reasons for this. The first reason can be found from the historical causes of China's unreasonable economic structure, the second reason can be analyzed from the impact of the two rounds of expanding domestic demand on economic structure in 1998 and 2008, and the third reason can be understood from the functions of the market mechanism.

First, we will analyze the historical causes of China's unreasonable economic structure.

At the beginning of liberation, New China was an agricultural country with an economic structure dominated by the traditional agriculture, had no independent and complete industrial system, and had a rather backward service industry. In 1952, the proportion of primary, secondary, and tertiary industries in China's GDP structure was 50.5:20.9:28.6,[1] and agriculture accounted for almost half of the national economy, resulting in a very unreasonable economic structure. It can be seen that the problem of China's economic structure was born with New China and is a historical problem. Therefore, soon after the establishment of New China and after the initial completion of the "one industrialization and three transformations", the economic structural reform and adjustment have been put on the important agenda of CPC and the government. This was the first large-scale economic structural adjustment of the People's Republic of China. In April 1956, Comrade Mao Zedong published "On the Ten Major Relationships". From this article, we can see that at that time, although the People's Republic of China had only been founded for a few years, there was already a large structural imbalance in the economy. The ten relationships mentioned in his article include: (1) the relationship between heavy industry on the one hand and light industry and agriculture on the other; (2) the relationship between industry in the coastal regions and industry in the interior; (3) the relationship between economic construction and defense construction; (4) the relationship between the state, the units of production, and the producers; (5) the relationship between the central and the local authorities; (6) the relationship between the Han nationality and the minority nationalities; (7) the relationship between Party and Non-Party; (8) the relationship between revolution and counter-revolution; (9) the relationship between right and wrong; and (10) the relationship between China and other countries. Among them, except for the three relationships listed in Items 7, 8, and 9, the other seven relationships are involved with the issue of economic structure as we discussed here. So as early as 1956, the Party Central Committee and Comrade Mao Zedong already attached great importance to the issue of economic structure and proceeded to make adjustments. It can also be seen that more than 60 years have passed since then, but we have not yet solved well the many economic structure problems that Comrade Mao Zedong raised in 1956. If the economic structure problems we faced in 1956 were left to us by the Old China, the unreasonable economic structure at that time was caused by historical reasons; and we had not enough time to solve such problems shortly after the founding of the New China—so, after so many years, why are there still so many problems with China's economic structure? Of course, such problems today are very different in content and nature from those of the 1950s. For example, the structure of China's economy in the 1950s was agricultural industry, heavy industry, and light industry, with the secondary and tertiary industries weak and backward; from 1970, the proportion of the secondary industry steadily exceeded that of the primary industry, with the proportions of the primary and secondary industries being 34.8% and 40.3%, respectively, in that year, and the proportion of the secondary industry has continued to rise since then;[2] and from 1985, the proportion of the tertiary industry began to exceed that of the primary industry, and since 2010, the proportion of the tertiary industry has exceeded that of the secondary industry (see Figure 7.3). The change in the structure of the three industries marks the development of China from an agricultural country to an industrialized and modernized economy. However, it goes without saying that most of the economic structure problems we face today are still those mentioned in "On the Ten Major Relationships". This calls for a serious rethinking.

The second large-scale economic structural adjustment after the founding of the People's Republic of China occurred from 1961 to 1965 after the three years of natural disasters. The natural disasters combined with man-made disasters at that time not only caused serious setbacks in economic development, but also led to serious structural imbalances in the economy. In 1961 and 1962, China's GDP and per capita GDP decreased in absolute terms compared with the previous year in turn, and the GDP and per capita GDP in 1964 had not yet recovered to the level in 1960 (see Table 11.1). This round of economic structural imbalance was characterized mainly by the high output, low quality, and low efficiency of industry produced by the "Great Leap Forward" in industry (for example, much of the iron and steel made during the Nationwide Large-scale Steelmaking Movement was unusable), the withering of agriculture and the sharp decline of grain production due to the widespread natural disasters, and the quantitative and structural imbalances between AD and AS caused by the boastfulness, arbitrary guidelines, and foolhardy acts of local governments. Under such a serious economic situation, the Chinese government had to make an economic adjustment. The main goal of this round of economic structural adjustment was to restore production and recover the economy.

At the beginning of reform and opening up, that is, in April 1979, the Party Central Committee put forward the policy of "adjustment, reform, rectification and improvement", and began the first round of large-scale economic structural adjustment after the reform and opening up. This round of economic structural adjustment aimed mainly at the stagnation of economic development and the imbalance of economic structure caused by the ten-year "Cultural Revolution".

In the 10th year of reform and opening up, that is, in September 1988, in response to the economic chaos, overheated investment, repeated construction, and worsening inflation, the Party Central Committee and the State Council put forward the policy of governance, rectification, and comprehensive and in-depth reform, and began the second large-scale economic structural adjustment after the reform and opening up. The period of this adjustment was roughly from 1988 to 1991.

The third large-scale economic structural adjustment after the reform and opening up began in 1998. This round of economic structural adjustment began in the textile industry by "limiting production and reducing spindles", with the aim of eliminating excess capacity in some traditional industries.

Table 11.1 China's GDP (1960–1965)

Year	*GNI*	*GDP*	*Per capita GDP (RMB/person)*
1960	1457.0	1457.0	218
1961	1220.0	1220.0	185
1962	1149.3	1149.3	173
1963	1233.3	1233.3	181
1964	1454.0	1454.0	208

The data in the Table are calculated according to the prices of the current year. Unit: RMB 100,000,000

Source: *A Compilation of 55 Years of Statistical Data of New China*. Beijing: China Statistics Press, 2005:9.

Starting from 2009, we have entered another period of large-scale economic structural adjustment for the fourth time since the reform and opening up. The background of this round of economic structural adjustment was that under the impact of the 2008 international financial crisis, the growth of domestic and external demand in China's economy slumped sharply, the economic growth rate dropped sharply, and China's GDP grew only 6.1% in the first quarter of 2009, highlighting the contradictions of economic structural imbalance. The 2009 Central Economic Work Conference proposed that it was urgent to change the mode of economic development, and we should focus on expanding domestic demand, especially increasing consumer demand, and based on promoting steadily urbanization, optimize the industrial structure, make significant progress in economic restructuring, and promote the optimization of the economic structure and enhance the pulling power of economic development by protecting and improving people's livelihood.

On November 10, 2015, General Secretary Xi Jinping proposed "strengthening supply-side structural reform" at the 11th meeting of the Central Leading Group on Financial and Economic Affairs, marking China's fifth large-scale economic structural reform and adjustment since the reform and opening up.

In the nearly 40 years since the reform and opening up, China has made five nationwide large-scale economic structural adjustments; plus the two nationwide large-scale economic structural adjustments before the reform and opening up, China has made a total of seven rounds of major economic structural adjustment since the founding of the People's Republic of China. It is not difficult to find that China's economic structural adjustment has a certain regularity, roughly once every 10 years on average. This suggests that structural imbalances in China's economy recur cyclically. It should also be noted that there have been some localized small-scale structural adjustments in each period of 10 years. Why is China's economic structure repeatedly, even cyclically, out of balance? Why have some economic structural problems remained unresolved for decades? Why do structural imbalances in China's economy seem to have become a chronic disease of China's economy? There are many things that need to be studied, and some of them are worthy of our deep thinking.

Economic structure, whether it is the structure of AD and AS, industrial structure, regional economic structure, or urban-rural economic structure, is a dynamic concept and it is always changing and evolving. Changes in technology, population, demand, systems, policies, and other factors will make some aspects of the economic structure change (for example, the Internet revolution has given rise to the information industry), while causing the fixed telephone, telegraph, postal, newspaper publishing, and printing industries to shrink. The influx of rural populations into cities has caused a lack of supply of public infrastructure such as urban housing, education, and health care, thus unbalancing the economic structure. Therefore, in a general sense, economic structural imbalance often occurs; it is a necessary stage or inseparable link of economic development, and an inevitable phenomenon in the process of economic development. This is just like a person who will have different physical discomfort or problems at different ages in the process of growing up. The rebalancing of an imbalanced economic structure is not a simple return to the original economic structure, but the optimization and upgrading of the original economic structure through economic structural adjustment, and the economic development will enter a new stage and new platform. Therefore, the imbalance and adjustment of economic structure to a new balance is the upgrading process of economic structure. Because of this, from the perspective of long-term development, the nature and content of each economic structural imbalance should be different rather than simply repetitive. If the economic structure repeatedly has similar imbalances, such as overheated investment, duplicated investment, and inefficient investment, some structural imbalances cannot be solved for a long time, such as the long-term supply shortage before China's reform and opening up and the long-term excess capacity in many industries in the manufacturing industry since the 21st century; then it obviously cannot be considered as a normal phenomenon in the process of economic development, but an economic disease.

For China's long-term unreasonable economic structure with the repeated occurrence of structural imbalances that require adjustment once every 10 years or so throughout the history of the economic development of the People's Republic of China, there are certainly historical and external reasons (such as the three-year natural disasters, the deterioration of China's relations with the Soviet Union, the impact of the international financial crisis), but the main reason is rooted in our economic system.

The first system reason is the influence and legacy of the planned-economy system. In the past, we have been practicing a highly centralized planned-economy system, in which the government controls and allocates resources and determines the scale, structure, and development speed of the economy; the market mechanism plays little role in resource allocation and economic structural adjustment. Although the traditional political economy theory tells us that capitalist commodity production is anarchic and the periodic outbreak of economic crisis of excess production is the inevitable companion of the capitalist economy, while the socialist planned economy is superior in that it can achieve "planned and proportional" development of the national economy, and thus the socialist economy will not suffer from economic structural imbalance and the economic crisis of excess production, but in fact, planned economy can achieve "planned" development, while it is difficult to achieve "proportional" development, because the various proportional relationships in the economy are determined by the needs of producers and consumers, and by the technical conditions and technical relationships, and these proportional relationships are dynamic and constantly changing; ultimately, these proportional relationships are determined by the behavior of countless consumers and producers, and are the result of their voluntary choices. Therefore, in order to achieve "proportional" economic development, the planner must know the needs and demands of consumers and producers, including the quantity and structure of demand, effective demand, and potential needs. However, under the planned-economy system, there is no mechanism to indicate these demands, and no signal or information may be provided to the planner in this regard. Therefore, the planner's attempt to achieve "proportionality" is tantamount to making an overall judgment on the basis of one-sided viewpoint. Since the planners do not have access to sufficient, timely, and dynamic demand information, the planned-economy system cannot achieve "proportional" production and resource allocation. Without the necessary demand information, planners can only allocate resources and determine the "content of production" and the "quantity of production" based on experience, exploration, and the economic goals they want to achieve. This will inevitably lead to a disconnect between production and consumption, and a mismatch between supply and demand. In addition, a planner is not an entrepreneur or an economic person, and does not need to make decisions and choices or determine the "content of production" and the "quantity of production" according to the principle of profit maximization or cost minimization. This will inevitably lead to resource misallocation, resource waste, and low economic efficiency. Thus, when the economic disproportion and economic structural imbalance accumulate to a certain extent and the economy can not run normally, a government-led national economic structure adjustment will have to be made every few years. Today's excess capacity and economic structural imbalance are still closely related to the influence and residue of the planned-economy system. From the point of view of the path dependence of the system, today's structural imbalance in China still has the historical reasons of the old system (planned-economy system). Although we have started the transition to a socialist market economic system since the mid-1990s, the transition is still far from complete and the influence of the planned-economy system is still present, but the degree of such influence is weakening.

The second system reason is the performance appraisal system of local governments and their principal officials, as discussed in Chapter 4 of this monograph. The behavior of Chinese local governments (officials) at the present stage is driven by dual incentives: on the one hand, it is the political incentive for official career promotion; on the other hand, it is the economic incentive for more local tax revenue to control more resources; the system for evaluating officials' political achievements integrates these two incentives for mutual reinforcement. In addition, many local government officials have a sense of mission and responsibility, which has created a strong driving force for local governments to promote economic development.

Since each local government plans GDP growth, local tax revenue growth, and foreign investment introduction growth from local or their own reality and interests, it is impossible for the whole country to consider economic structure issues, major proportional issues, and moderate growth issues in economic development in a holistic manner; as local government officials, they have no need to consider the whole national economic structure and proportional relationship coordination, and objectively, they do not have enough information to consider these issues, so this double incentive mechanism, coupled with our long-standing catch-up strategy, has over time resulted in the distortion of the proportional relations in the national economy, the imbalance of the economic structure, and the persistence of the following ten phenomena in economic and social life: "emphasis on production over life", "emphasis on accumulation over consumption", "emphasis on products over services", "emphasis on short-term over long-term ", "emphasis on construction over utilization", "emphasis on investment over effect", "emphasis on quantity over quality", "emphasis on speed over efficiency", "emphasis on aggregate over structure", and "emphasis on economy over people's livelihood". These imbalances are not only the manifestations of China's economic structural imbalance, but also the causes of China's economic structural imbalance. The main responsibility given to local governments for economic development and the main role of local governments in controlling and allocating resources are the system root of these imbalances.

Second, let's look at the impact of the two rounds of expanding domestic demand in 1998 and 2008 on the economic structure.

In 1998, in response to the negative impact of the Asian financial crisis on China's economy, China introduced an active fiscal policy to expand domestic demand. This policy has played a very positive role in stabilizing economic growth, increasing employment, and avoiding a further decline in the economy, and has also achieved very obvious results. However, we should also see that the implementation of this round of active fiscal policy to expand domestic demand has also produced a lot of economic structural problems. To sum up, there are at least the following four structural problems: First, heavy industry was once again growing at a high rate, and its proportion in the industrial structure has rebounded significantly. In 1990, the proportion of light and heavy industries in China was roughly equal, each accounting for 50%. Since 1999, heavy industry has shown a rapid growth momentum, and industrial growth has once again formed a pattern dominated by heavy industry. After 2002, the proportion of heavy industry in industrial added value rose rapidly, from 62.6% in 2002 to 69.0% in 2005, while light industry fell from 37.4% in 2002 to 31.0% in 2005. The proportion gap between the light industry and heavy industry has widened significantly, and the trend of heavy industrialization has become increasingly significant. Second, repeated construction and structural assimilation. In order to expand domestic demand, most provinces (municipalities directly under the Central Government and autonomous regions) throughout the country focused on investment and development of industries such as automotive, electronics, machinery, chemical, and construction industries as pillar industries, and among them, 22 provinces (municipalities directly under the Central Government and autonomous regions) took the automotive industry as a pillar industry, and the vast majority of provinces were producing complete vehicles. Third, structural imbalance and disproportion. There are two aspects of data here to illustrate the problems. One aspect of the data is that, according to the survey conducted by the Ministry of Commerce on the supply and demand of 600 major consumer goods, the proportion of oversupply of these goods in the first and second half of 1998 was 25.8% and 33.8% respectively, while in 2003 this proportion rose to 85.5% and 84.8% respectively. In other words, the result of expanding domestic demand is that the imbalance between supply and demand in China's domestic market has not been eased, but has become more serious. Another aspect of the data is that from 1998 to 2004, China's investment rate rose from 36.2% to 43.2%, while the consumption rate fell from 59.6% to 54.3%. The proportion of resident consumption in final consumption fell from 76.0% in 1998 to 73.4% in 2004; the proportion of government consumption rose from 24.0% to 26.6% over the same period. This indicates that in China's AD structure, the ratio of consumption to investment and the ratio of resident consumption to government consumption have become more unreasonable. Fourth, the economy is overheating. As a result of the continuous expansion of investment, the resulting AD was not fully absorbed by the increase in employment and GDP growth, the economy became overheated, and deflation turned into inflation. Starting from September 2003, the central government began to cool down the overheated economy and make structural adjustment.

Let's look at the impact of expanding domestic demand on economic structure in 2008. The main elements of this round of expanding domestic demand were the RMB 4 trillion economic stimulus plan, the Ten Plans for Expanding Domestic Demand and the Plan for Invigorating Ten Key Industries, together with the loose fiscal and monetary policies, this policy package did play a very good role in "maintaining growth and stabilizing employment", and China's economy soon resumed high growth after a short decline. However, this round of expanding domestic demand has also brought some negative effects on the economic structure. These negative effects mainly include the following: First, it intensified the imbalance between investment and consumption. In 2009, the total investment in fixed assets increased by 30.1% over the previous year, while total retail sales of consumer goods increased by only 15.5%, with the contribution of investment and consumption to economic growth being 8% and 4.6% respectively. It can be seen that China's economic recovery and economic growth since the outbreak of the international financial crisis have been mainly driven by investment. Second, it resulted in a new excess capacity. The excess capacity that began to appear in 2009 existed not only in the traditional industries such as steel and cement, but also in some new industries, such as wind power equipment, polysilicon, etc. In the first half of 2009, the output of China's wind power equipment increased by 545.5% year-on-year. At that time, the capacity of domestic polysilicon projects under construction or proposed was up to 140,000 tons, while the global demand for polysilicon was expected to be only about 80,000 tons in 2010—the production capacity greatly exceeded the demand. Third, the virtual economy bubble expanded. Due to system reasons and inadequate supervision, a vast amount of the RMB 4 trillion investment did not really enter the real economy, but flowed into the virtual economy, thus causing the falsely high prices in the securities market and the real estate market, especially housing prices, to rise at a faster speed after a brief decline in 2008.

The two rounds of expanding domestic demand in 1998 and 2008 were both led by the government, which intervened heavily in the economy. As a result, economic growth has been boosted and employment has been saved, but it has also brought many sequelae, especially the problem of economic structural imbalance and weakened economic growth momentum.

Finally, from the function of the market mechanism, why should the economic structural adjustment and optimization take the path of market-oriented reform?

As we saw through Chapter 4 of this monograph, in a mature market economy, the market (price) mechanism mainly has four functions: (1) Conveying information—to convey information about preferences, resource availability, and production possibilities via prices. (2) Providing incentives—to get people to adopt the lowest cost production methods and to use the available resources for the highest value purposes. (3) Distributing income—to decide who gets what and how much. Price provides incentives to people only because it is used to distribute income; people's income is linked to their contribution, which naturally motivates people to pay attention to the message conveyed by price, and motivates people to work hard to reduce costs. (4) Automatic removal and self-rehabilitation.

These functions of the market price mechanism have now been generally recognized, and this knowledge of microeconomics is now widespread. One of the reasons why we are changing from a highly centralized planned-economy system to a socialist market economic system is that the price mechanism has these functions and advantages.

The automatic removal function of the market mechanism means that the market mechanism has the function of removing excess capacity, backward products, backward technology, and backward enterprises; the self-rehabilitation function of the market mechanism means that when the various proportional relationships in the economy are out of balance, after a period of economic self-adjustment, these proportional relationships can gradually become reasonable and achieve a new balance; and the declined or recessed economic growth may automatically rebound and recover after a period of self-rehabilitation. This function of automatic removal and self-rehabilitation is mainly realized through the competitive mechanism of selecting the superior and eliminating the inferior and the interest mechanism of the economic parties to pursue the maximization of their own interests. This function of market mechanism is not only the function of spontaneous adjustment and automatic optimization of economic structure, but also the function of self-stabilization of economic fluctuations.

Today, we should understand economic crises or economic fluctuations under the market economy in a dialectical way.[3] On the one hand, every economic crisis or economic fluctuation will lead to the suspension or interruption of economic growth, the destruction of productivity, the destruction of some products, wealth, and production capacity, the bankruptcy and closure of some enterprises, and the unemployment of some or even thousands of workers; but on the other hand, the process of economic fluctuation or economic crisis is also the process of automatically removing excess products and excess capacity, the process of eliminating low-quality products, backward technology, and backward enterprises, and reshuffling various kinds of markets and economic structures. Therefore, if we say that the economic crisis destroys productivity, it mainly destroys backward productivity; if we say that it destroys production capacity, it mainly destroys backward production capacity. Therefore, we cannot regard economic crisis or economic fluctuation as an absolutely bad thing. Looking at the history of economic fluctuations in the past 200 years, we can see that after each economic crisis or economic fluctuation, there will be new changes in the economic structure, some new technologies, new products, new enterprises, and new industries appear in the economic life, while others gradually disappear; after each economic crisis or economic fluctuation, there is a period of economic recovery and prosperity. The market economy is evolving in this kind of fluctuations. Subjectively, we humans always expect the economy to develop smoothly or steadily, but objectively, economic fluctuations are inevitable. What we want to avoid is only large-scale economic fluctuations like those in the 1930s and 2008. Such fluctuations and crises often destroy the backward capacity together with the advanced capacity at that time.

From the perspective of theoretical analysis and practical experience, we can make this preliminary judgment: in terms of aggregate adjustment, the strength and efficiency of the market mechanism are not as good as the government regulation; in terms of structural adjustment, government intervention is usually lagging, passive, inaccurate, and difficult to put in place; from China's practical experience, the structural adjustment is often beyond the range if made by the government; while market adjustment may be made in a timely and appropriate manner, at any time and any place, and may be identified automatically. Which is better, government regulation or market regulation? We should discuss it separately according to the aggregate and structure, and treat it differently. The "visible hand" of the government has its advantages, while the "invisible hand" of the market also has its advantages. However, from the perspective of resource allocation and economic structural adjustment, the market mechanism has more advantages than government intervention.

II. How to promote marketization and government transformation

If the construction period of China's socialist market economic system is counted from the time when the Decision on Several Issues concerning the Establishment of a Socialist Market Economic System adopted at the Third Plenary Session of the 14th CPC Central Committee in November 1993, it is less than 30 years. The construction of a new system cannot be completed in just 30 years. China's socialist market economy system is still in the process of construction, still in the primary stage of construction, and is only a "semi-market economy". In the current semi-market economy, the market system and market mechanism are still in the process of growth and development; the market mechanism is still weak with insufficient strength of regulation, and cannot really play a decisive role in the allocation of resources and a leading role in the economic structural adjustment. The process of marketization of China's economy is still far from being in place, and we still need to further deepen the reform of the economic system and further promote marketization. The purpose of further marketization is to cultivate and improve the market system and market mechanism, and give full play to the function of market mechanism in allocating resources and adjusting the structure. In terms of the need for economic structural adjustment, the main contents of further marketization include at least the following: (1) full marketization of prices—prices truly reflect the degree of scarcity of resources, prices are determined by supply and demand rather than by an institution (such as price bureau), prices are determined by competitive forces rather than by monopolistic forces, and prices are elastic rather than rigid. (2) Free resource flow—resources (including labor) can flow freely between different industries, markets, and regions, and talents can move freely in the vertical direction. (3) Free access to markets—except for some special industries (markets) involving state secrets and military security, access to other markets should be barrier-free. At present, the marketization of prices in China's economy is not enough, for example, the prices of some of our resource-based products, agricultural and sideline products, and the prices of some labor (wages) do not fully reflect the relationship between supply and demand, and the degree of scarcity; China's interest rates are not yet fully marketized, and government control factors still play a great role in determining and adjusting the interest rate; China's current financial (capital) is not yet a financial market in the regulated or standard market economy, and cannot give full play to its function of resource allocation perfectly. In terms of free flow resources, there are still many restrictions and obstacles in China, and the freedom of resource flow between regions and industries is not high; the labor flow between urban and rural areas especially is still restricted by the household registration system (the reform of this system has just begun), social security system, children's school enrollment, and eligibility for house purchase, etc. Although our current resource flow is much freer than that under the planned-economy system, there are still some gaps compared with the requirements of the development of market economy. The free access to markets is linked to the free flow of resources. Only by lowering the threshold of market access and abolishing those unnecessary and artificially set market access conditions can we improve the degree of the free flow of resources. The degree of the free access to markets and the free flow of resources is positively related to the degree of competition in the market economy. And the degree of market competition is in turn positively related to the efficiency of resource allocation.

The direction of China's system reform and the construction of a socialist market economy is to "enable the market to play a decisive role in the allocation of resources and give better play to the role of the government". To achieve this reform orientation, we must further promote government reform and government transformation in the process of furthering market-oriented reform, and deepen the reform of our current government management system and government governance style. In other words, to establish a long-term mechanism for economic structural adjustment and optimization, on the one hand, we must further promote marketization; on the other hand, corresponding reforms and adjustments should be made to the status, functions, and role of our government in economic operation. Without the reform and transformation of the government system and government functions, marketization will not be realized appropriately, and the market mechanism will not be able to give full play to its decisive role in in resource allocation and economic structural adjustment.

The goal of government reform and government transformation is to transform the government under the planned-economy system into a government that is compatible with the socialist market economy system. To achieve this goal, China's government functions shall complete the following three transformations: (1) from a production-based government to a service-based government; (2) from an all-encompassing government to a limited government; and (3) from a government with unlimited power to a constitutional government.

At present, the Chinese government still undertakes too many production tasks and command and direction functions of economic activities. To put it simply, the transformation from a production-oriented government to a service-oriented government is to free the government from undertaking a large number of productive tasks and production commands and to switch to providing services for the production and business activities of individuals and enterprises. More normatively, a service-oriented government can be defined as one in which all organizations and officials at all levels of government are engaged in administration under the law and other system rules, providing services for the reasonable and lawful activities of citizens and for the creation of a fair and just competitive environment. This kind of service-oriented government is a rule-based government rather than a person-based government. A service-oriented government should include at least some of the following elements: (1) There is a clear division of powers and responsibilities of all levels of government and officials at all levels. (2) There is a set of standardized and scientific administrative rules and decision-making procedures. (3) Government departments and their officials provide public services rather than for-profit services. (4) If the market is compared to a sports field, government departments and their officials are only referees and attendants, and should not act as athletes. (5) Documents, files, and other records (such as statistics) are systematic, authentic, and well preserved, and they should be publicly available and accessible, except where confidentiality requires. (6) The work or services of the government and its officials should be sunny, transparent, and supervised, except for those involving national security and secrecy.

Government in a market economy differs from government in a planned economy in that the former is service-oriented, while the latter is command-oriented—the government directly issues planning indicators enterprises, gives orders to individuals and enterprises on what they should do and what they should not do, and decides what to produce, how to produce, and for whom to produce. The service-oriented government is the judge and protector of market rules; it only stipulates what enterprises and individuals should not do—i.e., it will formulate a negative list, but will not order them to do anything; and the question of what to produce, how to produce, and for whom to produce is mainly solved by the market or economic entities themselves.

The so-called limited government means that the scope of government acts is limited to protecting the rule of law, maintaining fairness, promulgating rules, making plans, supervising management, and serving citizens, etc. The scope of acts and activities of limited government is limited, not all-inclusive and indiscriminate, so the scale of government budget and expenditure is also limited;

except for special circumstances, government revenue and expenditure should be balanced.

Limited government is different from the minimal government or the weakest government advocated by extreme liberals; the latter type of government only assumes the function of "night watchman".[4] We believe that even in the most developed modern market economy countries, the market cannot automatically solve the problem of unequal distribution of income and wealth, nor can it solve the problem of inadequate supply of public goods through the market mechanism, nor can it overcome the problem of market failure, nor can it rely on the market mechanism to solve the problem of market regulation; therefore, the idea of the weakest government is unrealistic. If, considering that in the era of globalization, the international coordination function among national governments needs to be strengthened rather than weakened or eliminated, the idea of the weakest government is in fact a pipe dream and cannot become a reality.

The so-called constitutional government, known as the "law-based government" in China, means that in a market economy, the powers and acts of the government are limited to the extent that they are bound by constitutional rules that prevent the government from infringing on individual freedom. "The acts of private and public agents are subject to the law and to the constitutional limits in force".[5] Article 5 in Chapter I General Principles of the Constitution of the People's Republic of China stipulates that "all state organs and armed forces, all political parties and social organizations, and all enterprises and public institutions must abide by the Constitution and the law. Accountability must be enforced for all acts that violate the Constitution or laws". "No organization or individual shall have any privilege beyond the Constitution or the law". The CPC Central Committee has also repeatedly stressed that: "Stick to the principle that all people are equal before the law and no organization or individual is privileged to be beyond the Constitution. Any acts in breach of the Constitution shall be investigated".[6]

The proper functioning of a market economy is based on market order. From the perspective of the market order, a country's constitution establishes the basic rules for the behaviors of individual citizens, the market, and the government; and it defines the structure of the transactions between individuals and between the market and the government. A constitutional system can establish a political order that directs the self-interested behavior of individuals toward the common interests. Both individual economic activity and government intervention in economic activity must take place within the framework of the constitution. Neither the individuals nor governments can violate the constitution. If a country's governmental power is not subject to the constitution, or if the governmental power is above the constitution, the government is not a constitutional government or a law-based government. The constitutional system defines the boundaries and scope of the government's power, and establishes the procedures by which the government makes decisions and exercises its power. Market order can be formed and protected only if both individuals and the government can abide by and maintain the constitutional order. If the government can arbitrarily expand the scope of its power and the size of government, the market mechanism will not be able to fully perform its function of allocating resources and adjusting the economic structure.

III. The future model of China's socialist market economy

The "model" mentioned here mainly refers to how the relationship between the government and the market is positioned in China's socialist market economic system, and what role the government and the market play in resource allocation, economic structural adjustment, and optimization, respectively.

In terms of resource allocation and economic structural adjustment, the future model of China's market economy should change from a government-led to a market-led model.

Our future resource allocation and economic structural adjustment should be mainly undertaken by the market mechanism, with the government playing its guiding, complementary, and supplementary role. In China's future socialist market economic system, government intervention and regulation of economic activities will be needed. We cannot completely copy the "policy ineffectiveness" proposition of neoclassical macroeconomics and neoliberal policy propositions. Although the spontaneous and automatic regulation of the market mechanism has its advantages, it cannot always guarantee the achievement of full employment and the just distribution of income and wealth. In an era of objective monopoly and economic globalization, the completely laissez-faire economic activity is unrealistic.

The market mechanism has the function of automatically removing excess production and excess capacity and automatically repairing the imbalance between supply and demand, but the automatic regulation of the market mechanism cannot avoid or eliminate large-scale structural imbalances and economic fluctuations. There are some structural imbalances and economic fluctuations that are beyond the power of the market mechanism.

1. Structural imbalance caused by "animal spirits"

In his General Theory, M. K. John pointed out that in addition to speculation causing economic fluctuations, the characteristics of human nature may also contribute to economic instability. The characteristics of human nature he refers to are animal spirit. By animal spirit, he means that a large part of people's economic behavior and even social and political activities are driven by spontaneous optimism rather than by mathematical expectations of prospects; people tend to act on sentiment, whim and chance rather than rational decisions and actions. "In estimating the prospects of investment, we must have regard, therefore, to the nerves and hysteria and even digestion and reaction to the weather of those upon whose spontaneous activity it largely depends".[7]

The American economists G. A. Akerlof and R. J. Shiller in their book *Animal Spirits* (2012) further interpret Keynes' animal spirits as five factors that tend to govern people's behavior: confidence, fairness, corruption and bad faith, money illusion, and stories. Influenced by these factors, people's behavior tends to deviate from rationality by being capricious, following the trend ("Effect of Sheep Flock") and being blindly optimistic, thus causing economic fluctuations by over-investment and over-borrowing. Since people's confidence has a multiplier effect on investment, consumption, and other expenditures, this makes economic fluctuations be magnified and eventually leads to economic crisis.

In a market economy, investment decisions or economic activities are always subject to risk and uncertainty, and information is incomplete, which makes it difficult to make rational analysis or decisions based on mathematical expectations, so people tend to adopt the simplest decision-making model: following the majority action. This kind of following behavior often results in excess production and overinvestment, as exemplified by the 2008 subprime mortgage crisis in the United States and the subsequent international financial crisis.

For this kind of economic fluctuations triggered by people's psychological motivation and human characteristics, market mechanism is powerless.

2. Economic structural changes brought about by the scientific and technological revolution

The application of major scientific and technological achievements in the process of economic activities will inevitably cause major changes in the mode of labor, production, and lifestyle, resulting in a series of important changes in the supply–demand relationship, market structure, industrial structure, etc. Although the market mechanism can play an automatic role in regulating the imbalance between supply and demand and structural imbalance brought about by these changes, the process from imbalance to restoration of equilibrium may be longer, and the economy may suffer greater costs and pain. In particular, technological innovation often triggers structural unemployment, making involuntary unemployment and job vacancies coexist in the economy; technological innovation has given rise to new industries that require workers with new skills that the unemployed in traditional industries do not possess. The popular application of computer technology and modern communication technology has created many new industries and new markets, and accordingly created many new jobs, such as software engineers, network administrators, and big data analysis engineers, while the unemployed who are freed from traditional industries often do not have the skills required for these jobs, and cannot be allocated the new jobs. The market mechanism cannot coordinate this type of labor supply and demand, and government expansion of AD cannot eliminate this structural unemployment, which can only be eliminated by enabling workers to acquire new skills through vocational training.

3. Structural imbalances in an economy caused by external shocks

External shocks can cause structural imbalances in an economy and divert the economy from its steady-state growth path, such as the 1997 Southeast Asian financial crisis, the 2008 international financial crisis, and the impact of the COVID-19 epidemic on China's economy since 2020. External shocks may often cause international economic imbalances and possible deep imbalances, or even plunge some economies into depression. In the face of such imbalances, market mechanisms are often overwhelmed; even the independent intervention by an economy's government may not be effective, often requiring joint intervention and international cooperation of major economies.

These previously given reasons provide a rationale for government intervention, which is further reinforced by the socialist attributes of China's market economy. But government intervention and regulation of economic activities should be selective and scientific, and government intervention cannot replace the role of the market in the process of resource allocation and economic structural adjustment. The government can intervene in economic activities on the following occasions: (1) the economy suffers from large external shocks, which often occur unexpectedly and unpredictably, that is, the so-called "black swan events"; (2) when and in areas that cannot be regulated by the market mechanism and are not well regulated—for example, income and wealth distribution, economic activities that generate externalities, production of public goods, incomplete information, the existence of monopolies, and vacuum areas of regulation by market mechanisms; (3) major scientific and technological innovation and breakthrough; (4) support for the cultivation of emerging industries; (5) regional development and industrial development planning.

In the long run, for the purpose of constantly adjusting and optimizing China's economic structure to adapt to the development of science and technology and changes in demand to achieve stable, healthy and sustainable economic development, we need to choose the dual path of further marketization and government transformation. Through the supply-side structural reform, we aim to establish a socialist market economy model with Chinese characteristics, which is a "double-effect" model combining effective market and effective government. The so-called effective market means that the market is an effective competitive market, the market mechanism plays a decisive role in resource allocation and a leading role in economic structural adjustment, and the market mechanism is effective in resource allocation and economic structural adjustment. The so-called effective government means that the government, within the scope authorized by law, acts in the long-term interests of the country and the overall interests of the economy and society, innovates systems, increases the supply of effective systems, makes scientific decisions, scientific administration, and scientific governance, performs government intervention and macro control in accordance with the principles of efficiency and fairness and justice, and takes actions in a scientific and effective manner.

Notes

1 Department of Comprehensive Statistics of National Economy. (2005). *National Bureau of Statistics. A Compilation of 55 Years of Statistical Data of New China*. Beijing: China Statistics Press, 10.

2 The proportion of the secondary industry (36.9%) exceeded that of the primary industry (34%) for the first time in 1958, and further increased to 42.6% and 44.4% in 1959 and 1960, while the proportion of the primary industry dropped to 26.5% and 23.2% accordingly. However, from 1961 to 1969, except for 1966 when the proportion of the secondary industry (37.9%) was slightly higher than that of the primary industry (37.2%), the proportion of the secondary industry was again consistently lower than that of the primary industry in the remaining eight years.

3 Although the concepts of "economic crisis", "economic cycle", and "economic fluctuation" cannot be equated, since the 1980s, more and more economists tend to use the term "economic fluctuation" to refer to "economic cycle" or "economic crisis".

4 Ludwig Edler Von Mises and Robert Nozick are two representative figures who advocate the weakest government. According to Mises, government (the state) has only one task: to protect personal safety and health; to protect personal freedom and private property; and to defend against any violent encroachment and plunder. Any acts of government that go beyond this function are evil. By the weakest government, Nozick meant a government limited to the limited functions of preventing violence, theft, and deception, and enforcing the performance of contracts; he believed that any government with more functions would violate the individual's freedom rights. In the view of extreme liberals, the rights possessed by weakest government are conceded by the individual; beyond that, government itself possesses no rights.

5 [USA] Buchanan, J. (1988). *Liberty, Market and State*. Chinese Version 1. Beijing: Beijing College of Economics Press, 250.

6 *Decision of the Central Committee of the Communist Party of China on Several Major Issues Concerning Comprehensively Deepening Reforms*. Beijing: People's Publishing House, 2013, 32.

7 [UK] Keynes, John Maynrd (1999). *The General Theory of Employment, Interest and Money*, retranslated by Gao Hongye, Beijing: The Commercial Press, 166.

Conclusion

The analysis in this Monograph shows that this supply-side structural reform in China is essentially a new round of system reform, and a Chinese-style supply-side revolution. The term "supply-side structural reform" is just a specific name given to the comprehensively deepening reform, just like the name "household contract responsibility system" given to the rural system reform at the beginning of China's reform and opening up.

If the reform and opening up from 1979 to 1993 was the preliminary project of building a socialist market economic system in China, then the period from 1993 to 2013 may be deemed as the Phase I Project of building a socialist market economic system in China, and the period since the Third Plenary Session of the 18th Central Committee held in November 2013 may be deemed as the Phase II Project of building a socialist market economic system in China. This Phase II Project is to position the market mechanism to play a decisive role in the resource allocation, and to "form a system that is complete, scientific and standardized, and effective in operation, so as to make all aspects of the system more mature and more established" through comprehensively deepening reform.

The Phase II Project of transforming to a complete, scientific, standardized, and effective socialist market economic system is a more magnificent and arduous project, because it is an advanced stage in the construction of China's socialist market economic system and a deep water area for China's system reform. It touches on such deep-seated and sensitive issues as the relationship of ownership, the positioning of state-owned enterprises, the establishment of the boundary between the market and the government, and the readjustment and redistribution of interests of different groups. This makes the supply-side structural reform and comprehensively deepening reform more revolutionary.

The success of supply-side structural reform should be marked by the realization of four transformations: the transformation of resource allocation from government-led to market-determined; the transformation of the driving force of economic growth from relying mainly on resource inputs to relying mainly on technological progress; the transformation of the mode of economic growth from pursuing mainly quantitative growth to pursuing mainly quality improvement and sustainable growth; and the transformation of the goal of economic development from pursuing mainly GDP growth to pursuing the growth of national happiness index.

DOI: 10.4324/9781003367000-16

The effectiveness and the achievement of the expected goals of the supply-side structural reform, and whether China's economy can successfully break through the current dilemma, cross the middle-income trap, step into the track of sustainable development, and successfully achieve the goal of "two centenary goals", depend on the strength and depth of the system reform and on the effectiveness of the reform.

Adam Smith pointed out in *The Wealth of Nations* that everyone in real society has a desire to improve his or her own situation, and it is this individual desire for improvement that shapes people's qualities of hard work, frugality, advancement, and accumulation. This desire for improvement is also what we call today the people's yearning for a happy and good life. This desire or yearning for improvement is the motive power for people to trade and engage in economic activities and to engage in inventions and innovations, and thus the driving force behind wealth growth and social development. At present, China's economy is still under the dual pressure of a downward spiral and major structural imbalances, and the world economy is still in the midst of a recessionary winter. However, the desire for improvement is always there. As long as we continue to increase the supply of effective systems through deepening reforms, and turn people's desire for improvement into great enthusiasm for investment, production, invention, and innovation, another period of prosperity for China's economic growth and social development will come soon!

References

Abel, A. et al. (1989) "Assessing Dynamic Efficiency: Theory and Evidence", *The Review of Economic Studies*, 56(1), 1–20.

Akerlof, G. A., & Shiller, R. J. (2012) *Animal Spirits* [M], translated by Huang Zhiqiang, Xu Weiyu and Jin Lan. Beijing: CITIC Press.

Aoki, S. H. (2012) "A Simple Accounting Framework for the Effect of Resource Misallocation on Aggregate Productivity", *Journal of the Japanese and International Economies*.

Buchanan, J. (1988) *Liberty, Market and State* [M], translated by Wu Liangjian et al. Beijing: Beijing College of Economics Press.

Buera, F. J., & Yongseok, S. (2013) "Financial Frictions and the Persistence of History: A Quantitative Exploration", *Journal of Political Economy*, 121(2), 221–272.

Caballero, R. J. et al. (2008)" Zombie Lending and Depressed Restructuring in Japan", *American Economic Review*, 98(5), 1943–1977.

Cooper, et al. (1988) "Coordinating Coordination Failures in Keynesian Models", *Quarterly Journal of Economics*.

Decision of the Central Committee of the Communist Party of China on Several Major Issues Concerning Comprehensively Deepening Reforms. (2013) [M]. Beijing: People's Publishing House.

Depalo, D. et al. (2015) "Public—Private Wage Differentials in Euro-area Countries: Evidence from Quantile Decomposition Analysis", *Empirical Economics*, 49(3), 985–1015.

Dewar, R. D., & Dutton, J. E. (1986) "The Adoption of Radical and Incremental Innovations: An Empirical Analysis", *Management Science*, 32(11), 1422–1433.

Diamond, P. A. (1981) "Mobility Costs, Frictional Unemployment, and Efficiency", *Journal of Political Economy*, 89(4), 798–812.

Diamond, P. A. (1982) "Aggregate-Demand Management in Search Equilibrium", *Journal of Political Economy*, 90(5), 881–894.

Fang, F. Q. (2009) "Shorten the Policy Time Lag and Improve the Level of Macroeconomic Control [J]", *Teaching and Research*, (7).

Fang, F. Q. (2014a) *Main Schools of Modern Western Economics* [M]. 2nd Edition. Beijing: China Renmin University Press.

Fang, F. Q. (2014b) "Reconstruction of China's Macro-economic Control System from the Perspective of Great Reform [J]", *Economic Theory and Business Management*, (5).

Fang, F. Q. (2015) "China's Economy is Undergoing Five Transformations [J]", *People's Tribune*, (12).

Fang, F. Q., & Ma, X. J. (2016) "The Reason and Way out of Slowdown for China's Economy [J]", *Journal of Renmin University of China*, (6).

Friedman, M. (1962) *Capitalism and Freedom*. Chicago: University of Chicago Press.

Ge, Q. G, et al. (2013) "Labor Market Distortion, Structural Transformation and China's Labor Productivity [J]", *Economic Research Journal*, (5).

Gilder, G. (1985) *Wealth and Poverty* [M], translated by Chu Yukun et al. Shanghai: Shanghai Translation Publishing House.

Gustafsson, B., & Li, S. (2000) "Economic Transformation and the Gender Earnings Gap in Urban China", *Joural of Population Economics*, 13(2), 305–329.

Hailstones, T. J. (1982) *A Guide to Supply-side Economics*. Richmond, VA: Robert F. Dame.

Han, G. Z., & Li, G. Z. (2015) "Factor Misallocation and China's Industrial Growth [J]", *On Economic Problems*, (1).

Hayashi, F., & Prescott, E. C. (2008) "The Depressing Effect of Agricultural Institutions on the Prewar Japanese Economy", *Journal of Political Economy*, 116(4), 573–632.

Hirschman, A. O. (1958) *The Strategy of Economic Development*. New Haven: Yale University Press.

Hirschman, A. O. (1991) *The Strategy of Economic Development [M], translated by Pan Zhaodong and Cao Zhenghai*. Beijing: Economic Science Press.

Hsieh, C. T., & Klenow, P. J. (2009) "Misallocation and Manufacturing TFP in China and India", *Quarterly Journal of Economics*, 1403–1448.

Jeong, H., & Robert, T. (2007) "Sources of TFP Growth: Occupational Choice and Financial Deepening", *Society for the Advancement of Economic Theory (SAET)*, 32(1), 179–221.

Jin, R. Q. (2006) *Science Development and Fiscal Policy in China* [M]. Beijing: China Financial & Economic Publishing House.

Kasper, W., & Streit, M. E. (2002) *Institutional Economics: Social Order and Public Policy* [M]. Beijing: The Commercial Press.

Keynes, J. M. (1999) *The General Theory of Employment, Interest and Money* [M], retranslated by Gao Hongye. Beijing: The Commercial Press.

Maddison, A. (2003) *The World Economy: A Millennial Perspective*, translated by Wu Xiaoying, etc. Beijing: Peking University Press.

Mankiw, N. G. (2016) *Macroeconomics*. 9th Edition, translated by Lu Yuanzhu. Beijing: China Renmin University Press.

Marx. (2004) *Capital*. Vol. 3 [M]. Beijing: People's Publishing House.

Marx & Engels (1973) *Collected Works*. Vol. 26 [M]. Beijing: People's Publishing House.

Marx & Engels (1995) *Collected Works*. Vol. 30 [M]. Beijing: People's Publishing House.

Marx & Engels (2001) *Collected Works*. Vol. 44 [M]. Beijing: People's Publishing House.

Marx & Engels (2003) *Collected Works*. Vol. 46 [M]. Beijing: People's Publishing House.

Marx & Engels (2012) *Selected Works*. Vol. 2 [M]. Beijing: People's Publishing House.

Miller, T. et al.(2018) *2018 Index of Economic Freedom*. Beijing: The Heritage Foundation.

Milton, F. (2001) *The Essential of Friedman. Volume 1. Chinese 1st Edition*. Beijing: Capital University of Economics and Business Press.

Mueller, R. E. (1998) "Public-private Sector Wage Differentials in Canada: Evidence from Quantile Regressions", *Economics Letters*, 60(2), 229–235.

Munshi, K., & Rosenzweig, M. (2016) "Networks and Misallocation: Insurance, Migration, and the Rural-urban Wage Gap", *American Economic Review*, 106(1), 46–98.

Petty, W. (1981) *The Economic Writings of Sir William Petty*, translated by Chen Dongye, Ma Qinghuai and Zhou Jinru. Beijing: The Commercial Press.

Phelps, E. S. (1961) "The Golden Rule of Accumulation: A Fable for Growthmen", *The American Economics Review*, 51, 638–643.

Robert, S. (1956) "A Contribution to the Theory of Economic Growth", *Quarterly Journal of Economics*, 70(1), 65–94.

Samuelson, P. A., & Nordhaus, W. D. (2014) *Economics* [M]. 19th Edition, translated by Xiao Chen et al. Beijing: The Commercial Press.

Say. (1963) *A Treatise on Political Economy*, translated by Chen Fusheng and Chen Zhenhua. Beijing: The Commercial Press.

Selected Papers on Modern Foreign Economics (5). (1984) [M], compiled by The Commercial Press. Beijing: The Commercial Press.

Selected Papers on Modern Foreign Economics (17). (1997) [M], compiled by The Commercial Press. Beijing: The Commercial Press.

Shi, Z. F. (2013) *Extraordinary Growth: China's Economy from 1979 to 2049* [M]. Shanghai: Shanghai People's Publishing House.

Smith, A. (2001) *The Wealth of Nations* [M], translated by Yang Jingnian. Xi'an: Shaanxi People's Publishing House.

Stefano, E. D., & Marconi, D. (2016) *Structural transformation and allocation efficiency in China and India*. Temi di Discussion (Economic Working Paper), No. 1093.

Stefano, E. D., & Marconi, D. (2017) *Structural Transformation and Allocation Efficiency in China and India*. Social Science Electronic Publishing.

Xi Jinping's Speech at the 11th Meeting of the Central Leading Group on Financial and Economic Affairs on November 10, 2015 [N]. *People's Daily*. (1).

Xi, J. P. (2017). *Securing a Decisive Victory in Building a Moderately Prosperous Society in All Respects, and Striving for the Great Success of Socialism with Chinese Characteristics for a New Era—Report to the 19th CPC National Congress*. Beijing: People's Publishing House, 28.

Xi Jinping's Speech at a Ceremony Marking the Centenary of the Communist Party of China on July 1, 2021, People's Daily, July 2, 2021.

Index

Printed in the United States
by Baker & Taylor Publisher Services